A PRODUCT MANAGER'S JOURNEY IN ESG SOFTWARE DEVELOPMENT

DR. JAYAKUMAR INDRACANTI

notionpress.com

INDIA • SINGAPORE • MALAYSIA

ISBN 979-8-89556-364-9

Dedicated to my parents

Contents

Preface

In the early 2000s, I was a young PhD student working as a Research Associate at a university. As part of my program, I had the opportunity to contribute to developing a pioneering product. At that time, real-time remote monitoring of air pollution and posting data to the internet were revolutionary concepts. Internet connectivity was limited, with bandwidths around 2 MB or less, and we relied on dial-up connections to get online. Despite these constraints, given our resources, technology, and opportunities, I was fortunate to be involved in one of the most ambitious product development initiatives of that era.

The initial goal was to build a minimum viable product (MVP) capable of real-time air pollution monitoring, capturing data from the surrounding environment, including weather variables such as temperature, humidity, wind speed, and wind direction. We also aimed to integrate particulate matter (PM 2.5) measurements using a Bruel and Kjaer PM meter and sound level monitoring, striving for a cost-effective solution compared to market leaders whose products cost upwards of Rs. 15 lakhs—a prohibitive price for most universities, especially when considering scalability across multiple locations.

Our project team worked tirelessly and was led by an exceptional architect whose intelligence and problem-solving skills enabled us to progress significantly within our limitations. We assembled the system within a computer CPU, incorporating small rotor pumps to draw in air for monitoring. Over several months, we conducted rigorous testing of the electrolytic sensors sourced from the UK, often working around the clock and closely tracking our advancements.

Access to modern product management tools or sophisticated systems is necessary for us to rely on our collaborative efforts among the university, an instrument company, and the regional Pollution Control Board.

We developed custom software to collect air samples at designated intervals and compute averages over specific periods. The software then used a modem to dial into the internet and post the data to a simple HTML-based webpage, displaying pollution metrics alongside air quality limits at regular intervals. After extensive effort, we successfully set up an ambient air quality monitoring station in Punjagutta, Hyderabad. The project received excellent media coverage, positive reviews, and recognition, including the best presentation award at a local competition. This success was a moment of great pride for the team, and for me, it provided the foundation to defend my thesis and author meaningful research papers based on the collected data.

However, as time passed, new challenges emerged. When the Central Pollution Control Board announced a proposal to set up real-time pollution monitoring stations across India, our university eagerly submitted a bid. Unfortunately, our proposal was not approved, and the contract was awarded to an imported product from a competitor. It soon became apparent that our celebrated system had a critical flaw: the electrochemical sensors we relied on had accuracy limitations. Although marketed as suitable for ambient air monitoring, these sensors did not perform reliably under real-world conditions. While our technology for data collection, internet posting, and ASP.NET-based web display was robust, the core sensor system fell short.

This setback was deeply frustrating. We had invested significant effort into perfecting the product, even developing a mobile van equipped with the sensor system. The realization of this flaw prompted a reevaluation of our approach and a series of questions: Who decides which sensors are appropriate for air pollution monitoring? Should we use UV-based sensors or electrolytic sensors that are susceptible to moisture? What criteria determine sensor selection? These questions led me to an essential product lesson: no matter how skilled the engineering or technology team is, a product's success ultimately hinges on delivering value and meeting the end user's needs.

From that moment onward, I prioritized thoroughly assessing the end use and practical functionality of any product I developed. This experience highlighted that our reliance on sensor provider brochures and marketing input, rather than a deeper analysis of success criteria, had impacted the project's outcome. This pivotal lesson has stayed with me, influencing my approach to product development and ensuring that end-user value is always at the forefront of my work.

The journey I embarked on during that project laid the groundwork for my later focus on many EHS, Sustainability Product development, and now the ESG (Environmental, Social, and Governance) application development. The lessons I learned from that experience, including the importance of aligning technology with user needs and understanding the broader context of product use, have informed my work and the insights shared in this book. Here, I narrate the development journey not as a dry, technical recount but as an evocative story that captures the adventurous nature of creating impactful products.

Throughout this book, I use a blend of metaphors, historical references, and real-life stories to illustrate the multifaceted challenges product managers face when developing a product from the ground up. These narrative elements help frame the key message: the path to building successful, meaningful technology is rarely straightforward. By sharing these stories, I aim to transform what can often be perceived as a dry or daunting topic into an engaging and relatable one.

Each chapter draws from the reality of those early challenges and the lessons learned, guiding readers through turning initial ideas into products that fulfill their intended purpose and resonate with end users. Whether the stories are symbolic, historical, or based on real-life experiences, they emphasize the complexities and the persistent questions that define the product development process.

This book is an exploration of my past work and a testament to the universal truths about product development. The narrative underscores the importance of understanding user value, the balance of innovation and practicality, and the resilience needed to navigate unexpected outcomes. I hope readers find inspiration and practical takeaways for their journeys in ESG application development and beyond.

Jayakumar
22.11.2024

Foreword

It is an honor and a privilege to write this foreword for a book that showcases the technical intricacies of product development and shares the human journey behind it. I have enjoyed working alongside Jayakumar for 20 years in environmental health and safety (EHS) and sustainability. I can attest firsthand to the deep commitment and passion that drives their work.

Developing ESG (Environmental, Social, and Governance) applications is a complex, multifaceted process that requires technical prowess, strategic thinking, and an unwavering focus on user impact. In this book, Jayakumar has masterfully woven their journey—one marked by early triumphs, unexpected challenges, and profound lessons—into a story that educates and inspires.

Jayakumar's early experiences, highlighted in this book, set the stage for an ongoing dedication to creating solutions that address real-world problems while focusing on end-user value. Their background in building pioneering air pollution monitoring systems with limited resources exemplifies the resilience and ingenuity needed in product development. These experiences, shared in an evocative and narrative style, transform the potentially dry subject of ESG application development into a rich, relatable journey filled with insights.

As someone who has witnessed Jayakumar's growth and the evolution of his approach to problem-solving over two decades, I can confidently say that this book is not just a technical guide but a testament to the realities faced by product managers and developers. It reminds us that behind every innovation is a story of dedication, hard work, collaboration, and continuous learning.

This book will serve as an educational resource and a source of inspiration for field professionals, aspiring product developers, and those passionate about ESG initiatives. Its lessons underscore the importance of aligning product design with user needs, navigating unforeseen obstacles, and understanding that the path to successful development is as much about resilience as it is about innovation.

I am proud to introduce this compelling work by my long-time colleague and friend, whose experiences and reflections have enriched the sustainability and ESG fields and continue to push the boundaries of impactful product development.

Dr. Mohana Chetlapally

Acknowledgments

I am deeply grateful to the many people who have supported and inspired me as I have written this book and in my other work over the years.

First and foremost, I want to thank my family—my wife, Madhuri, and my daughter, Lasya. Your unwavering support, patience, and encouragement have been the foundation of all my endeavors. Madhuri, your belief in my work and constant motivation kept me going during the most challenging moments. Lasya, your boundless energy and joy reminded me of the importance of perseverance and balance.

To my childhood friend Dillesh, my twin brother Vijaya, family members, and Friend Suresh, your camaraderie and thoughtful conversations have inspired and strengthened me. Your friendship has enriched my journey in ways words cannot fully express.

I also want to extend my heartfelt thanks to my colleagues, Sree Nallagatla, Abhishek Banerjee, and Santhana Selvan. Your collaboration, insights, and shared passion for innovation have made every project a rewarding experience. Working alongside such talented individuals has been a privilege.

A special thanks goes to my manager, Laszlo Gyorky, whose guidance and support have been instrumental in my professional growth. Your leadership and trust gave me the confidence to pursue ambitious goals and tackle complex challenges.

To all of you, thank you for sharing this journey with me and for helping me turn my vision into reality. Your influence and encouragement are woven into the pages of this book, and I am forever grateful.

Jayakumar

Chapter 1

The Spark of an Idea

In the heart of Amsterdam's Dam area, surrounded by historic architecture and the hum of modern business, you are seated at a Starbucks coffee shop, sipping a rich espresso. The day has been long at the DPW Procurement Conference, with meetings and discussions about the latest industry trends and witnessing great products. As the sun sets, you finally have a moment to reflect.

Your mind drifts to the European regulations that had been the center of many conversations at the conference. The E.U. is ramping its focus on environmental, social, and governance (ESG) standards, demanding more company transparency and accountability. As a management consultant, you've seen how businesses struggled to meet stringent requirements like the ECHA REACH regulatory standards nearly 16 years ago. The weight of compliance was not just a bureaucratic burden but a challenge that required a fundamental shift in how companies operated and reported their activities.

The café's radio plays softly in the background, occasionally interrupted by the clinking of cups and the chatter of patrons. As you gaze out the window, a headline on a discarded newspaper catches your eye: 'France introduces one of the world's first greenwashing laws.' You know how massive the fines for greenwashing are: major corporations are penalized. Intrigued, you reach over and pick it up. The article details fines of up to 80% of the false promotional campaign cost, a correction on billboards or in media, and a

30-day clarification on the company website for greenwashing. You know how several high-profile companies are exaggerating their environmental efforts, resulting in substantial fines and a loss of consumer trust. It is a stark reminder of the growing importance of genuine ESG commitments.

Your thoughts are interrupted by a notification on your phone. An industry report from the Gartner Market Research agency you have been waiting for has just been published. It contains an in-depth analysis of how the new wave of transformation focuses on ESG evolving from a product/service focus to a social focus, driven by climate change, declining political trust, and transparency. You remember reading research on 'The State of ESG Disclosures and a CFO's View on ESG Measures that Matter' just a few days ago. You skim through the report, noting the challenges and opportunities it highlights. Companies are eager to improve their ESG performance but need more breadth and depth of tools to do so effectively. There is a clear need for a solution that could simplify the process, ensure compliance, and protect against the risks of greenwashing.

As you sit there, the pieces begin to fall into place. The European regulations, the penalties for greenwashing, and the insights from the industry report highlighting the new wave of transformation focusing on ESG all point to a glaring gap in the market. What if there was a way to help companies navigate the complex world of ESG management? What if you could develop software that ensures compliance with regulations, provides a transparent and verifiable way to report ESG activities, and sets a strategic roadmap to mitigate the risk?

The idea begins to take shape. This software could integrate with existing applications and business processes, collect and analyze data, and generate reports that meet regulatory standards. It would offer real-time insights, highlighting areas where companies could improve and helping them avoid the pitfalls of greenwashing. More importantly, it would build trust with stakeholders, showing that the company's ESG commitments were genuine and impactful.

Excitement surges through you. The development of software is more than just a business opportunity; it is a chance to make a real difference. You quickly pull out your digital notebook, jotting ideas and sketching features and functionalities. The possibilities seem endless, and the potential impact is profound. At that moment, amid the fading light and the gentle murmur of the café, the spark of an idea ignites a fire within you. You know you have found your next big project: developing ESG management software that could transform how companies approach sustainability, governance, and social responsibility. And with that, you finish your espresso, gather your things, and head out into the evening.

As you guessed, in the scenario above, I was sitting in an Amsterdam Starbucks Café after attending the DPW Procurement Conference! I felt a surge of excitement. What if I could create a software solution to help companies manage their ESG (Environmental, Social, and Governance) responsibilities more effectively? I am fully aware of the efforts it takes to develop and implement software to meet the moving regulatory target—reflecting upon my experience with SAP REACH Compliance software and an in-house software development architecture proposal given to a chemical major to meet their Mandatory Reporting of GHG Rule.

It took us many years to find a stable solution for the previous situation. During this time, ECHA improved its draft regulations by introducing tools for data integration and SDS generation. In a later scenario, we witnessed first-hand the complexity of getting the correct data from multiple sources inside the organization and its vast silos of processes and procedures with various versions of data. It was a perfect recipe for a scenario with different countries and multiple legal and voluntary requirements, and a software application capable of meeting ESG would be a great opportunity.

This idea consumed my thoughts for days. I envisioned a tool that would simplify compliance and provide valuable insights for companies to improve their sustainability practices. My mind raced with possibilities and knew I had to turn this vision into reality. I needed to run—not simply run, but in the right direction while facing hurdles. I recounted the phrase from the book 'Where to Play: Commercializing Innovative Ideas is a Constant Run. But where to start?'

Inspiration from My Experience: ECHA REACH Regulation and SAP Solution

So, I was at the crossroads of opportunity and uncertainty. It was a typical Thursday afternoon at an Information Technology consulting firm when our capability leader for PLM and EHS called me to a meeting. They had an exciting yet daunting task for my colleague and me: start working on REACH compliance and SVT to meet the E.U. ECHA regulatory requirements. Little did I know that this project would be a rollercoaster of highs and lows, testing my patience and perseverance at every turn.

To give you some context, SAP has just rolled out its version, SAP REACH Compliance 1.1. At the same time, ECHA, the European Chemicals Agency, had provided tentative timelines for implementation based on the chemical quantities companies were importing or manufacturing within Europe. However, the essential tools from ECHA, IUCLID, and CHESAR, as well as the interpretation of the legal text, were still under development. Setting up the software meant we were navigating uncharted waters with incomplete maps.

The requirements were massive. Companies had to identify substances exceeding certain tonnage bands, figure out their use cases, communicate effectively along the supply chain, implement controls, and create an extended safety data sheet. To say the task was huge would be an understatement; even the SAP software didn't have all the features to meet these regulatory requirements. It was like trying to build a puzzle with pieces from different sets.

One of the significant challenges was volume tracking via Substance Volume Tracking (SVT). It had limitations, especially in assessing Only Representative and bonded warehouse scenarios. But giving up wasn't an option. We rolled our sleeves and set up our sandbox environment to demonstrate the tool. It took immense effort to keep the software up-to-date with the latest patches and updates released by SAP, which was constantly evolving to keep up with the moving regulatory requirements.

During this journey, I witnessed something extraordinary. SAP created a collaboration hub for SAP REACH Compliance, bringing together industry experts, software developers, and the SAP team. They were all trying to find answers to our numerous questions. Dr. Marko Lange was at the forefront of SAP communication, providing guidance and insights. It wasn't just about developing software; it was like running a marathon while the track was being laid.

There were moments of success—like when we finally managed to get the software running smoothly in our sandbox, demonstrating its potential to our stakeholders. Those moments were exhilarating and motivated us to push forward. But there were also moments of failure—like when we hit roadblocks with the SVT limitations or when the regulatory requirements shifted yet again, and we had to pivot and adapt.

Through it all, I learned invaluable lessons. I knew the importance of resilience and adaptability in the face of ever-changing requirements. I learned the power of collaboration and how collective efforts can overcome even the most daunting challenges. Most importantly, I knew that success isn't always about having all the answers from the start but the determination to find those answers along the way.

Working on REACH Compliance and SVT was one of my career's most challenging yet rewarding experiences. It was an actual test of character and capability, and I emerged from it with newfound confidence and a treasure trove of lessons I carry with me to this day.

Navigating the Complexity of Mandatory GHG Requirements: A Journey to Delaware

Back in 2010, I found myself in an exciting yet challenging situation. I was working for a leading Information Technology Services company. My manager, who was always supportive and encouraged me to take on new challenges, set me on a path that would provide invaluable insights into the complexities organizations face when implementing regulatory compliance measures. This journey involved understanding and addressing the US EPA's Mandatory Greenhouse Gas (GHG) Requirements.

One day, I received a call from our USA leadership team. They needed me to visit Delaware to conduct a workshop to understand our client's GHG reporting requirements. The goal was to gather accurate carbon emissions data from multiple sources within the organization and develop a robust system to manage this data effectively.

When I first arrived in Delaware, the scale of the challenge struck immediately. The organization was grappling with several significant issues, and it was clear that we had our work cut out for us. Many processes were manually carried out, leading to inefficiencies and increasing the risk of errors. I immediately saw that automating these tasks would save time and reduce mistakes. I remember thinking how much smoother things could run with the right automation.

Another major issue was data integration. Data was scattered across multiple sources, often containing different versions of the same information. It was like trying to piece together a puzzle where none of the pieces quite fit. The inconsistency made it difficult to understand the organization's overall performance. Finding a way to bring all this data together consistently and reliably would be crucial.

The team managing this wide array of tasks was small. The team was stretched thin, with only a few handling critical tasks. It was a classic case of too much to do and needing more hands. Seeing their struggle first-hand, I knew we needed to find a solution to help them manage their workload more effectively.

The organization also relied on outdated and isolated software applications, including manual spreadsheets, Lotus Notes-based applications, and older versions of SAP. These systems didn't communicate with each other, making it hard to get a comprehensive view of anything. The lack of communication between systems was a significant barrier to efficiency and accuracy, and it was clear that we needed to modernize and integrate these tools.

Compiling data from all these different sources into a single source of truth was another enormous challenge. It required a lot of time, effort, and a clear strategy to ensure that all the data was accurate and current. The enormity of this task was daunting, but I knew that solving it would be a significant step forward.

We also faced the limitations of early cloud storage. Since cloud storage was still in its infancy, we had to rely on on-site storage systems. Database volume added another layer of complexity, as managing and maintaining these systems required significant resources and expertise. Despite the challenges, I saw the potential benefits of a more modern solution.

We focused on automating manual processes, integrating data sources, and creating a cohesive strategy to manage our resources effectively.

As I navigated these challenges, I learned valuable lessons that would later inform my approach to developing ESG management software. The experience underscored the importance of flexibility, adaptability, and a clear, strategic vision. These insights became the foundation for the framework I would use to guide my product development journey, ensuring that I could create a tool that truly met the needs of its users.

The workshop in Delaware provided a first-hand look at the real-world challenges organizations face when complying with complex regulations. Gathering requirements, understanding the existing infrastructure, and developing a viable solution was enlightening. It was clear that implementing an effective GHG reporting system required more than just technology; it demanded a thorough understanding of the organizational processes, a commitment to change, and a collaborative approach to problem-solving.

Moving Forward with ESG Compliance

As we move forward with ESG compliance, these lessons from my Delaware experience are more relevant than ever. Organizations need robust systems that not only meet regulatory requirements but also adapt to the ever-changing landscape of ESG regulations. By understanding the challenges and leveraging modern technology, we can develop solutions that drive efficiency, accuracy, and sustainability. In conclusion, my experience with REACH Compliance & SVT, my journey to Delaware, and subsequent challenges provided a deep understanding of the complexities involved in regulatory compliance and my ability to navigate the complexities of ESG regulations to develop effective, sustainable strategies. These insights are invaluable as we continue to navigate the evolving world of ESG, ensuring that we meet requirements and drive positive change and sustainable practices within organizations.

Books, Books, and Books!

For the next few months, I embarked on an intensive reading journey, immersing myself in the rich world of digital product management. I surrounded myself with some of the most influential books on Product Management, each offering a treasure trove of insights, recommendations, and cautionary tales to guide my path.

One of the first books I picked up was *Inspired: How to Create Products Customers Love* by Marty Cagan. Cagan's emphasis on understanding customer needs and building products that solve their problems resonated deeply with me. I took meticulous notes, jotting down every nugget of wisdom about product discovery, agile practices, and the importance of a strong product culture. The book's real-life case studies of successful product launches were inspiring and enlightening, giving me a clearer picture of what my ESG management software could achieve. It reminded me of my time working on REACH Compliance and SVT, where understanding the evolving regulatory landscape was crucial to developing a relevant and effective solution.

Next, I dove into *Lean Product and Lean Analytics* by Ben Yoskovitz and Alistair Croll. This book introduced me to the idea of using data to drive product decisions. I learned about key performance indicators (KPIs), metrics that matter, and how to pivot based on data insights. I visualized the dashboards and analytics features my software could offer as I read, helping companies track their ESG performance in real-time and make data-driven improvements. This insight was especially relevant to my experience in Delaware, where integrating diverse data sources into a single, reliable system was a significant challenge.

The Lean Startup by Eric Ries became another cornerstone of my reading list. Ries's approach to building and scaling startups through continuous innovation and validated learning was exactly what I needed. I filled pages of my notebook with ideas on how to apply the lean methodology to my product development process, from creating a minimum viable product (MVP) to conducting rapid iterations based on user feedback. Developing products iteratively was a concept I had seen first-hand during the Delaware project, where we had to adapt quickly and iteratively to meet the complex GHG reporting requirements.

I also immersed myself in *Escaping the Build Trap* by Melissa Perri. Perri's insights into product strategy and aligning product development with business goals were invaluable. She highlighted common pitfalls that product managers face, such as building features that don't add value or failing to meet customer needs. Her practical advice on avoiding these traps and ensuring that every feature contributes to the overall vision of the product was eye-opening. This reminded me of the challenges I faced during the REACH Compliance project, where ensuring each feature met the regulatory requirements was a constant balancing act.

When it came to discovering market opportunities, I turned to *Where to Play: 3 Steps for Discovering Your Most Valuable Market Opportunities* by Marc Gruber and Sharon Tal. This book provided a systematic approach to identifying and evaluating new market opportunities. The Market Opportunity Navigator framework was particularly helpful as it allowed me to strategically assess where my ESG software could make the most significant impact. It helped me focus on high-potential areas with measurable risks and promising returns, much like how we had to strategically prioritize the various aspects of GHG data collection and reporting in Delaware.

I became utterly engrossed in these books as the days turned into weeks and months. I would often stay up late into the night, lost in the pages, imagining the potential of my ESG management software. I dreamed of a platform that would revolutionize how companies approached their environmental, social, and governance responsibilities. I envisioned dashboards filled with real-time data, automated compliance reports, and tools to help companies avoid greenwashing and build genuine, sustainable practices. These dreams were vivid and exhilarating. I saw the positive impact my product could have on the world, helping businesses become more transparent, accountable, and sustainable. The excitement of this vision kept me motivated, pushing me to learn more and refine my ideas.

However, amidst these dreams, I often overlooked the practical aspects of turning a product vision into a saleable product. The books provided insights but highlighted the complexity and challenges of product management. The reality of product development was much more than just having a great idea; it involved meticulous planning, market research, user testing, and a deep understanding of the competitive landscape.

I realized I needed to bridge the gap between my visionary ideas and the practical steps required to bring them to life. Allocating the right resources and clearly defining roles within the team is essential for effective ESG task management. This approach ensures the team operates efficiently and meets ESG goals and compliance requirements. It was a humbling realization but also a crucial one. The journey from vision to reality is filled with obstacles, but with the knowledge and insights I had gained from these books, I felt better equipped to navigate them.

A Journey of Discovery: Learning from Industry Experts

The journey of developing my ESG management software continued beyond books. As the weeks passed, I realized I needed to go beyond theoretical knowledge to truly understand the market and create a product that would resonate with its users. I needed to talk to the people who lived and breathed ESG daily. So, I embarked on a new journey phase, seeking out industry experts for their invaluable insights. I began by diving into LinkedIn, the professional network that connected me to thought leaders, practitioners, and innovators in the ESG space. I followed their posts, engaged with their content, and started to understand the pulse of the industry. These experts shared their experiences, challenges, and successes, providing a real-world perspective that complemented my book learning.

I reached out to these professionals one by one. Some were high-ranking executives in sustainability roles, while others were consultants with years of experience helping companies navigate the complex landscape of ESG regulations. I crafted thoughtful messages, explaining my vision and asking if they could spare time for a one-on-one interview. To my delight, many responded positively, willing to share their knowledge and insights, but only some politely recommended reaching out to others, or they were not the right SMEs.

The interviews were enlightening. I spoke with ESG managers in the trenches, dealing with the day-to-day realities of implementing sustainability initiatives. They shared the challenges they faced with existing tools – the inefficiencies, the lack of integration, and the constant struggle to ensure data accuracy. I learned about the regulatory pressures that kept them awake at night and the ESG risks that loomed over their efforts.

One conversation stood out. I spoke with a sustainability director at a major corporation who had been navigating ESG for over a decade. He described the evolution of ESG from a niche concern to a critical business imperative. His insights into the changing regulatory landscape were eye-opening. He emphasized the need for a tool to manage compliance and drive strategic decision-making, helping companies proactively improve their ESG risks and performance. These conversations also highlighted the gaps in the market. Many experts mentioned the need for a comprehensive, user-friendly platform and the ability to take data from diverse sources that could integrate with their existing systems and provide real-time analytics. They desired a solution that was a reporting tool and a strategic partner in their ESG journey.

The feedback I received was both encouraging and constructive. It validated many of my ideas while pointing out areas needing refinement. The experts appreciated the vision of an all-encompassing ESG management software but emphasized the importance of making it adaptable to different industries and scales of operation. Engaging with these professionals was more than just a learning experience; it was a co-creation process. Their initial feedback helped me to iterate on my ideas, refine the features, and prioritize the functionalities that would be most valuable to the end-users. The conversations were rich with practical advice, from the necessity of intuitive user interfaces to the importance of robust data security measures.

In addition to these one-on-one interactions, I spent considerable time on LinkedIn reading blogs and articles related to ESG and product management. I immersed myself in the insights shared by industry leaders and followed discussions in various professional groups. This interaction helped me gauge the initial pulse of the market and understand the broader conversations around ESG. I also started writing my blogs (www.digitalesgpro.com), sharing my thoughts and ideas about ESG management. These posts sparked discussions and feedback from the LinkedIn community, providing me with diverse perspectives. It was a valuable exercise in testing the waters and refining my ideas based on the reactions and comments from professionals in the field.

Browsing product roadmaps from established companies became another crucial part of my research. I analyzed how successful products evolved, the features they prioritized, and how they responded to market needs and regulatory changes. The provided guidance served as a blueprint for creating a robust roadmap for my ESG management software, ensuring it was both innovative and aligned with industry standards and best practices.

Exploring ESG Product Roadmaps: Insights from Leading Software Organizations

While diving into sustainability solutions, I explored offerings from several major players to understand what's out there. Many well-known companies are making significant strides in this area, and I found their innovative and inspiring approaches. Starting with SAP, their solutions stand out because they integrate ESG practices seamlessly into everyday business operations. For example, their 'Record, Report, Act' framework transforms sustainability from a vague goal into actionable steps. By recording actual data instead of relying on averages, businesses can gain a clear, precise picture of their environmental and social impact. This data is then meticulously reported to meet various regulatory standards, and the actionable insights help embed sustainability deeply into business processes. Data management is a critical aspect of sustainability, and SAP excels here by managing and integrating data from multiple sources to ensure accuracy and reliability. This approach goes beyond meeting compliance requirements; it's about maintaining data integrity through built-in audit and assurance mechanisms.

Navigating the plethora of ESG frameworks and standards can be overwhelming, but SAP simplifies this with a solid foundation that supports over 600 frameworks. Their solutions are tailored to specific industries, helping each sector optimize its sustainability practices. The Sustainability Control Tower (SCT) from SAP is like a command center for sustainability. It provides real-time insights, tracks ESG performance, and even allows for scenario planning and forecasting. This proactive approach helps businesses set and achieve their sustainability goals.

I also explored IBM's sustainability solutions, which leverage their strengths in AI and blockchain to enhance transparency and efficiency in ESG reporting. IBM's offerings focus on providing comprehensive insights and fostering collaboration across the supply chain to drive sustainable practices.

Enablon, another key player, offers robust software for managing environmental performance, health and safety, and operational risk. Their platform helps businesses comply with regulations, manage risks, and improve overall sustainability performance. Sphera specializes in integrated risk management software and information services, assisting organizations in managing and mitigating environmental, health, safety, and operational risks. Their tools provide comprehensive insights and ensure compliance with various regulatory requirements.

In my exploration, I found that each of these companies brings something unique. SAP's comprehensive integration of ESG into business processes, IBM's innovative use of AI and blockchain, Enablon's focus on risk management, and Sphera's robust compliance tools all offer valuable solutions for driving sustainability. These diverse approaches broadened my perspective on harnessing different technologies and strategies to create more sustainable businesses. No one-size-fits-all solution exists; organizations committed to positively impacting the planet must tailor a rich landscape of tools and techniques to meet their specific needs.

As I synthesized the insights from these interviews, blogs, and product roadmaps, I felt a growing sense of confidence and clarity. The pieces of the puzzle were coming together. The theoretical knowledge from the books I had read and the real-world insights from industry experts and the LinkedIn community shaped my vision into a concrete plan. The journey was far from over, but with each conversation, blog post, and roadmap analysis, I felt more equipped to tackle the challenges ahead. The input from these industry leaders and the LinkedIn community was valuable feedback and a source of inspiration and motivation. I was no longer working in isolation but was part of a broader community striving toward the same goal: to make ESG management more effective, transparent, and impactful.

With renewed determination and a wealth of knowledge, I continued my journey, ready to turn my vision into a reality that would revolutionize how companies approached their ESG responsibilities. The path was challenging, but the support and insights from these industry experts and the LinkedIn community were invaluable, guiding me every step of the way.

This book is more than just a recounting of my experiences; it's a treasure map designed to equip you with the knowledge and tools you need to succeed in your product development journey. Following my framework, you can assess market opportunities, understand your customers, create a strategic roadmap, and bring your product to life confidently and clearly. Whether you're a seasoned product manager or a budding entrepreneur, this book aims to inspire and empower you to turn your vision into a reality.

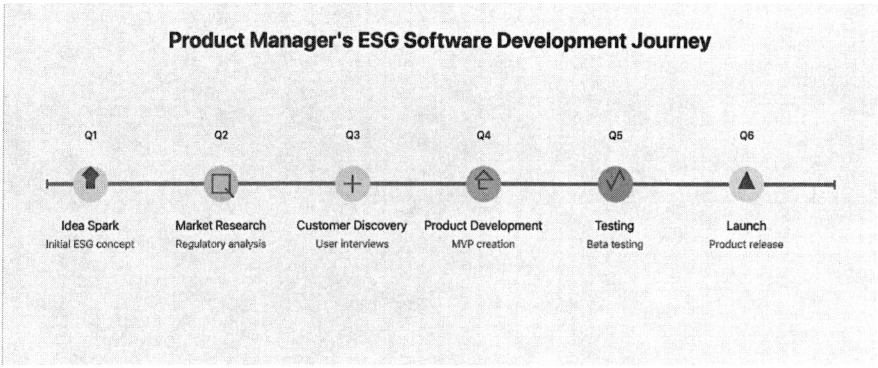

Chapter 2

ESG Regulations: An Overview

At the beginning of my entrepreneur adventure, I was sitting at a small, dimly lit desk in my house, watching my wall-mounted TV play the SAP Sustainability Day virtual session, highlighting how SAP acts as an enabler, creating sustainable business value. With a glimmer in my eyes, the goal was clear: create an ESG management tool to transform how businesses view environmental, social, and governance metrics. But one question loomed: who were our customers, and what did they need? Building the right product is not a stroke of genius that strikes like lightning; it is a meticulous discovery process. This process begins with a deep dive into customer discovery, as described in Steve Blank's 'The Four Steps to the Epiphany.' Understanding our customers, their problems, preferences, and buying behavior was not just about creating a product but about crafting a solution that resonated deeply with them.

When I embarked on this journey, it was like a treasure hunt. There were two crucial stages to this treasure hunt: The first leg of my trip was about asking fundamental questions. Is this a problem? We had to confirm if the issues we thought our prospective clients were experiencing were their own. This process involved extensive market research, conducting interviews, and analyzing industry trends. I attended online conferences, joined webinars, and networked with industry experts using LinkedIn to gather insights. I also immersed myself in the world of our potential customers, understanding their day-to-day challenges and workflows. The journey to understand the ESG landscape felt like piecing together a massive, global puzzle. Every piece was critical; missing even one could derail our entire strategy.

The next question was, is this the solution? I had to determine if the proposed solution addressed these issues effectively. Over the next three months, I immersed myself in an iterative strategy formulation and refinement process. I deeply dove into the complex and dynamic world of ESG (Environmental, Social, and Governance) regulations and software strategy. I started by understanding the various ESG regulations worldwide, highlighting their evolution and impact on organizations. Then, I spent time assessing the strategic direction to meet these regulations and the capabilities required to comply, using a framework based on the breadth of requirements and pressure to act. Following this, a detailed analysis of select ESG software vendors in the market, evaluating their strengths and weaknesses, was carried out to develop an initial roadmap designed to fit our customer value proposition, ensuring that our ESG management application meets the market's needs.

This period was about experimenting, gathering feedback, and refining our approach. We spoke to industry experts, potential customers, and early adopters, constantly iterating on our North Star vision and value proposition to better meet their needs. I will leverage the subsequent chapters to walk you through the various aspects of strategy identification, strategy selection, strategy implementation, and policy identification that I derived from the activity.

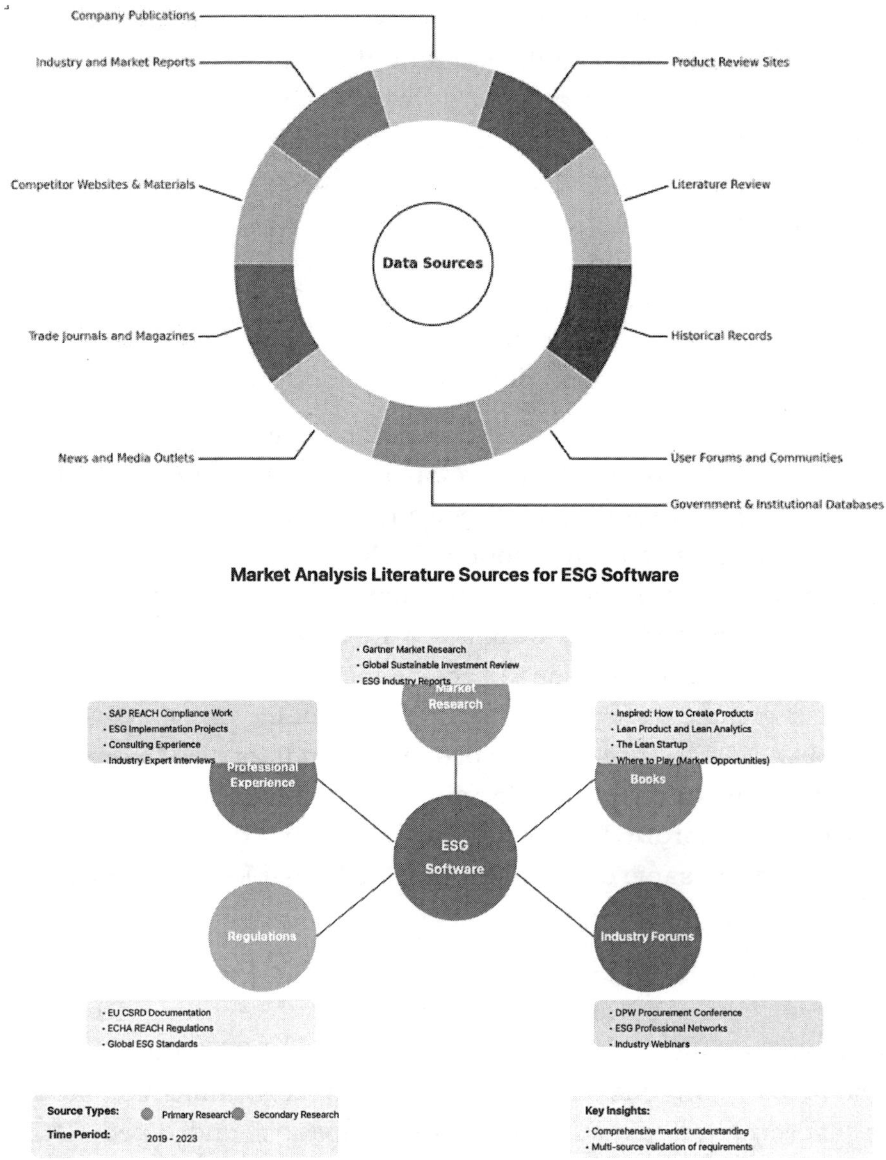

Figure 2.1 Different sources of market analysis literature used for assessment

Understanding the ESG Landscape

The first step is understanding a fundamental question: Are we solving a real problem? Determining whether our potential customers genuinely experience the issues we perceive is vital to this process. It's about understanding the market pain points and identifying the specific customers who experience these issues. The journey started with extensive market research. We immersed ourselves in ESG compliance, studying industry reports, regulatory requirements, and market trends. But data alone wasn't enough. We needed to get close to our potential customers and walk a mile in their shoes. Achieving this required conducting in-depth interviews, surveys, and focus groups with compliance managers, sustainability officers, and data experts.

In the early days of ESG, companies voluntarily reported their sustainability efforts to enhance their reputation and meet the growing expectations of socially conscious investors and consumers. This voluntary approach allowed companies to choose the metrics and standards they wanted to follow, leading to a lack of consistency and comparability in ESG reporting. However, as the impacts of climate change became increasingly evident and the need for greater transparency and accountability grew, regulatory bodies worldwide began to implement mandatory ESG reporting requirements to ensure uniformity and comparability. This shift aimed to standardize ESG disclosures, ensuring that all companies adhered to the same criteria and provided reliable and comparable data.

The first ESG regulation I looked into was CSRD, the European Union's Corporate Sustainability Reporting Directive (CSRD). Promulgated in 2020 and enacted in 2022, this directive demanded comprehensive disclosures on environmental, social, and governance factors from large companies and listed SMEs across the E.U. Only after introducing CSRD did companies start embarking on a mandatory reporting path. The level of detail required was staggering, covering everything from sustainability risks to opportunities, and it impacted the entire European Union. The CSRD requires companies to report approximately 1,178 data points across the 12 ESRS standards. Interestingly, about half of these data points (612) focus on ESRS 2, ESRS E1, and ESRS S1 standards. What's more, around 72% of the CSRD information is narrative. About 22% of the data points are voluntary and depend on the materiality assessment.

Next, I turned my attention to the United States, where the SEC's ESG Disclosure Proposal was gaining traction. Announced in 2021 and expected to come into force by 2024, this regulation targeted public companies listed on US stock exchanges. It mandated detailed disclosures on climate-related risks, governance structures, and the impacts on business operations. The impending changes signaled a significant shift in how American companies would need to operate, focusing more heavily on transparency and sustainability. Much like CSRD, many of the SEC's requirements are narrative – about 70% of the information reported is detailed narratives. Additionally, some disclosures are voluntary and depend on the company's specific materiality assessment, which makes up roughly 20% of the total data points.

The Task Force on Climate-related Financial Disclosures (TCFD) was already making waves in the United Kingdom. Since its promulgation in 2017 and enforcement in 2021, it required large companies and financial institutions to report on climate-related financial risks and opportunities. The UK's proactive stance on ESG was evident and provided a blueprint for other regions. There are numerous data points to report on, focusing on areas like governance, strategy, risk management, and metrics and targets. Much of this information is narrative – about 70% of the disclosures involve detailed descriptions and explanations. Around 20% of the TCFD requirements are voluntary and depend on the company's materiality assessment.

Japan's Corporate Governance Code, promulgated in 2015 and enacted in 2018, encouraged listed companies to integrate ESG information into their governance practices. This regulation highlighted Japan's commitment to sustainable corporate governance, influencing companies to adopt more transparent and responsible practices. Key focus areas include board composition, shareholder rights, and transparency in financial and non-financial disclosures. Of these, a significant portion is narrative – around 65% of the disclosures involve detailed descriptions and explanations. Additionally, about 25% of the data points are voluntary and depend on the company's assessments and circumstances, such as materiality assessments and stakeholder engagement practices.

Australia, too, was stepping up its game. The ASX Corporate governance principles, last revised in 2020, recommended that companies listed on the Australian Securities Exchange disclose their ESG risks and governance practices. Australia's approach was more advisory than mandatory, but it reflected a growing recognition of the importance of ESG transparency. A significant portion of these data points – about 70% – are narrative, requiring detailed descriptions and explanations. Additionally, around 20% of the data points are voluntary, based on the company's specific materiality assessments and circumstances. These guidelines promote transparency, accountability, and responsible business practices among ASX-listed companies.

A Global Mosaic: Summary of Key ESG Regulations

1. Global Regulations:

    - **GRI (Global Reporting Initiative):** Established in 1997, this initiative provides standards for sustainability reporting. A critical requirement is comprehensive sustainability reporting on environmental, social, and governance impacts. The central IT challenge is integrating data from multiple sources to ensure accuracy. The reports need to follow GRI standards, and the data typically comes from internal company records, environmental monitors, and HR systems. A market gap exists in the integration and standardization of diverse data sources.

    - **SASB (Sustainability Accounting Standards Board):** Since 2011, it has focused on disclosing information on financial material sustainability specific to industries. The challenge is aligning financial and non-financial data. Reports must be industry-specific, with data sourced from financial and operational systems. There is a gap in customization for industry-specific metrics.

2. European Union:

   - **NFRD (Non-Financial Reporting Directive):** Enforced since 2014, the directive requires large entities to report on environmental, social, employee, human rights, anti-corruption, and diversity matters. The challenge is standardizing non-financial data. Reports cover a variety of non-financial factors, using data from internal records and supply chains. Better standardization and comprehensive coverage of non-financial data are needed.
   - **CSRD (Corporate Sustainability Reporting Directive):** Effective 2021, this directive expands on the NFRD and includes more companies and detailed reporting standards. It demands detailed sustainability reporting, which challenges meeting the expanded scope and ensuring consistency. The gap here is in scalability and audit readiness for detailed reporting.
   - **E.U. Taxonomy Regulation:** Introduced in 2020, it classifies sustainable economic activities. Companies must align their business activities with taxonomy criteria, which is challenging. Reports must be taxonomy-aligned, using financial and operational data. Detailed activity classification is a market gap.

3. United Kingdom

   - **UK Modern Slavery Act:** Since 2015, it has mandated reporting on steps to prevent slavery and trafficking in operations and supply chains. The main challenge is collecting supply chain data transparently. Reports must detail actions taken, sourced from supply chain data and audits. Comprehensive supply chain transparency is needed.

- **SECR (Streamlined Energy and Carbon Reporting):** This system was implemented in 2019 and requires annual energy and carbon reporting. Accurate data collection on energy use and emissions is essential. Reports must cover energy use, emissions, efficiency measures, and data from energy meters and carbon tracking systems. A gap exists in the real-time integration of energy and carbon data.

4. United States

- The **Dodd-Frank Act,** which was passed in 2010, includes conflict minerals disclosure. The challenge is supply chain traceability. Reports need to detail sources and due diligence efforts, using data from supply chains and audits. Traceability and compliance verification for conflict minerals are gaps.
- **California Transparency in Supply Chains Act 13:** Since 2010, this act has required disclosure on efforts to eliminate slavery and trafficking. Transparent supply chain data collection is challenging. Reports must detail efforts sourced from supply chain data and audits. Detailed reporting on supply chain transparency is required.
- **GHGRP (Greenhouse Gas Reporting Program):** Since 2009, it has mandated reporting greenhouse gas emissions for significant sources. Accurate GHG data collection is a challenge. Reports cover emissions, using data from emission monitoring systems. However, real-time GHG tracking and detailed reporting are gaps.

5. Canada

- **CBCA (Canada Business Corporations Act):** Amended in 2019, it requires diversity and ESG factors disclosures. Collecting and standardizing diversity and ESG data is challenging. Reports cover diversity policies and ESG practices, with data from HR records and audits. There is a gap in the comprehensive diversity data integration of diversity data.

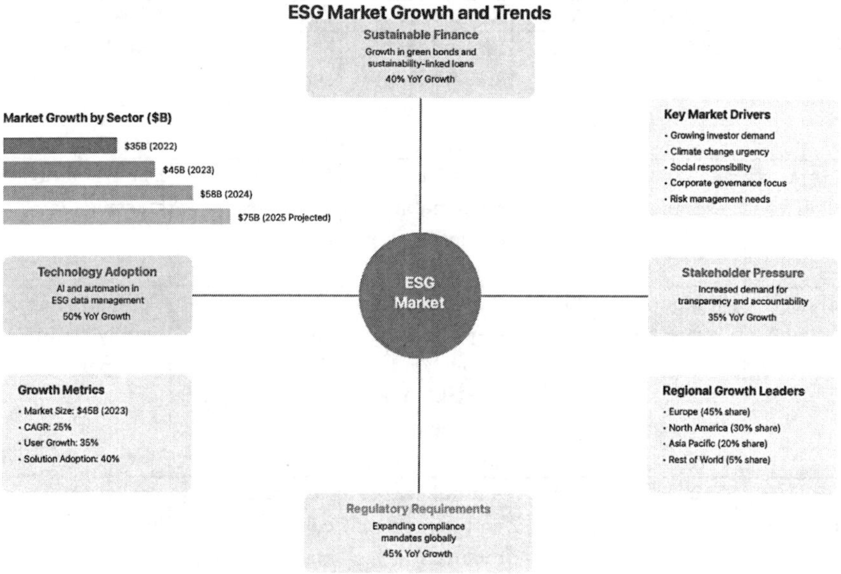

Table 2.1 Regulatory mosaic comparison across the world

Country	Regulation	Year	Key Focus	Key Challenge	Market Gap
Global	GRI	1997	Sustainability reporting on environmental, social, and governance impacts	Integrating data from multiple sources to ensure accuracy	Integration and standardization of diverse data sources
Global	SASB	2011	Industry-specific financial material sustainability disclosure	Aligning financial and non-financial data	Customization for industry-specific metrics
European Union	NFRD	2014	Reporting on environmental, social, employee, human rights, anti-corruption, and diversity matters	Standardizing non-financial data	Standardization and comprehensive coverage of non-financial data

(*Contd.*)

Country	Regulation	Year	Key Focus	Key Challenge	Market Gap
European Union	CSRD	2021	Expanded and detailed sustainability reporting	Meeting expanded scope and ensuring consistency	Scalability and audit readiness for detailed reporting
European Union	E.U. Taxonomy Regulation	2020	Classifying sustainable economic activities	Aligning business activities with taxonomy	Detailed activity classification
United Kingdom	UK Modern Slavery Act	2015	Reporting on steps to prevent slavery and trafficking in operations and supply chains	Collecting supply chain data transparently	Comprehensive supply chain transparency
United Kingdom	SECR	2019	Annual energy and carbon reporting	Accurate data collection on energy use and emissions	Real-time integration of energy and carbon data
United States	Dodd-Frank Act	2010	Conflict minerals disclosure	Supply chain traceability	Traceability and compliance verification for conflict minerals
United States	California Transparency in Supply Chains Act	2010	Disclosure of efforts to eliminate slavery and trafficking	Transparent supply chain data collection	Detailed reporting on supply chain transparency
United States	GHGRP	2009	Greenhouse gas emissions reporting	Accurate GHG data collection	Real-time GHG tracking and detailed reporting
Canada	CBCA	2019	Diversity and ESG factors disclosures	Collecting and standardizing diversity and ESG data	Comprehensive diversity data integration
Australia	Modern Slavery Act	2018	Annual reporting on modern slavery risks in operations and supply chains	Supply chain data collection	Effective risk management reporting

Country	Regulation	Year	Key Focus	Key Challenge	Market Gap
Japan	Corporate Governance Code	2015	Disclosure of ESG information, particularly climate risks	Aligning governance data with ESG metrics	Alignment of management and climate risk data
China	Green Finance Guidelines	2018	Environmental information disclosure	Collecting and standardizing environmental data	Integration of ecological data with finance criteria
India	BRSR	2021	ESG reporting for top-listed companies	Comprehensive ESG data collection	Consistent ESG reporting
Brazil	Instruction CVM 480	2009	Disclosure of ESG practices for listed companies	Standardizing ESG data collection	Standardization and integration of ESG data
South Africa	King IV Code	2016	Integrated reporting on governance and ESG performance	Integrating financial and non-financial data	Comprehensive data integration for reporting

6. Australia

    - **Modern Slavery Act:** Since 2018, it has mandated annual reporting on modern slavery risks in operations and supply chains. Supply chain data collection is challenging. Reports must describe risks and mitigation efforts based on supply chain data and audits. Effective risk management reporting is needed.

7. Japan

    - **Corporate Governance Code:** Since 2015, it has encouraged disclosure of ESG information, particularly climate risks. Aligning governance data with ESG metrics is challenging. Reports cover governance and ESG information using data from governance records and climate assessments. However, there is a gap in the alignment of management and climate risk data.

8. China

    - **Green Finance Guidelines:** Since 2018, they have encouraged environmental information disclosure. Collecting and standardizing environmental data is challenging. Reports cover environmental impacts and green finance initiatives, using data from monitoring systems and financial records. However, there is a gap in integrating ecological data with finance criteria.

9. India

    - **BRSR (Business Responsibility and Sustainability Report):** Introduced in 2021, it mandates ESG reporting for top-listed companies. Comprehensive ESG data collection is challenging. Reports detail environmental, social, and governance performance, with data from internal assessments. Consistent ESG reporting is needed.

10. Brazil

    - **Instruction CVM 480:** Since 2009, Brazil has required disclosure of ESG practices for listed companies. Standardizing ESG data collection is challenging. Reports cover ESG practices and outcomes using data from internal records and audits. However, there are gaps in the standardization and integration of ESG data.

11. South Africa

    - **King IV Code**: Effective 2016, it promotes integrated reporting on governance and ESG performance. Integrating financial and non-financial data is challenging. Reports cover governance, strategy, and ESG performance, with data from internal records and assessments. Comprehensive data integration for reporting is needed.

Market Growth and Size

The global ESG market has taken off recently. It's incredible to see how much awareness around sustainability has grown. People are starting to care more about these issues, putting pressure on regulations and sparking demand from investors who want to put their money into responsible ventures. I came across this fascinating stat from the Global Sustainable Investment Review (GSIR): sustainable investing assets hit a whopping $35.3 trillion in 2020! That's 36% of all professionally managed assets across the big markets. This shift highlights how vital sustainability has become these days.

Key Trends in the ESG Market:

1. Integration of ESG Factors into Investment Decisions.
    - Report: Sustainable Investing: Resilience Amid Uncertainty (Morningstar)
    - Insight: Investors are increasingly integrating ESG factors into their decision-making processes to identify long-term risks and opportunities. This trend is driven by the recognition that ESG factors can significantly impact financial performance and risk management.
2. Regulatory Developments and Reporting Requirements
    - Report: The Road Ahead: The KPMG Survey of Corporate Responsibility Reporting
    - Insight: Governments and regulatory bodies worldwide are introducing new ESG reporting requirements, leading to greater corporate transparency and accountability. For example, the European Union's Corporate Sustainability Reporting Directive (CSRD) mandates comprehensive ESG disclosures from large companies.
3. Growth of Sustainable Finance
    - Report: Sustainable Finance Report (World Economic Forum)
    - Insight: Sustainable finance is gaining momentum, with many financial institutions incorporating ESG criteria into their lending and investment practices. Green bonds, social

bonds, and sustainability-linked loans are examples of financial instruments supporting ESG initiatives.

4. Corporate ESG Performance and Disclosure
   - Report: State of Green Business Report (GreenBiz)
   - Insight: Companies are enhancing their ESG performance and disclosure practices to meet stakeholder expectations and regulatory requirements. The report highlights improvements in areas such as carbon emissions reduction, diversity and inclusion, and supply chain sustainability.
5. Impact Investing
   - Report: Global Impact Investing Network (GIIN) Annual Impact Investor Survey
   - Insight: Impact investing proliferates, aiming to generate positive social and environmental impact alongside financial returns. The survey reveals that impact investors focus on renewable energy, healthcare, and education sectors.
6. Advancements in ESG Data and Analytics

   Report: The Future of ESG Data (JP Morgan)
   - Insight: The availability and quality of ESG data are improving, enabling better analysis and decision-making. Technological advancements, such as artificial intelligence and machine learning, enhance the ability to assess ESG risks and opportunities.
7. Stakeholder Pressure and Corporate Accountability
   - Report: Sustainable Signals: Asset Owners Embrace Sustainability (Morgan Stanley)
   - Insight: Stakeholders, including investors, customers, and employees, pressure companies to adopt sustainable practices. This pressure leads to greater corporate accountability and a shift toward more responsible business models.

8. Sectoral and Regional Variations
   - Report: Global ESG Benchmark for Real Assets (GRESB) Reports
   - Insight: ESG performance and priorities vary across sectors and regions. For example, the real estate sector focuses on energy efficiency and green building certifications, while the financial industry emphasizes ESG risk management in lending and investment.

Direction of the ESG Market:

Experts expect the ESG market to continue growing, with several vital directions emerging:

1. Standardization and Harmonization of ESG Reporting.
   - Efforts to standardize ESG reporting frameworks are intensifying, with initiatives such as the International Financial Reporting Standards (IFRS) Foundation's work on global sustainability standards. Enhancing the comparability and reliability of ESG data will be the result.

Table 2.2 Key Trends, Direction, and Opportunities in the ESG Market

Trend	**Direction**	**Opportunity**
Standardization and Harmonization of ESG Reporting	Inward toward consistent global standards	It enhanced the comparability and reliability of ESG data across global markets.
Integration of Climate Risk into Financial Regulation	Inward toward integrating climate risk into financial reporting	It improved financial risk management by incorporating climate considerations
Expansion of ESG Investing in Emerging Markets	Companies are turning inward toward expanding ESG investments, particularly in emerging markets	There are new investment opportunities in sectors like renewable energy and sustainable agriculture

(Contd.)

Trend	Direction	Opportunity
Technological Innovation and ESG Solutions	Inward toward leveraging advanced technologies for better ESG reporting	It has increased efficiency and transparency in ESG reporting and supply chain tracking
Focus on Social and Governance Issues	Inward, toward emphasizing social and governance factors	A holistic approach to sustainability, focusing on human rights and governance, is becoming increasingly important

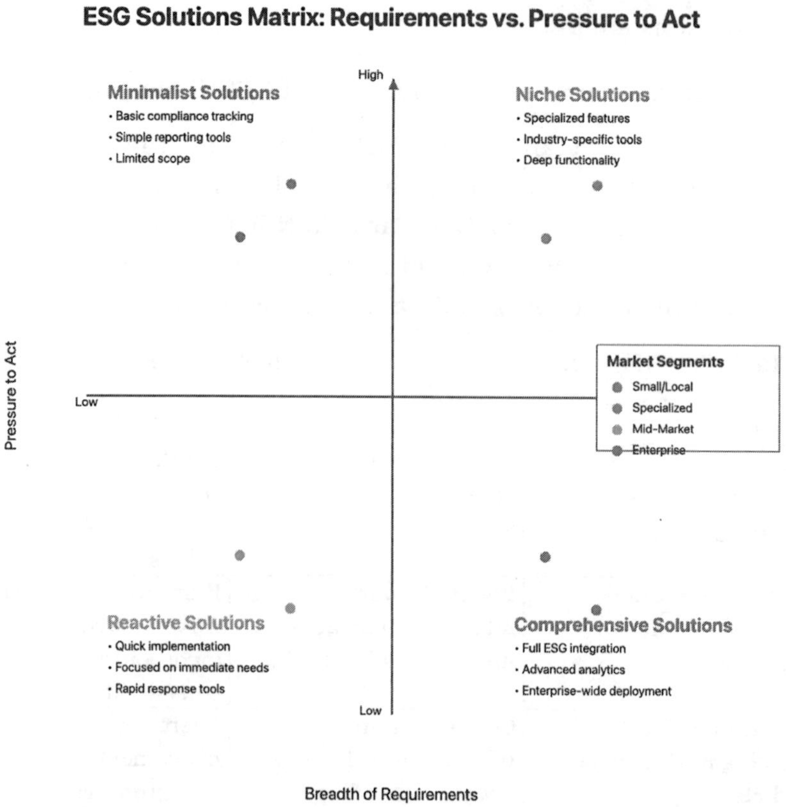

Figure 2.2 Requirements and pressure to act - ESG solutions matrix

2. Integration of Climate Risk into Financial Regulation
   - Regulators are increasingly recognizing the financial risks posed by climate change. The Task Force on Climate-related Financial Disclosures (TCFD) framework is becoming a benchmark for climate risk reporting, influencing regulatory policies worldwide.
3. Expansion of ESG Investing in Emerging Markets
   - Emerging markets are becoming significant players in the ESG space. As ESG awareness and regulatory frameworks develop in these regions, investment opportunities are expanding, particularly in renewable energy and sustainable agriculture.
4. Technological Innovation and ESG Solutions
   - Technology is crucial in advancing ESG practices. Innovations in data analytics, blockchain, and IoT enable more efficient and transparent ESG reporting and better tracking of supply chain sustainability.
5. Focus on Social and Governance Issues

   While environmental issues have dominated the ESG agenda, there is a growing emphasis on social and governance factors. Topics such as human rights, labor practices, and corporate governance are gaining prominence in ESG assessments and strategies.

Table 2.2 visually represent the converging trends in ESG reporting and regulation centered around 'ESG Management.' Key trends include the standardization of ESG reporting, driven by global standards like those from the IFRS Foundation, and the integration of climate risk into financial regulations, heavily influenced by the TCFD framework. Emerging markets are also becoming significant players in the ESG space, offering new investment opportunities, particularly in renewable energy. Technological innovations such as data analytics, blockchain, and IoT revolutionize ESG reporting and supply chain tracking. Additionally, there is an increasing focus on social and governance issues, reflecting a more holistic approach to sustainability.

Unveiling the ESG Market

With a comprehensive understanding of the regulatory landscape, I began to map out the ESG market and its key segments. It was like watching a fog lift, revealing a vast and dynamic terrain. The global ESG market was booming. Experts value the market at approximately $30 billion in 2020 and project it will soar to $50 billion by 2025. Increasing regulatory requirements and a surging demand from investors for sustainable practices drove this growth. The market's expansion was not just a trend but a seismic shift in how businesses operated and investors allocated capital.

Let's talk about the different players in the ESG market and what they're up to. It's a diverse group, and each segment has unique challenges and needs. First, we have large enterprises. These multinational corporations have the resources to dedicate to ESG initiatives. They need comprehensive, integrated ESG management solutions to handle complex reporting requirements. But it's not all smooth sailing. These big companies often need help to navigate diverse regulatory environments and integrate ESG into their corporate strategies.

Then there are small to mid-sized enterprises (SMEs). These often need more resources than their larger counterparts, but they feel pressure to enhance their ESG performance. They need affordable, user-friendly tools that simplify compliance and reporting. Their biggest challenge? Limited budgets and expertise in ESG are significant challenges. It's a tough spot, but many SMEs are finding innovative ways to meet these demands.

Next, we have financial institutions—banks, asset managers, and insurance companies. This segment increasingly focuses on ESG data and analytics to inform investment decisions and manage risks. They need tools that ensure data accuracy and help integrate ESG factors into financial models. However, the challenge lies in consistently guaranteeing reliable and effectively integrated data.

Let's remember the public sector and NGOs. Government agencies and non-governmental organizations are crucial in promoting ESG compliance and sustainability initiatives. They need robust tools for monitoring and promoting ESG compliance. Their challenges are significant, too: They must deal with diverse stakeholder needs and often have limited funding.

Each segment navigates the ESG landscape, and the dynamics are continuously evolving. Understanding their unique needs and challenges helps paint a clearer picture of the ESG market. It is fascinating to see how each player contributes to the bigger picture of sustainability and responsible governance.

The ESG market is dynamic and rapidly evolving, driven by regulatory developments, investor demand, and technological advancements. Companies and investors recognize the importance of integrating ESG considerations into their strategies to mitigate risks, capitalize on opportunities, and contribute to a more sustainable future. As we move forward, the standardization of reporting, the incorporation of climate risk into financial regulation, and the expansion of ESG investing in emerging markets will shape the future of the ESG landscape.

Emerging Trends and Drivers of Growth in ESG

The journey of developing ESG management software involved understanding the present landscape, anticipating future trends, and identifying growth drivers. The dynamic nature of the ESG market made this both challenging and exhilarating. Here's how I navigated these emerging trends and growth drivers, turning insights into strategic opportunities.

One of the most significant trends I uncovered was the increasing integration of ESG factors into investment decisions. According to Morningstar's Sustainable Investing: Resilience Amid Uncertainty report, investors were no longer content with just financial returns; they wanted their investments to reflect their values and contribute positively to society and the environment.

Table 2.3 Emerging Trends, Key Insights and Growth Drivers for ESG

Emerging Trend	**Key Insight**	**Growth Driver**
Integration of ESG Factors into Investment Decisions	Investors increasingly incorporate ESG criteria into decision-making, recognizing its impact on financial performance	There is a growing recognition of ESG's influence on financial returns
Regulatory Developments and Reporting Requirements	New regulations require companies to enhance transparency, increasing demand for robust ESG management tools	They are facing increasing regulatory requirements globally
Growth of Sustainable Finance,	Sustainable finance is growing, with green bonds and sustainability-linked loans becoming mainstream	The financial sector is increasingly embracing ESG principles
Corporate ESG Performance and Disclosure	Companies are improving ESG performance and disclosure, driving demand for sophisticated management tools	ESG has become strategically crucial in shaping corporate behavior
Impact Investing	Impact investors seek investments that generate positive social and environmental impacts, creating new opportunities	The rising popularity of investments aligning with profit with purpose reshapes the market

Emerging Trend	Key Insight	Growth Driver
Advancements in ESG Data and Analytics	Technological advancements in AI and data analytics enhance the ability to assess ESG risks and opportunities	Technology is enhancing data accessibility and actionability, making it more effective for decision-making
Stakeholder Pressure and Corporate Accountability	Stakeholders demand more sustainable business practices, pushing companies to integrate ESG principles	They are intensifying pressure from stakeholders for sustainability
Sectoral and Regional Variations	ESG performance varies by sector and region, with tailored solutions needed to address specific challenges	Regional and sectoral differences are the development of tailored ESG solutions

I recall reading about how large asset managers, representing trillions of dollars in assets, incorporated ESG criteria into their investment processes. This wasn't just a fad; it marked a fundamental change. Companies began using ESG principles to identify long-term risks and opportunities, ultimately impacting investment decisions on a massive scale. The growing recognition that ESG factors could significantly influence financial performance and risk management drove this trend.

Regulatory Developments and Reporting Requirements

Another powerful growth driver was the wave of regulatory developments sweeping across the globe. The Road Ahead: The KPMG Survey of Corporate Responsibility Reporting provided a detailed analysis of these changes. Governments and regulatory bodies were introducing new ESG reporting requirements, compelling companies to enhance transparency and accountability.

The European Union's CSRD, the United States SEC ESG Disclosure Proposal, and the UK's TCFD were just a few examples. These regulations increased the burden of compliance and elevated the importance of ESG in corporate strategy. Companies had to disclose detailed information on their ESG practices, risks, and impacts, which meant robust ESG management tools were in high demand.

Growth of Sustainable Finance

Another trend that caught my attention was the rise of sustainable finance. The World Economic Forum's Sustainable Finance Report highlighted how financial institutions increasingly adopted ESG criteria. Green bonds, social bonds, and sustainability-linked loans were becoming mainstream, providing new avenues for financing ESG initiatives.

I was particularly intrigued by how banks and asset managers used ESG data to inform their lending and investment decisions. This shift toward sustainable finance was about being ethical and recognizing that ESG factors could affect creditworthiness and investment returns. The financial sector's embrace of ESG principles was a powerful driver of market growth.

Corporate ESG Performance and Disclosure

Corporate behavior was also changing. The State of Green Business Report by GreenBiz revealed that companies were making significant strides in improving their ESG performance and disclosure practices. From reducing carbon emissions to enhancing diversity and inclusion, businesses took concrete steps to meet stakeholder expectations and comply with regulatory demands. I remember reading about a major corporation that had slashed its carbon footprint by 50% in five years, becoming a benchmark for others. Such stories were not isolated; they reflected a broader trend of companies recognizing the strategic importance of ESG and investing in sustainable practices. This shift created a ripple effect, driving demand for sophisticated ESG management tools.

Impact Investing

Impact investing was another trend that stood out. The Global Impact Investing Network (GIIN) Annual Impact Investor Survey provided a wealth of data on this growing field. Impact investors were not just looking for financial returns; they wanted their investments to generate positive social and environmental impacts.

I was fascinated by the stories of investors funding renewable energy projects, healthcare initiatives, and educational programs in underserved communities. Impact investing was bridging the gap between profitability and purpose, attracting new investors who believed their capital could drive meaningful change. This trend created new opportunities for ESG management solutions tailored to impact measurement and reporting.

Advancements in ESG Data and Analytics

Technological advancements were also crucial. JP Morgan's Future of ESG Data report underscored improved ESG data quality and availability. Innovations in data analytics, artificial intelligence, and machine learning enhanced the ability to assess ESG risks and opportunities.

I recall a conversation with a data scientist who explained how their team used AI to analyze vast amounts of ESG data, providing unimaginable insights. These technological innovations made ESG data not only more accessible but also more actionable, enabling better decision-making for both companies and investors.

Stakeholder Pressure and Corporate Accountability

The Sustainable Signals: Asset Owners Embrace Sustainability report by Morgan Stanley highlighted the growing pressure from stakeholders. Investors, customers, employees, and regulators demanded more sustainable and responsible business practices. This pressure pushed companies to be more accountable and transparent, driving further integration of ESG principles into their operations.

I remember a meeting with a corporate client who shared how their employees advocated for more substantial ESG commitments. This internal pressure and external demands from investors and customers created a powerful impetus for change. Companies realized that embracing ESG was not just good for their reputation; it was essential for their long-term success.

Sectoral and Regional Variations

The Global ESG Benchmark for Real Assets (GRESB) Reports provided insights into how ESG performance varied across sectors and regions. For instance, the real estate sector focused on energy efficiency and green building certifications, while the financial industry emphasized ESG risk management.

The regional differences also struck me. Europe was leading the charge with stringent regulations and high levels of ESG integration, while emerging markets were beginning to catch up, driven by regulatory developments and investor interest. These variations underscored the need for tailored ESG solutions that could address specific regional and sectoral challenges.

The ESG market is dynamic and rapidly evolving, driven by regulatory developments, investor demand, and technological advancements. Companies and investors recognize the importance of integrating ESG considerations into their strategies to mitigate risks, capitalize on opportunities, and contribute to a more sustainable future. As we move forward, the standardization of reporting, the incorporation of climate risk into financial regulation, and the expansion of ESG investing in emerging markets will shape the future of the ESG landscape.

A Summary of ESG Ratings and Rating Agencies

When it comes to evaluating a company's environmental, social, and governance (ESG) performance, there are a few big names in the game that you should know about. These ratings help investors, regulators, and stakeholders understand companies' performance in these critical areas. First up, we have MSCI ESG Ratings. They're thorough in analyzing how companies handle ESG risks and opportunities. Imagine a report card where companies get grades from AAA to CCC based on how well they manage industry-specific ESG risks. This platform is a go-to resource for institutional investors, with thousands of users relying on it to make intelligent, responsible investment choices.

Then there's Sustainalytics, which focuses on ESG risk ratings. They review over 10,000 companies and rate them on how much ESG risk they have yet to manage. Companies are labeled anywhere from negligible to severe risk. If you're an investor trying to dodge risky bets, Sustainalytics, which many financial institutions use, is super helpful.

FTSE Russell offers another layer of insights with its ESG ratings and data models. It covers around 7,200 companies and scores them from 0 to 5 across 14 ESG themes. Asset managers and financial institutions often rely on these ratings to build and assess their portfolios, making it a vital tool for a broad user base.

Moody's ESG Solutions, famous for credit ratings, also investigates ESG scores. They blend ESG factors into their credit ratings and offer standalone ESG scores. Credit analysts and investors use this tool to understand how ESG issues might impact financial health across the financial sector.

S&P Global is also in the mix, rating companies on a scale from 0 to 100 based on their ESG practices. They cover a wide range of companies—over 7,300! These scores help investors and analysts benchmark and compare how thriving companies are doing on the ESG front, serving many users globally.

Last but not least, we have ISS ESG. They focus on corporate governance and provide a numerical score from 1 to 10 based on crucial ESG factors. Institutional investors and corporate boards often use these insights to guide their decisions and improve their governance practices, making it a vital resource for many corporate users.

So, what's trending in the ESG rating world? Well, these ratings are becoming more critical than ever. Investors are starting to care about how companies manage ESG issues. There's also a big push to make these ratings more standardized and transparent so everyone's on the same page. But it's not all smooth sailing. Rating agencies have different ways of scoring things, which can be confusing. Getting accurate data—especially from smaller companies—can be tricky. And let's not forget that the regulations around ESG reporting are constantly evolving, which keeps everyone on their toes. Many studies highlight the role of ESG indicators in motivating organizations to set and prioritize sustainability goals. These indicators influence the effort companies put into achieving specific outcomes. However, there's a catch: the abundance and complexity of these indicators can make it hard to assess organizational performance consistently.

Summary of Selected ESG Rating Agencies

One significant finding is that ESG indicators are less specific in governance than environmental and social domains. This lack of specificity can make it harder for organizations to adopt a holistic approach to sustainability. The researchers examined ratings, rankings, and indexes from 130 rating agencies, identifying and categorizing 237 unique ESG indicators. They found that most rating agencies focus primarily on investors, influencing the type of information provided and the priorities highlighted.

Interestingly, the study reveals that while ESG ratings aim to assess corporate performance, they often need to catch up in encouraging organizations to integrate sustainability into their core strategies genuinely. Instead, companies might focus more on meeting external expectations rather than pursuing meaningful internal goals. The research suggests that for ESG indicators to be truly effective, they must be more balanced and transparent, providing more explicit guidance on what businesses need to improve. By doing so, rating agencies can better support organizations in achieving sustainable development goals.

In conclusion, while ESG indicators have the potential to drive positive change, greater clarity and balance in how they are defined and applied are needed. Aligning strategies more closely with sustainability goals will help businesses foster genuine and integrated corporate social responsibility efforts.

Chapter 3

Customer Segmentation and Targeting

With a thorough understanding of the ESG landscape, I was ready to dive into market research and analysis. This phase was crucial for identifying unmet needs and gaps in the market. The goal was to turn these insights into strategic opportunities that would guide the development of our ESG management software. Armed with the knowledge of ESG regulations and trends, I journeyed to map out the market. I started by gathering data from various sources, including industry reports, market surveys, and stakeholder interviews.

As I delved deeper into the data, patterns began to emerge. As ESG investing grew significantly, experts recognized that they needed to fully address several unmet needs and gaps to unlock the market's potential. Here are some key findings:

1. Complexity and Fragmentation of ESG Data
    - Insight: One of the most significant challenges faced by companies and investors was the complexity and fragmentation of ESG data. Different standards, metrics, and reporting frameworks made comparing and aggregating data difficult.
    - Unmet Need: There was a clear need for standardized, reliable, and easily accessible ESG data. Companies required

tools that could streamline data collection, integration, and reporting.

2. Lack of ESG Expertise in SMEs
    - Insight: Small to mid-sized enterprises (SMEs) often lacked the expertise and resources to implement robust ESG practices. Unlike large corporations, SMEs did not have dedicated sustainability teams or the budget to hire external consultants.
    - Unmet Need: Affordable, user-friendly ESG management solutions tailored to the needs of SMEs were in high demand. These tools are needed to simplify compliance and reporting without requiring extensive expertise.
3. ESG Integration in Investment Decisions
    - Insight: While many investors were integrating ESG factors into their decision-making processes, they needed better tools to assess and manage ESG risks and opportunities. Financial institutions require sophisticated analytics and data integration capabilities.
    - Unmet Need: The investment community needed advanced ESG analytics and risk management tools that could seamlessly integrate with existing financial models and platforms.
4. Transparency and Accountability in Supply Chains
    - Insight: Companies faced increasing pressure to ensure transparency and accountability in their supply chains. This challenge was particularly significant for sectors with complex, global supply chains, such as manufacturing and retail.
    - Unmet Need: Solutions that provided end-to-end visibility and traceability in supply chains, enabling companies to monitor and report ESG performance at every stage, were critically needed.

5. Employee and Stakeholder Engagement
   - Insight: Many organizations faced the challenge of engaging employees and other stakeholders in ESG initiatives. Effective communication and involvement were necessary to drive meaningful change and foster a culture of sustainability.
   - Unmet Need: Platforms facilitating stakeholder engagement, education, and collaboration on ESG initiatives were in demand. To ensure broad participation, these tools needed to be interactive and accessible.

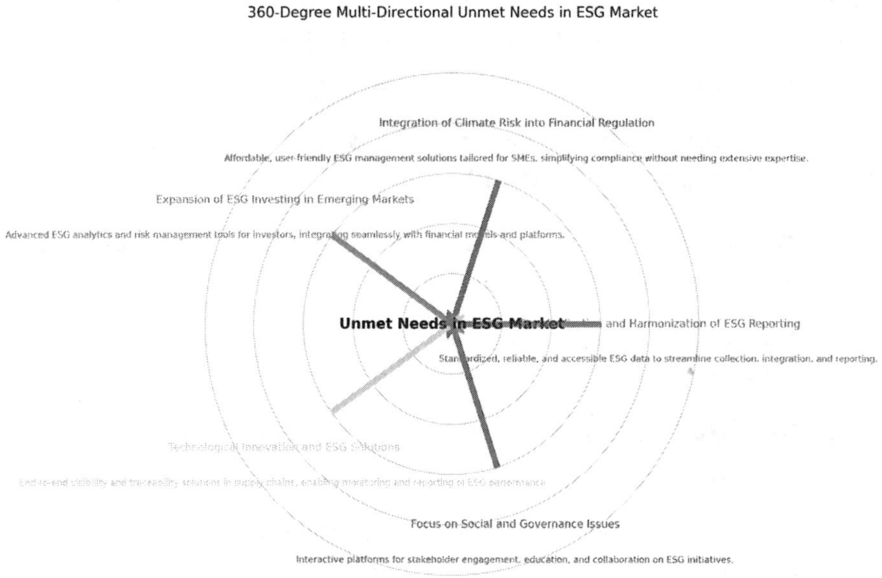

Figure 3.1 360 Visualization of Multi-directional Unmet Needs in the ESG Market

The Four-Quadrant Analysis - Breadth of Requirements vs Pressure to Act

In the rapidly evolving field of ESG management, selecting the right software solution is crucial for meeting regulatory requirements and achieving sustainability goals. To guide our decision-making process, we thoroughly assessed ESG software needs, evaluating them based on two critical dimensions: the breadth of requirements and the pressure to act. Plotting these dimensions in a four-quadrant matrix gave us valuable insights into how different solutions align with our needs and strategic priorities.

The breadth of requirements refers to the comprehensive nature of ESG criteria that a software solution must address, including capabilities such as data collection, analysis, reporting, and compliance with various regulatory frameworks. On the other hand, the pressure to act represents the urgency and external pressures organizations face to implement effective ESG practices, driven by factors like regulatory deadlines, stakeholder expectations, and competitive pressures.

By analyzing software capabilities within this framework, we identified four distinct quadrants:

1. **Minimalist Solutions**: Low breadth of requirements and low pressure to act.
2. **Niche Solutions**: High breadth of requirements and low pressure to act.
3. **Reactive Solutions**: Low breadth of requirements and high pressure to act.
4. **Comprehensive Solutions**: High breadth of requirements and high pressure to act.

Scenario 1: High Pressure to Act, Broad Requirements

Imagine you're under immense pressure to act on ESG initiatives. Investors, regulators, and customers are watching. The requirements are diverse and expansive. It would be best to have a software solution like a Swiss Army knife, handling everything from detailed reporting and compliance to sophisticated data analytics and stakeholder engagement.

Key Software Capabilities:

- **Comprehensive Data Integration:** The ability to pull data from various sources, including IoT sensors, supply chains, and financial systems.
- **Advanced Analytics:** Tools for in-depth data analysis, predictive modeling, and trend identification.
- **Detailed Reporting:** Extensive reporting capabilities to meet regulatory and stakeholder requirements.
- **Compliance Tracking:** Real-time monitoring and alerts for compliance with multiple standards and regulations.
- **Stakeholder Management:** Tools to engage and communicate with stakeholders, including investors, regulators, and customers.

Scenario 2: High Pressure to Act, Narrow Requirements

In this scenario, the pressure to act is intense, but the scope of what you must address is more focused than in broader, less urgent situations. Imagine spotlighting a few critical areas—maybe carbon emissions and supply chain ethics. It would be best to have specialized software that excels in these vital areas.

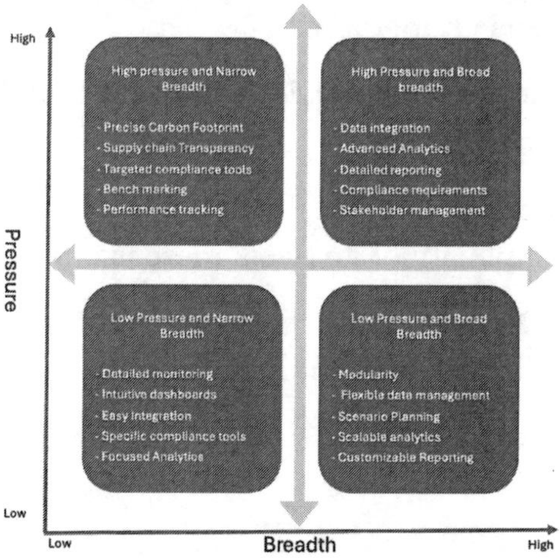

Figure 3.2 Visualization of Pressure to Act

Key Software Capabilities:

- **Precise Carbon Footprint Calculation:** Detailed tracking and reporting of carbon emissions across various operations.
- **Supply Chain Transparency Tools:** Capabilities to trace, monitor, and report on supply chain activities and ethics.
- **Targeted Compliance Modules:** Specialized compliance tools tailored to specific regulations relevant to your focused areas.
- **Benchmarking and Performance Tracking:** Tools to measure and compare performance against industry standards and best practices.

Scenario 3: Low Pressure to Act, Broad Requirements

The urgency is low, but the requirements range still needs improvement. You have time to contemplate your ESG strategy and build a comprehensive approach. Your software should be versatile and future-proof, able to grow and adapt as your ESG initiatives evolve.

Key Software Capabilities:

- **Modular Capabilities:** Flexible modules that can be added or removed as needs change.
- **Flexible Data Management:** Systems that handle various data types and sources.
- **Scalable Analytics:** Analytics that can scale up as the volume of data and complexity of analysis increases.
- **Customizable Reporting:** Reporting tools that can be tailored to different audiences and changing requirements.
- **Scenario Planning:** Tools for simulating different ESG scenarios and outcomes.

Scenario 4: Low Pressure to Act, Narrow Requirements

Finally, picture a situation where the pressure is low, and the requirements are specific. You're not in a rush and have a clear focus on a few key areas. The software you choose should be highly effective in these domains without overwhelming you with unnecessary features.

Key Software Capabilities:

- **Detailed Monitoring and Reporting:** Focused tools that provide in-depth insights into specific areas of interest.
- **Intuitive Dashboards:** Easy-to-use interfaces that visualize key metrics and data.
- **Easy Integration:** Seamless integration with existing systems and workflows.
- **Specific Compliance Tools:** Targeted compliance features for the specific regulations you must address.
- **Focused Analytics:** Analytical tools that offer deep insights into narrowly defined areas.

These tailored capabilities ensure that your software solution aligns perfectly with your organization's unique ESG and sustainability needs, guiding you toward the best choices for your specific scenario.

Segmenting the Market

To effectively segment the market, I used a combination of techniques:

- Demographic Segmentation: Dividing the market based on organizational characteristics, such as industry, size, and geographical location.
- Behavioral Segmentation: We segment based on how organizations approach ESG management, their readiness to adopt new technologies, and their existing ESG practices.

- Needs-Based Segmentation: Identifying segments based on specific needs and pain points related to ESG management and reporting.

  Selecting the most attractive segments for ESG Software – using these techniques, I identified the most attractive segments for my ESG software:

- Large Enterprises in High-Regulation Industries: These organizations often face stringent ESG reporting requirements and have complex data needs, making them ideal candidates for comprehensive ESG management solutions.

  Financial Services: With increasing pressure from stakeholders and regulatory bodies, financial institutions are actively seeking robust ESG solutions.

- Technology and IT Companies: These companies are typically early adopters of new technologies and are keen on integrating ESG practices into their operations.
- Manufacturing and Industrial Firms: The significant environmental impact of these firms pressures them to improve their ESG performance and reporting.

Market Segmentation Analysis for ESG Management Software

1. By Industry:

1. Large Financial Institutions: These institutions operate on a large-scale and have complex risk management needs. They face high regulatory scrutiny and extensive reporting requirements, requiring comprehensive ESG reporting, advanced risk management tools, and robust stakeholder communication features. We position them in the upper right of the matrix, where they experience high pressure to act and have broad requirements.

2. Mid-sized Manufacturing Companies: These firms face moderate regulatory pressure and focus on sustainability in their supply chains. They need scalable solutions that grow with their ESG initiatives, emphasizing cost-effective compliance and stakeholder engagement. They occupy the middle of the matrix with moderate pressure and requirements.
3. Technology Firms: Operating globally with high data privacy and ethical governance concerns, technology firms need flexible solutions that adapt to rapid changes in technology and regulations. They require data privacy modules, governance tools, and environmental impact tracking. Positioned in the upper middle of the matrix, they face high pressure but have moderate requirements.
4. Healthcare Organizations: With high regulatory and compliance demands, healthcare organizations have significant social impact considerations. They need tools for social impact management, sustainability tracking, compliance management, and community engagement. They span the matrix's upper middle to upper right, facing high pressure with moderate to broad requirements.
5. Small Businesses: At the initial stages of ESG implementation, small businesses often need more resources and budgets. They need simple, affordable, easy-to-implement solutions with basic reporting and compliance functionalities. Positioned in the matrix's lower left to the middle, they experience low to moderate pressure with narrow to moderate requirements.

2. By Company Size:

Large Enterprises: Multinational corporations with complex ESG requirements requiring comprehensive reporting and management tools.

- Mid-sized Companies: Firms needing scalable solutions that grow with their ESG initiatives and regulatory compliance needs.

- Small Businesses: Enterprises seeking cost-effective, easy-to-implement solutions to initiate and manage their ESG efforts.

3. By Geographic Region:

- North America: Driven by regulatory requirements and investor pressure, particularly in the US and Canada.
- Europe: Strong focus on sustainability and stringent ESG regulations, especially in the E.U. and UK.
- Asia-Pacific: Growing interest in ESG due to regulatory changes and increasing investor awareness, with significant activity in China, Japan, and Australia.
- Latin America: Emerging focus on ESG, driven by regional regulations and multinational corporate practices.
- Middle East & Africa: There is a nascent but growing interest in ESG, with opportunities in emerging markets and regional hubs like the UAE and South Africa.

4. By Function:

- ESG Reporting and Disclosure: Tools for tracking and reporting ESG metrics to meet regulatory and stakeholder requirements.
- Risk Management: Solutions to identify, assess, and mitigate ESG-related risks.
- Sustainability Management: Platforms to manage sustainability initiatives, carbon footprint tracking, and resource optimization.
- Governance and Compliance: Modules focusing on ethical governance, regulatory compliance, and corporate social responsibility.
- Stakeholder Engagement: Tools for engaging with investors, employees, customers, and communities on ESG issues.

5. By User Type:

- C-Suite Executives: Focused on strategic ESG goals, risk management, and stakeholder communication.
- ESG Managers and Analysts: These require detailed data collection, analysis, and reporting capabilities.
- Compliance Officers: Need tools to ensure regulatory compliance and manage ESG-related risks.
- Sustainability Officers: Focused on managing sustainability projects and initiatives across the organization.

Investors and Shareholders: Interested in ESG performance data and impact metrics for investment decisions.

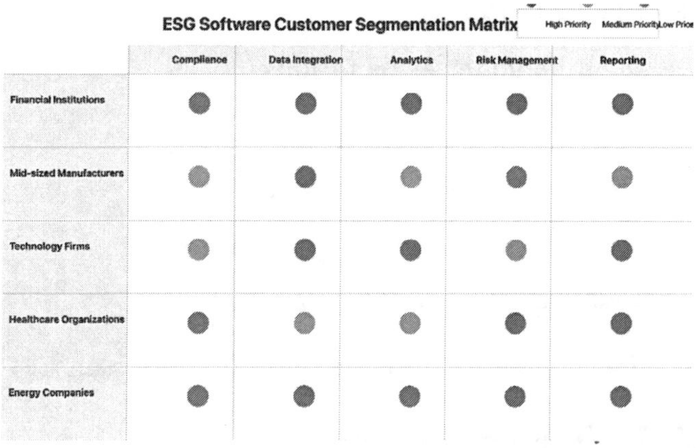

Cluster Analysis for ESG Management Software

Cluster 1: Large Financial Institutions

Characteristics:

- High regulatory scrutiny
- Extensive reporting requirements
- Large-scale operations with complex risk management needs
- Strong focus on investor relations and transparency

Needs:

- Comprehensive ESG reporting
- Advanced risk management tools
- Integration with financial and compliance systems
- Robust stakeholder communication features

Cluster 2: Mid-sized Manufacturing Companies

Characteristics:

- Moderate regulatory pressure
- Focus on sustainability in supply chain operations
- Resource constraints
- Diverse stakeholder expectations

Needs:

- Scalable sustainability management tools
- Supply chain tracking and optimization
- Cost-effective compliance solutions
- Tools for engaging suppliers and customers on ESG issues

Cluster 3: Technology Firms

Characteristics:

- Rapid innovation cycles
- High data privacy and security concerns
- Global operations with varying regulatory requirements
- Strong emphasis on ethical governance

Needs:

- Data privacy and security modules
- Governance and compliance tools

- Environmental impact tracking
- Flexibility to adapt to rapid changes in technology and regulations

Cluster 4: Healthcare Organizations

Characteristics:

- High regulatory and compliance demands
- Significant social impact considerations
- Focus on sustainability in operations and resource management
- Public and community engagement

Needs:

- Social impact management tools
- Sustainability tracking and reporting
- Compliance management
- Community and stakeholder engagement features

Cluster 5: Small Businesses Across Various Industries

Characteristics:

- Limited resources and budgets
- Initial stages of ESG implementation
- Simple operations with fewer complex ESG needs
- Growing awareness and commitment to sustainability

Needs:

- Cost-effective, easy-to-implement ESG solutions
- Basic reporting and compliance tools
- Scalable options for future growth
- Education and training on ESG practices

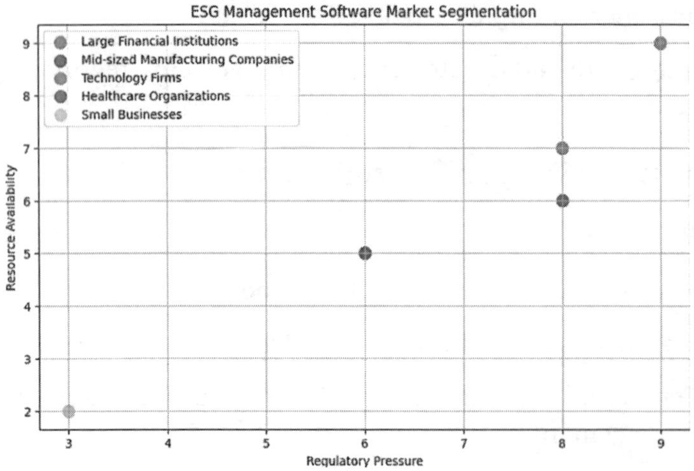

Figure 3.3 Customer Matrix Analysis: Pressure to Act vs. Breadth of Requirements

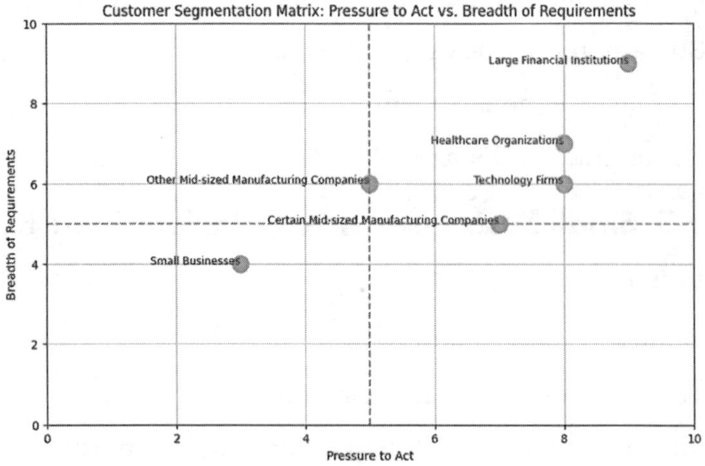

Figure 3.4 Customer Segmentation Matrix

By positioning the ESG management software according to the Customer Segmentation matrix, we can better address each market segment's specific needs and pressures, ensuring targeted and practical solutions.

3. Positioning the Product

Developing a Unique Value Proposition

Developing a unique value proposition was essential to stand out in the competitive landscape. I based my ESG software's unique value proposition on the following:

- Comprehensive Data Management: Offering advanced data collection, integration, and analytics capabilities to handle complex ESG data needs.
- Regulatory Compliance: Ensuring compliance with global and industry-specific regulations through automated reporting and robust data validation.
- Customization and Flexibility: Providing customizable dashboards and indicators to meet the specific needs of diverse organizations.
- User-Friendly Interface: Combining robust features with an intuitive interface to ensure ease of use across different organizational roles.
- Scalability: Supporting organizations of various sizes, from small enterprises to large multinational corporations.

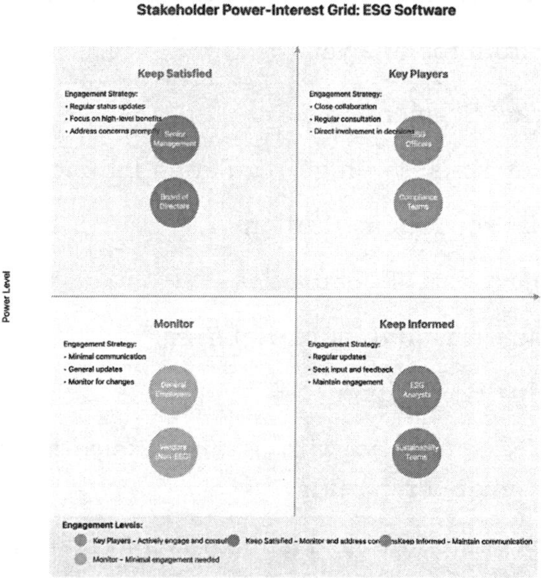

Figure 3.5 Stakeholder Power – Interest Grid

Crafting a Positioning Statement that Resonates with the Target Market

Crafting a compelling positioning statement was crucial to resonate with the target market. Here's the positioning statement for my ESG management software:

"Empowering organizations to lead in sustainability with our comprehensive, customizable, and user-friendly ESG management software. Our platform integrates advanced data analytics and regulatory compliance features, ensuring you can navigate the complexities of ESG reporting with ease and confidence."

This detailed analysis and strategic approach laid a strong foundation for developing my ESG software. By understanding where to play, segmenting the market effectively, and positioning my product uniquely, I was well-prepared to enter the market and make a significant impact. The journey ahead was promising, filled with opportunities to drive sustainability and create value for organizations worldwide.

Summary of Analysis and Recommendations

Key outcomes from the analysis:

1. Target Market Segments:
    - Large enterprises in high-regulation industries
    - Financial services institutions
    - Technology and IT companies
    - Manufacturing and industrial firms
2. Unique Value Proposition:
    - Simplifies compliance with comprehensive data management and automated reporting
    - Provides customizable dashboards and real-time insights
    - Ensures regulatory compliance and robust integration capabilities

3. Market Positioning:
    - Positioned as a high-value solution for organizations with complex ESG needs
    - Emphasizes ease of use, customization, and advanced analytics

Set Recommendations:

1. Focus on High-Priority Segments: Prioritize large enterprises and financial services institutions with the highest demand and compatibility with strengths.
2. Enhance User Experience: We will continue refining the user interface to keep it intuitive and user-friendly, even as we add new features.
3. Expand Market Presence: Invest in marketing and partnerships to increase market presence, particularly in regions with high regulatory pressures.
4. Leverage Automation and Analytics: Strengthen automated data collection and advanced analytics capabilities to maintain a competitive edge.
5. Tailor Solutions for Specific Industries: Develop industry-specific modules to address the unique challenges of different sectors, enhancing the overall value proposition.

Market Entry Barriers and Customer Adoption Challenges

As I delved deeper into developing our ESG application, I realized that targeting specific market segments would be pivotal to our success. However, each segment posed a unique set of risks that required careful consideration. Drawing on the insights and data we've discussed, let me walk you through the critical dangers of targeting these segments.

Starting with market entry barriers, it became clear that penetrating specific industries and substantial financial institutions was no small feat. These institutions operate within highly regulated environments and are accustomed to working with well-established vendors. For a new entrant like us, gaining their trust and meeting their stringent compliance requirements posed significant challenges. We had to ensure that our ESG application was robust in functionality and fully compliant with the various regulations these institutions adhered to, like the GRI, SASB, and TCFD frameworks. The sheer complexity of the compliance landscape was a barrier in itself, and we needed to demonstrate that our software could seamlessly integrate with their existing systems without causing disruptions.

Another significant risk revolved around customer adoption challenges. For mid-sized manufacturing companies and small businesses, adopting an ESG application could be seen as a daunting task. These companies often operate with tight budgets and limited resources, making them hesitant to invest in new technology, especially if it's perceived as complex or challenging to implement. We had to design our application to be user-friendly and scalable, ensuring that even companies with minimal technical expertise could quickly adopt and integrate it into their existing workflows. Additionally, we recognized that these companies might be reluctant to change their current processes, so we needed to provide clear and compelling reasons for them to switch to our platform—whether it was through demonstrating cost savings, improved efficiency, or enhanced compliance capabilities.

Resource allocation was another critical area of risk. As a startup, we had limited resources and needed to allocate them strategically. Targeting large enterprises, for example, required significant investment in developing advanced features, building a robust support infrastructure, and ensuring we had the necessary certifications to meet their compliance needs. On the other hand, focusing on smaller companies meant we needed to keep our costs low while still delivering a high-quality product. Balancing these competing demands was a delicate act. We had to make tough decisions about where to invest our time, money, and effort to maximize our impact and ensure that our product could serve both ends of the market.

Additionally, there was the risk of overextending ourselves by trying to cater to too many segments simultaneously. We had to resist the temptation to be everything to everyone. Instead, we needed to focus on segments where we could leverage our strengths—like comprehensive data management and regulatory compliance—and where we could make the most significant impact. This required us to be disciplined, constantly revisiting our strategy to ensure we stayed on course and didn't dilute our efforts by chasing opportunities outside our core competencies.

Lastly, market dynamics posed a continuous risk. The ESG landscape was rapidly evolving, with new regulations, standards, and stakeholder expectations emerging frequently. We needed to stay ahead of these changes to ensure our application remained relevant and practical. This meant keeping a close eye on industry trends, engaging with regulatory bodies, and continuously updating our software to incorporate the latest requirements and best practices.

In reflecting on these risks, I realized that developing an ESG application wasn't just about creating a product—it was about understanding the intricacies of the market, anticipating the challenges our customers might face, and being agile enough to adapt to a constantly changing environment. By taking these risks into account from the outset, we were better positioned to navigate the complexities of the ESG landscape and deliver a solution that indeed met the needs of our target market.

Chapter 4

Market Assessment and Competitive Analysis

We must align our efforts with our core strengths as we move forward. The market segments we target should be those where our capabilities genuinely shine. By doing this, we can deliver exceptional value and carve out a distinct place in the market. It's not just about what we can offer; it's also about ensuring that our potential customers are ready and eager to adopt the new technologies we're bringing to the table. Targeting these segments means smoother implementation and higher adoption rates, making our software more impactful right from the start.

With these criteria in mind, we can strategically choose the segments where we can leverage our strengths and make a significant impact. This approach positions us for success and ensures we provide genuine, meaningful value to our customers.

But before all this, one of the most critical steps was defining our company's strategic direction. These strategies aren't just lofty ideals but the guiding principles that influence every decision, action, and behavior within our organization. They are the foundation of our identity and the compass that guides us toward our vision.

Criteria for Selecting the Right Market Segments

We used Mintzberg 5P analysis, SWOT, PESTLE, Porter's Five Forces, and Benchmarking analysis of existing software tools to define the playing field. These tools helped me assess the internal and external market factors and align them with my company's strengths and capabilities.

- Mintzberg's 5P Model: Used to evaluate the strategic perspectives and define an overarching approach to strategy.
- SWOT Analysis: Identified my company's internal strengths and weaknesses, as well as external opportunities and threats.
- PESTLE Analysis: Evaluated the macro-environmental factors (Political, Economic, Social, Technological, Legal, and Environmental) influencing the ESG market.
- BENCHMARKING Analysis: To identify the current software landscape and the most attractive segments for the ESG software.

Exploring Strategic Perspectives Using Mintzberg's 5P Model

When I first encountered Mintzberg's 5P Model of strategy, I realized it was more than just a theoretical framework; it was a lens through which I could view the complexities of strategic decision-making, particularly in developing our ESG application. Each dimension of Mintzberg's strategy offers a unique approach to creating, positioning, and executing a product that meets the market's needs and stands out in a crowded field.

1. Strategy as a Plan: The Blueprint for ESG Success

In the context of our ESG application, strategy as a plan is about laying out a clear, purposeful course of action. This isn't just about dreaming big; it's about meticulously designing a roadmap that guides us from concept to market launch. We need to think about leveraging our deep industry expertise to craft a solution that directly addresses the pain points we've identified. Our plan must be forward-thinking, incorporating features like real-time compliance monitoring and advanced data integration—relevant capabilities today. It will remain as regulations and market expectations evolve.

The planning stage also involves considering our financial constraints and finding ways to overcome them. We might plan to bootstrap the initial development or seek targeted funding from investors who understand the value of specialized ESG solutions. A well-crafted plan will help us navigate these challenges, ensuring that our strategy is not just a wish list but a practical guide to achieving our goals.

2. Strategy as a Ploy: Tactical Moves in a Competitive Arena

Strategy as a ploy refers to the tactical maneuvers we can employ to outwit our competitors and secure a favorable position in the market. In the highly competitive ESG software landscape, this could mean finding ways to differentiate our product in the short-term. For instance, we could offer a limited-time pilot program that allows potential clients to experience the value of our solution with minimal risk. This not only attracts attention but also builds trust and credibility.

Another tactical move could be to focus on underserved markets—perhaps smaller enterprises that larger competitors overlook. We can carve out a niche where competition is less intense by tailoring our messaging and offerings to meet their needs. These ploys, while tactical, align with our broader strategy, helping us gain traction in the market and setting the stage for long-term success.

3. Strategy as a Pattern: The Emerging Blueprint

Sometimes, strategies are about more than what we plan but what unfolds. Strategy as a pattern refers to the consistent behaviors and actions that emerge, often unexpectedly, as we respond to real-world challenges. Developing our ESG application might mean recognizing and capitalizing on emerging trends we didn't initially plan for, such as a sudden shift in regulatory focus or a new technological advancement.

For example, as we engage with early clients, we might discover that they're using our application in ways we hadn't anticipated—perhaps for integrating ESG data into broader corporate governance frameworks. If this pattern emerges, we should be flexible enough to adapt our strategy, perhaps by enhancing features that support these new use cases. This emergent strategy, driven by real-world feedback and patterns, can be as powerful as a deliberate plan, helping us stay relevant and responsive in a rapidly changing market.

4. Strategy as a Position: Finding Our Place in the ESG Ecosystem

Positioning our ESG application within the broader market environment is critical. Strategy as a position involves understanding the external factors — market conditions, competition, technological advancements, and regulatory landscapes — that shape our industry. It's about aligning our internal strengths, like our subject matter expertise, with these external realities to create a sustainable competitive advantage.

Given the competitive nature of the ESG software market, our strategic position must emphasize our unique strengths, such as our deep understanding of industry-specific compliance needs. We should also be aware of our weaknesses, like limited financial resources, and find ways to mitigate them through strategic partnerships or collaborations that enhance our capabilities without requiring significant capital outlay.

Our position should also reflect the opportunities and threats we've identified. For instance, while there is a growing demand for ESG solutions, the presence of established players means we need to position ourselves as not just another option but the best option for specific, underserved market segments.

5. Strategy as a Perspective: The Shared Vision for ESG Impact

Finally, strategy as a perspective speaks to the collective mindset and shared vision that drive our organization. It's about more than just plans and positions; it's about cultivating a shared understanding of our goals and the value we bring to the ESG space. This perspective is crucial for fostering unity and collaboration within our team and ensuring everyone is aligned with our strategic objectives.

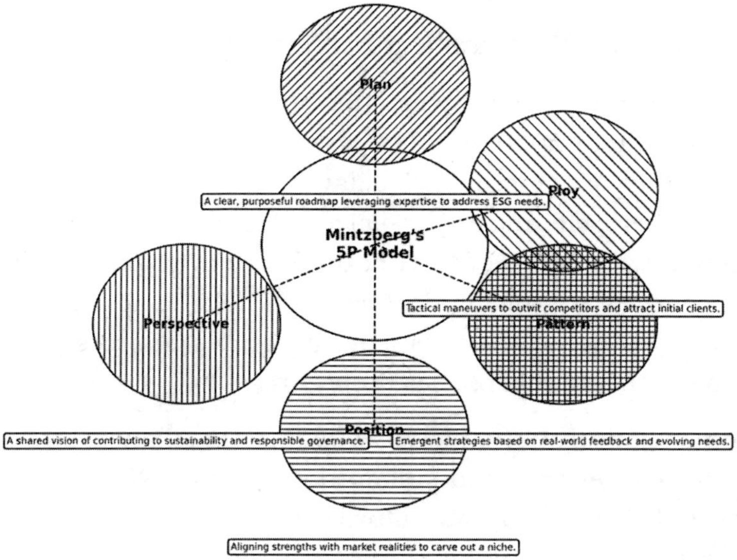

Figure 4.1 Mintzberg's 5P Model

For our ESG application, this shared perspective might center on the belief that we are not just building software but contributing to a larger mission of sustainability and responsible governance. By instilling this perspective throughout our organization, we can inspire our team to go beyond the technical aspects of development and consider the broader impact of our work.

This perspective also extends to how we communicate with our clients and stakeholders. By framing our strategy in terms of the positive change we aim to create, we can build stronger relationships and a more engaged user base. This strategic perspective is not just a backdrop; it is the guiding principle that informs every decision we make, from product development to marketing to customer support.

SWOT Analysis Results:

I remember the day I decided to develop ESG management software. The market was bustling with potential, and the demand for robust

ESG solutions was skyrocketing. I dove into the leading market research reports for ESG Management and Reporting Software, a comprehensive resource that would guide my journey.

The Beginning: Discovering Strengths

As I sifted through the pages, the strengths of my envisioned software started to crystallize. The research documents emphasized the importance of comprehensive data management. Our software would excel here, offering unparalleled capabilities for collecting and managing a wide range of ESG data, from environmental metrics to social and governance indicators. This holistic approach would allow users to consolidate data from various sources, ensuring comprehensive and reliable ESG reporting.

Another critical strength was regulatory compliance. By aligning with major frameworks and standards such as GRI, SASB, TCFD, and the E.U. Taxonomy, our software would simplify the complex web of regulations, making compliance easier for organizations. This feature alone would build immense trust and credibility with stakeholders.

The analysis highlighted the necessity of advanced analytics and reporting. I envisioned a platform offering basic reporting, advanced analytics, scenario planning, and benchmarking capabilities. Customizable dashboards allow users to monitor progress against their goals and industry benchmarks, making data-driven decisions to improve their ESG performance.

Another strength emerged as support for third-party verification. This feature would enhance the credibility of the data, meet regulatory requirements, and establish the software as a reliable tool for ESG reporting.

The Challenges: Facing Weaknesses

However, as I delved deeper, I realized the journey wouldn't be without its challenges. High implementation costs could be a significant barrier. Integrating the software with various data sources and systems would require substantial investment, potentially deterring smaller organizations. The software's complexity was another concern. Its comprehensive nature would necessitate extensive user training and support, which could slow down adoption and effective use. I needed to find a balance between robustness and user-friendliness.

Accurate data input was crucial for the software's effectiveness. Inconsistent or inaccurate data from external sources could undermine its reliability, and ensuring high data quality would be a constant challenge.

The Horizon: Spotting Opportunities

Despite these challenges, the opportunities were vast. The growing market demand for ESG solutions was undeniable. With increasing emphasis on sustainability and regulatory pressure, organizations across industries were seeking robust tools to manage and report their ESG performance. Technological advancements presented exciting possibilities. Leveraging AI and machine learning for predictive analytics and automated data collection could enhance the software's capabilities, setting it apart in the market.

Another promising avenue was forming strategic partnerships with consulting firms, IT providers, and other software vendors. These collaborations could expand the software's ecosystem, providing additional value to users through integrated solutions. Supporting multiple languages and regional regulations would allow the software to cater to a global market, tapping into diverse industries and geographies.

The Storm: Anticipating Threats

However, the guide also warned of potential threats. The ESG management software market was becoming increasingly crowded, and competition was fierce, ranging from startups to established enterprise software vendors. Engaging in such actions could lead to price wars and constant pressure to innovate.

Regulatory changes were another significant threat. Rapid shifts in ESG regulations and reporting requirements could necessitate frequent updates to the software, challenging our ability to stay current and compliant. Data security and privacy concerns loomed large. Handling large volumes of sensitive ESG data increases the risk of data breaches and cyber-attacks. Ensuring robust data security measures would be crucial to maintaining user trust. Economic uncertainty was the final hurdle. Economic downturns or budget constraints within organizations could reduce spending on new software solutions, impacting market growth and adoption rates.

The Findings: Data-Driven Insights

The market analysis provided invaluable insights into critical vendors and their capabilities. It was fascinating to see how various vendors excelled in data collection, emissions calculations, materiality assessments, and scenario planning. These insights became benchmarks for our software, helping me identify areas for differentiation. Understanding user needs and trends was another critical takeaway. CIOs prioritized capabilities such as enhanced environmental data collection, third-party verification, custom dashboards, and benchmarking. This knowledge guided the development of features that would meet these demands.

The team also highlighted implementation best practices. Successful ESG software implementations focused on aligning with corporate taxonomies, ensuring data quality, and providing flexible reporting capabilities. Incorporating these best practices would improve user adoption and satisfaction.

- Strengths: Advanced data analytics capabilities, strong expertise in regulatory compliance, and robust API integrations.
- Weaknesses: Limited market presence, high complexity for smaller organizations.

- Opportunities: Growing demand for ESG solutions, increasing regulatory pressures, and potential for market expansion.
- Threats: Intense competition, rapid technological changes, and evolving regulations.

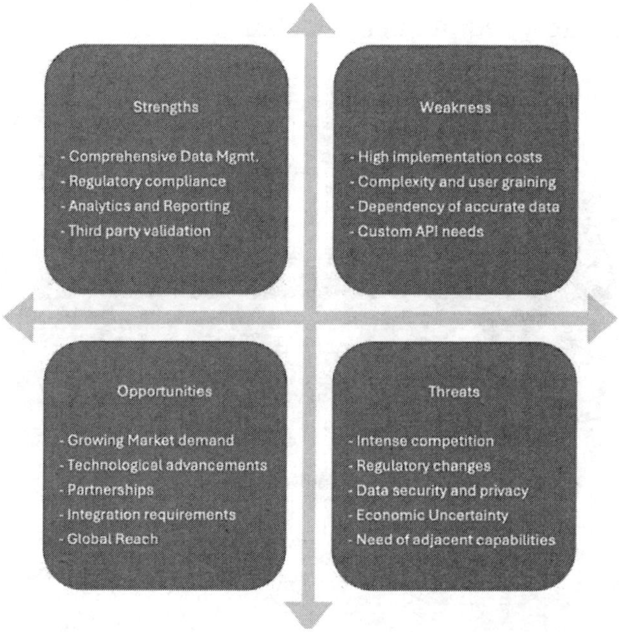

Figure 4.2 SWOT Analysis for ESG Management Software

PESTLE Analysis

The Beginning: Political Landscape

As I embarked on developing the ESG management software, the political landscape was one of the first aspects I needed to consider. Governments worldwide increasingly focus on sustainability, implementing policies to promote transparency and accountability in ESG practices. Regulations like the E.U.'s Corporate Sustainability Reporting Directive (CSRD) and the US SEC's proposed climate disclosure rules have driven companies to adopt robust ESG reporting practices.

These political pressures were both a challenge and an opportunity. On one hand, they created a complex regulatory environment that my software would need to navigate. On the other hand, they drove demand for solutions to help companies comply with these regulations efficiently. This understanding shaped the compliance features of my software, ensuring it could adapt to various regulatory requirements globally.

P	Political	• Governments worldwide increasingly focusing on Sustainability • Implementation of policies to promote transparency and accountability in ESG practices • Regulations such CSRD and SEC in US, driving companies to adopt robust ESG reporting • Political stability in key markets continue to ensure growth and opportunity
E	Economic	• The cost of developing and maintaining software • Economic uncertainty posing threat that might be hesitant to invest • Growing emphasis on sustainability driving in sustainability initiatives • Recognition of long-term benefits of adhering to sustainability
S	Social	• Stakeholder demanding transparency and accountability • Increased awareness and concern for issues such as climate change, social justice • Availability of skilled manpower to develop the software
T	Technological	• Technological advancements in AI, Data, cloud computing • Integration with diverse sources like ERP, HCM, Finance • Cyber security and data sensitive requirements in Europe and other countries • Availability of technology and its scalability
L	Legal	• Compliance with global, regional and local ESG regulations requires software to be updated periodically • Protecting intellectual property including proprietary algorithms • Liability of risk to avoid any legal challenges for ESG risk management
E	Environmental	• Sustainability trends to ensure need for comprehensive ESG solution • The need to address climate change and emission management • Resource efficiency by identifying waste and inefficiencies in operation

Figure 4.3 PESTLE Analysis of ESG Software Market

The Economic Climate: Navigating Uncertainty

Another critical factor was the economic landscape. The world was recovering from the financial impacts of the COVID-19 pandemic, and many organizations were tightening their budgets. This economic uncertainty posed a potential threat, as companies might hesitate to invest in new software solutions.

However, there was a silver lining. The growing emphasis on ESG was driving investment in sustainability initiatives. Companies recognized that robust ESG practices could lead to long-term financial benefits, such as improved risk management, enhanced brand reputation, and better access to capital. By positioning my software as a tool that could deliver these economic benefits, I aimed to overcome budgetary constraints and demonstrate its value.

Social Dynamics: Shifting Expectations

Social dynamics were changing rapidly, with stakeholders demanding greater transparency and accountability from organizations regarding their ESG practices. Consumers, employees, investors, and communities were increasingly concerned about climate change, social justice, and ethical governance issues.

These shifting expectations presented a significant opportunity for my software. Providing comprehensive and transparent ESG reporting capabilities could help organizations meet stakeholder demands and enhance their social license to operate. I focused on features enabling companies to report on various social metrics, such as diversity, equity, inclusion, supplier sustainability, and community engagement.

Technological Advancements: Leveraging Innovation

The technological landscape evolved quickly, offering exciting opportunities to enhance the capabilities of my ESG management software. Advances in artificial intelligence, machine learning, and big data analytics could revolutionize ESG data collection, analysis, and reporting.

By integrating these technologies, my software could offer predictive analytics, automated data collection, and real-time reporting, providing users with deeper insights and more efficient processes. Additionally, the rise of cloud computing enabled seamless integration with other enterprise systems, ensuring that my software could fit smoothly into existing IT infrastructures.

Legal Considerations: Ensuring Compliance

Legal considerations were paramount in developing ESG management software. The evolving regulatory landscape meant that my software needed to be flexible and adaptable to comply with various laws and standards.

The Gartner Market Guide emphasized supporting significant frameworks and standards such as GRI, SASB, TCFD, and the E.U. Taxonomy. Ensuring my software could handle these diverse requirements was crucial to its success. I also needed to consider data privacy and security laws, ensuring that my software protected sensitive ESG data from breaches and unauthorized access.

Environmental Factors: Driving Sustainability

Environmental factors were at the core of ESG management. The increasing awareness of climate change and ecological degradation drove organizations to adopt more sustainable practices.

Our software is needed to support comprehensive environmental data management, including tracking greenhouse gas emissions, water usage, waste management, and resource conservation. By providing tools for detailed environmental reporting and scenario planning, my software could help organizations minimize their environmental impact and contribute to global sustainability goals.

Porters

The Journey Forward

With a thorough understanding of the political, economic, social, technological, legal, and environmental factors shaping the ESG landscape, I felt equipped to develop a software solution that would meet the market's needs. These elements presented unique challenges and opportunities, guiding the features and capabilities I prioritized in my software.

The journey was complex and multi-faceted, but staying attuned to these external factors made me confident that my ESG management software would comply with regulations and drive positive change. As I continued this journey, I remained committed to creating a tool to empower organizations to achieve their ESG goals and build a more sustainable future.

This PESTLE analysis story highlights the various external factors that influenced the development of the ESG management software and provides a comprehensive view of the considerations and strategies involved.

Benchmarking Analysis - Existing ESG Software and Data Solution Market Assessment

As I embarked on my journey to explore the landscape of ESG management and reporting software, I was stepping into a world of innovation, complexity, and intense competition. To understand the capabilities, I looked into the company website, market reports, demonstration videos on YouTube, software help documents, and software review sites like Gartner, Forrester, McKinsey, and GetApp UK. Each vendor in this space had unique strengths and weaknesses; understanding these nuances was crucial for anyone making an informed decision. I have anonymized their names here to avoid legal implications.

My first stop was EcoPlan. Picture this: a platform with comprehensive dashboards and analytics tailored to support major frameworks like B Corp, CDP, GRI, and SASB. EcoPlan's flexibility allowed for customizable indicators and seamless data integration through a REST API. However, despite its robust capabilities, EcoPlan faced challenges. It had a limited market presence compared to its larger counterparts and primarily focused on a few regions. Yet, for small—to medium enterprises seeking a customizable ESG solution, EcoPlan stood out as a promising contender.

Next, I encountered SecureGuard Technologies. SecureGuard's strength lies in integrating enterprise risk management with ESG capabilities. Supporting a wide range of frameworks, it offered customizable ESG metrics and robust API integration. But here's the catch—while SecureGuard excelled in risk management, it fell short in environmental capabilities compared to its peers and had limited deployment regions. SecureGuard positioned itself as an ideal choice for organizations with complex risk profiles looking to integrate ESG into their risk management processes.

GreenSuite ESG

As I continued my exploration, I came across GreenSuite, a leading solution for process-level management for ESG, EHS, Quality, and Supply Chain Risk. With extensive global framework support and seamless data integration, GreenSuite caters to large enterprises that need comprehensive digital systems. However, its complexity made it a daunting choice for smaller organizations. For those needing an all-encompassing solution, GreenSuite was a formidable option.

GreenSuite ESG is like an old but reliable friend. It started strong with data management and sustainability reporting. Now, it offers advanced features like AI for risk management and IoT integration, which make gathering real-time data from various sources easier. Its mobile app integration ensures you can manage ESG metrics on-the-go.

Gaps: They could quickly enhance their data integration capabilities. Predictive analytics would be a great addition in the mid-term. Long-term, real-time compliance monitoring will be essential.

Opportunity:

- **Near-Term**: We can develop enhanced data integration capabilities to handle more diverse and complex data sources seamlessly.
- **Mid-Term**: We can introduce advanced predictive analytics to provide deeper insights and future trend predictions, which current solutions might lack.
- **Long-term:** Real-time compliance monitoring can be a game-changer, allowing businesses to remain ahead of regulatory requirements continuously.

By addressing these gaps, we can offer a more comprehensive and future-proof solution that outperforms GreenSuite ESG.

SustainCloud

The story took a turn when I explored SustainCloud. This vendor had acquired multiple companies to bolster its sustainability software solutions, offering centralized workflows for ESG data collection and reporting. SustainCloud supported major frameworks and boasted strong API capabilities. Yet, the integration complexity posed a challenge. SustainCloud positioned itself as a versatile provider with strong industry support that is ideal for medium to large enterprises.

SustainCloud has been around for a while, focusing on comprehensive data collection and regulatory compliance. It offers detailed sustainability reporting and advanced analytics to track performance. Its tools are excellent for managing compliance and predicting risks.

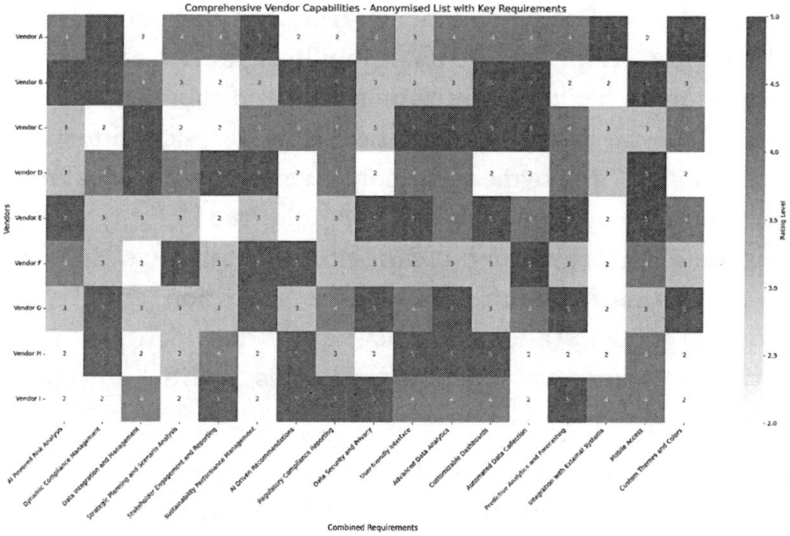

Figure 4.4 Comprehensive Vendor Capabilities Assessment.

Gaps: They should focus on improving integration capabilities in the near-term. In the mid-term, we need better reporting customization. In the long-term, more advanced AI-driven insights would be beneficial.

Opportunity:

- **Near-Term**: Improve integration capabilities to ensure seamless data flow from various sources.
- **Mid-Term**: Develop enhanced reporting customization features that allow users to tailor reports to their needs.
- **Long-Term**: Integrate advanced AI-driven insights to provide more nuanced and actionable intelligence for sustainability performance.

We can position our software as a more flexible and intelligent option that is capable of meeting the evolving needs of sustainability management.

DataEco ESG Management System

Then came DataEco, a niche player focused on regulatory compliance and supply chain sustainability. DataEco's strength was its integration with significant frameworks and robust supply chain sustainability and finance capabilities. However, its limited market penetration and deployment regions were notable weaknesses. DataEco was a niche provider that delivered for organizations needing detailed regulatory compliance. DataEco is one of the newer players, streamlining ESG data collection and reporting aligned with global standards. They've got risk identification and mitigation tools and customizable workflows for ESG processes.

Gaps: Expanding data collection features in the near-term would help. In the mid-term, they need enhanced risk management tools. In the long-term, integrating IoT data will be crucial.

Opportunity:

- **Near-Term**: Expand data collection features to include more granular and real-time data points.
- **Mid-Term**: Enhance risk management tools to offer more robust and proactive risk mitigation strategies.

- **Long-Term**: Integrate IoT data to provide real-time insights and a more dynamic view of ESG performance.

These improvements will make our software stand out as a comprehensive and real-time ESG management leader.

GovernSense ESG

GovernSense emerged next with its automated data retrieval and standardization capabilities. Supporting extensive frameworks and partnering with consulting firms, GovernSense was strong in the North American and European markets. Its primary weakness was its limited geographical focus. Nevertheless, GovernSense was a key player for global enterprises seeking robust ESG management and reporting solutions.

GovernSense ESG combines data from various sources, focusing on governance and compliance management. Their analytics help track governance and compliance and offer AI for risk assessment.

Gaps: They should enhance governance analytics in the near-term. In the mid-term, better AI-driven compliance tools are needed. The goal is long-term, real-time risk management.

Opportunity:

- **Near-Term**: Develop enhanced governance analytics to provide deeper insights into governance practices.
- **Mid-Term**: Introduce better AI-driven compliance tools to automate and streamline compliance processes.
- **Long-Term**: Focus on real-time risk management to help businesses anticipate and mitigate risks promptly.

Addressing these areas, we can create a more sophisticated and proactive ESG management tool.

InsightAI

The journey continued with InsightAI, a giant in enterprise IT solutions. InsightAI's ESG Suite featured customizable dashboards and data health check capabilities, with strong integration with external systems. Yet, its primary focus on large enterprises could be a drawback. InsightAI positioned itself as a customizable ESG dashboard and scenario forecasting provider, which is ideal for large enterprises. InsightAI ESG is a recent addition to the market, with strong data integration and advanced analytics using AI. They provide detailed reporting tools and ensure compliance with various standards.

Gaps: They need to enhance data integration in the near-term, introduce more predictive analytics in the mid-term, and focus on real-time compliance and scenario planning in the long-term.

Opportunity:

- **Near-Term**: Enhance data integration to support a broader range of data sources and formats.
- **Mid-Term**: Develop more predictive analytics capabilities to offer forward-looking insights.
- **Long-Term**: Implement real-time compliance and scenario planning features to help businesses stay ahead of changes.

We can offer a more integrated, forward-thinking solution that helps businesses manage and anticipate ESG challenges.

SustainControl

The journey brought me to SustainControl, known for its integrated sustainability data management and extensive scenario planning capabilities. However, the complexity of its solutions made it less suitable for smaller organizations. SustainControl positioned itself as an enterprise application software provider with a strong focus on integrated sustainability data management. Its tool integrates

ESG data across enterprise systems with real-time monitoring and compliance tracking. Its advanced analytics track sustainability performance, and AI helps with predictive insights.

Gaps: In the near-term, they should focus on real-time data tracking. In the mid-term, better AI-driven analytics are needed. Long-term, advanced scenario planning will be essential.

Opportunity:

- **Near-Term**: Focus on real-time data tracking to provide up-to-the-minute insights.
- **Mid-Term**: Enhance AI-driven analytics to deliver more precise and actionable intelligence.
- **Long-Term**: Develop advanced scenario planning tools to help businesses navigate potential future challenges.

We can provide a more dynamic and strategic ESG management platform by filling these gaps.

EcoFlow ESG Management

EcoFlow showcased substantial data collection and reporting automation with extensive integration capabilities. Primarily focused on large enterprises, EcoFlow positioned itself as a cloud-based platform with robust data collection and integration capabilities. EcoFlow centralizes ESG data and offers detailed reporting and compliance tracking. Its analytics tools assess ESG performance and enhance stakeholder engagement.

Gaps: We need better data centralization in the near-term. In the mid-term, we need to focus on improving stakeholder engagement. Long-term, real-time compliance monitoring will be a game-changer.

Opportunity:

- **Near-Term**: Enhance data centralization capabilities to ensure all ESG data is easily accessible and manageable.

- **Mid-Term**: Improve stakeholder engagement tools to foster better communication and collaboration.
- **Long-Term**: Introduce real-time compliance monitoring to keep businesses compliant with minimal effort.

These improvements will help us build a more user-friendly and comprehensive ESG management solution.

RiskSphere

RiskSphere is impressed with its extensive support of industry-specific guidelines and robust data mining capabilities. However, its primary focus on North American and European markets was a limitation. RiskSphere positioned itself as a comprehensive ESG software provider with industry-specific solid support. It focuses on managing environmental, health, safety, and sustainability data. RiskSphere offers robust reporting and tools for identifying and mitigating ESG risks, with AI for predictive insights.

Gaps: They need to enhance supply chain tracking in the near-term. In the mid-term, better risk management analytics are required. Long-term, advanced AI-driven risk mitigation will be essential.

Opportunity:

- **Near-Term**: Enhance supply chain tracking for more detailed and transparent insights.
- **Mid-Term**: Develop better risk management analytics to offer more proactive risk mitigation strategies.
- **Long-Term**: Integrate advanced AI-driven risk mitigation tools for more effective and efficient risk management.

We can offer a more robust and proactive ESG management platform by focusing on these areas.

SpeedoEHS

SpeedoEHS provided substantial compliance and regulatory support with robust integration capabilities. Its complexity was a barrier for smaller organizations. SpeedoEHS positioned itself as an ESG and EHS software provider with solid compliance and regulatory support. SpeedoEHS provides real-time monitoring, risk management, and compliance tracking. Their tools help manage environmental, health, safety, and sustainability metrics with AI for predictive analytics.

Gaps: We need to improve real-time monitoring in the near-term, enhance predictive analytics tools in the mid-term, and implement advanced compliance tracking in the long-term.

Opportunity:

- **Near-Term**: Improve real-time monitoring capabilities to provide immediate insights and alerts.
- **Mid-Term**: Enhance predictive analytics tools to offer more accurate and actionable forecasts.
- **Long-Term**: Develop advanced compliance tracking features to ensure continuous regulatory compliance.

These enhancements position our software as a real-time and predictive ESG management leader.

EnviroHub

EnviroHub offers integrated financial and ESG data management with extensive reporting capabilities. However, its primary focus on large enterprises needed to be improved. EnviroHub is a professional information and software solutions provider that provides integrated solid data management. It offers comprehensive data collection, advanced analytics, and compliance management. Its tools help manage sustainability insights and risk assessments, and AI provides better insights.

Gaps: They should enhance data integration in the near-term. Mid-term, improved AI-driven analytics are needed. Long-term, real-time risk, and compliance management will be essential.

Opportunity:

- **Near-Term**: Enhance data integration capabilities to support a broader range of data sources and formats.
- **Mid-Term**: Develop improved AI-driven analytics to provide deeper insights and more accurate predictions.
- **Long-Term**: Focus on real-time risk and compliance management to help businesses stay ahead of challenges.

We can offer a more integrated and proactive ESG management solution by addressing these gaps.

ReportWise

Finally, I arrived at ReportWise, known for its automated data collection and extensive partner network. ReportWise's primary focus was on North American and European markets, and its strong reporting capabilities supported this focus. ReportWise positioned itself as a cloud-based compliance and reporting solutions provider with automated, solid data collection. It streamlines data collection and management for ESG reporting. It also provides collaborative analytics and reporting tools, with AI for data insights and compliance tracking.

Gaps: We need better data management tools soon, and improved collaborative analytics are essential in the mid-term. In the long-term, advanced AI-driven compliance tracking will be a game-changer.

Opportunity:

- **Near-term**: Develop better data management tools to streamline data collection and organization.

- **Mid-Term**: Enhance collaborative analytics to foster better teamwork and data sharing.
- **Long-Term**: Introduce AI-driven compliance tracking to automate and streamline compliance processes.

These enhancements will help us create a more collaborative and intelligent ESG management platform.

As I concluded my journey, I realized that each vendor brought something unique. The key was to match the right solution to the organization's specific needs. This exploration has revealed a dynamic and evolving landscape in ESG management and reporting software.

Table 4.1 Comparative Vendor Analysis*

Vendor	Strengths	Gaps	Opportunities
GreenSuite	Comprehensive digital systems, extensive global framework support, seamless data integration, AI for risk management, and IoT integration	Complexity for smaller organizations needs enhanced data integration, predictive analytics and real-time compliance monitoring	Enhanced data integration, predictive analytics, and real-time compliance monitoring
SustainControl	Centralized workflows, strong API capabilities, comprehensive data collection, regulatory compliance, and advanced analytics	Integration complexity, need for better reporting customization and advanced AI-driven insights	Improved integration capabilities, enhanced reporting customization, and advanced AI-driven insights

(*Contd.*)

Vendor	Strengths	Gaps	Opportunities
DataEco ESG Management System	Regulatory compliance, supply chain sustainability, customizable workflows, risk identification, and mitigation	Limited market penetration, need to expand data collection, enhance risk management and integrate IoT data	Expanded data collection, enhanced risk management tools, IoT data integration
GovernSense ESG	Automated data retrieval, standardization, strong partnerships with consulting firms, and a strong North American and European market presence	Limited geographical focus, need to enhance governance analytics, AI-driven compliance tools and real-time risk management	Enhanced governance analytics, AI-driven compliance tools, real-time risk management
InsightAI	Customizable dashboards, data health checks, strong data integration, and advanced analytics	The primary focus is on large enterprises that need to enhance data integration, predictive analytics, real-time compliance and scenario planning	Enhanced data integration, predictive analytics, real-time compliance and scenario planning
SustainControl	Integrated sustainability data management, extensive scenario planning, real-time monitoring, and compliance tracking, AI for predictive insights	Complexity for smaller organizations needs real-time data tracking, better AI-driven analytics and advanced scenario planning	Real-time data tracking, AI-driven analytics, and advanced scenario planning

Vendor	Strengths	Gaps	Opportunities
EcoFlow ESG Management	Robust data collection and reporting automation, extensive integration capabilities, detailed analytics, and stakeholder engagement	Better data centralization, the need for improved stakeholder engagement tools, and real-time compliance monitoring	Data centralization, improved stakeholder engagement, and real-time compliance monitoring
RiskSphere	Industry-specific guidelines, robust data mining, AI for predictive insights, and strong reporting capabilities	The primary focus is on North American and European markets, and there is a need to enhance supply chain tracking, risk management analytics and AI-driven risk mitigation	Supply chain tracking, risk management analytics, AI-driven risk mitigation
SpeedoEHS	Real-time monitoring, compliance tracking, strong integration capabilities, AI for predictive analytics	Complexity for smaller organizations needs improved real-time monitoring, predictive analytics and advanced compliance tracking	Real-time monitoring, predictive analytics and advanced compliance tracking
EnviroHub	Integrated financial and ESG data management, extensive reporting, compliance management, and advanced analytics	The primary focus is on large enterprises, which need to enhance data integration, AI-driven analytics, and real-time risk and compliance management	Data integration, AI-driven analytics, real-time risk, and compliance management

(*Contd.*)

Vendor	Strengths	Gaps	Opportunities
ReportWise	Automated data collection, extensive partner network, robust reporting capabilities, collaborative analytics, and AI for compliance tracking	The primary focus is on the North American and European market's need for better data management tools, collaborative analytics and AI-driven compliance tracking	Better data management, collaborative analytics, AI-driven compliance tracking

* Software vendor names have been anonymized.

Key Outcomes from the Market Analysis:

1. Data Management

    - **Key Capabilities:** Most leading ESG software solutions offer robust data integration capabilities, enabling companies to pull data from various sources, including IoT sensors, financial systems, and supply chain data. Advanced data management features ensure data accuracy and consistency.

    - **Assessment:** These tools are highly available and mature. They are well-developed and widely implemented, providing a solid foundation for ESG data collection and management.

2. Reporting and Compliance

    - **Key Capabilities:** Comprehensive reporting features, including customizable templates and automated report generation for standards like GRI, SASB, TCFD, and more. Compliance tracking with real-time alerts and audit trails.

    - **Assessment:** Moderately mature. While most solutions offer robust reporting capabilities, the customization and integration with specific regulatory requirements can vary. Continuous improvements are needed to keep up with evolving standards.

3. Advanced Analytics and Insights

    - **Key Capabilities:** Tools for advanced data analysis, predictive modeling, and scenario analysis. AI and machine learning integration to provide deeper insights and automated recommendations.
    - **Assessment:** These features are increasingly available and continue to be enhanced as they emerge and evolve. There's significant potential for growth in predictive analytics and AI-driven insights.

4. Stakeholder Management and Engagement

    - **Key Capabilities:** Tools for managing stakeholder communications, engagement activities, and feedback collection. Features for real-time collaboration and information sharing.
    - **Assessment:** Our team can improve interactivity and real-time engagement features. While basic capabilities are present, we can further develop them.

5. Supply Chain Management and Transparency

    - **Key Capabilities:** Detailed monitoring and reporting of supply chain activities, ethical sourcing verification, and sustainability performance tracking.
    - **Assessment:** Growing. These features are becoming more prevalent, but the depth and integration of supply chain transparency tools can vary across solutions.

6. Audit Management

    - **Key Capabilities:** Internal and external audit management tools, comprehensive audit trails, version control, and automated compliance checks.
    - **Assessment:** Strong and improving. Most leading software solutions provide robust audit management features, though ease of use and integration with other systems can vary.

7. Risk Management
    - **Key Capabilities:** Identify and assess ESG-related risks, risk mitigation strategies, and continuous monitoring tools.
    - **Assessment:** Increasing focus. These tools are evolving to provide more comprehensive risk management capabilities, driven by growing regulatory and stakeholder expectations.
8. Disclosure Management
    - **Key Capabilities:** Tools for preparing and publishing sustainability reports, financial disclosures, and other required communications with stakeholders.
    - **Assessment:** Well-established but evolving. Disclosure management tools are generally robust, with ongoing improvements to meet diverse reporting requirements and ensure transparency.

Overall Roadmap of Software Vendors

Leading ESG software vendors are focusing on several key areas to enhance their offerings and better meet market demands:

1. Integration and Interoperability
    - Enhancing integration capabilities with various data sources and enterprise systems to ensure seamless data flow and comprehensive ESG reporting.
2. Advanced Analytics and AI
    - Investing in AI and machine learning to provide more advanced analytics, predictive modeling, and automated insights helps companies make more informed decisions than traditional methods.
3. User Experience and Customization
    - Improve user interfaces and offer more excellent customization options to tailor the software to specific industry needs and regulatory requirements.

4. Regulatory Compliance Updates
    - Continuously updating compliance modules to align with new and evolving regulations, ensuring companies remain compliant without significant manual effort.
5. Real-Time Monitoring and Reporting
    - Developing capabilities for real-time data monitoring and instant reporting to provide up-to-the-minute insights and enable swift action on ESG issues.
6. Supply Chain Transparency
    - Expanding tools for detailed supply chain visibility, ethical sourcing, and sustainability performance tracking to ensure transparency.
7. Stakeholder Engagement and Collaboration
    - Enhancing features for stakeholder engagement, including real-time collaboration tools, feedback mechanisms, and interactive reporting dashboards.

A SIPOC (Suppliers, Inputs, Processes, Outputs, Customers) diagram visualizes the process involved in ESG management. This diagram provides a high-level view of the critical elements involved in ESG management software, illustrating the flow from data providers and integration partners to the end-users, who are typically large enterprises, medium enterprises, industry-specific organizations, regulatory bodies, and internal stakeholders.

Table 4.2 SIPOC Chart for ESG Software

Element	**Description**
Suppliers	- Data Providers (e.g., Environmental data sources, Regulatory bodies)
	- Integration Partners (e.g., API providers, IoT device manufacturers)
	- Technology Vendors (e.g., AI, Analytics, Cloud services providers)
	- Consulting Firms (e.g. Implementation partners, Regulatory consultants)
Inputs	- ESG Data (e.g., Environmental metrics, Social performance, governance practices)
	- Regulatory Requirements (e.g. CSRD, TCFD, GRI standards)
	- Risk Management Data (e.g. supply chain risks, compliance risks)
	- Integration Data (e.g., Real-time IoT data, API data feeds)
	- Frameworks (e.g., Global ESG standards, Industry-specific guidelines)
Process	- Data Collection (e.g. automated data retrieval, IoT integration)
	- Data Integration (e.g. consolidation of ESG data from various sources)
	- Analysis & Reporting (e.g. predictive analytics, sustainability reporting)
	- Compliance Monitoring (e.g. real-time compliance tracking, governance analytics)
	- Risk Management (e.g. AI-driven risk assessment, Scenario forecasting)
Outputs	- ESG Reports (e.g., Compliance reports, Sustainability performance reports)
	- Risk Mitigation Strategies (e.g. AI-driven insights, Scenario planning)
	- Compliance Status (e.g., Real-time compliance updates, governance analytics)
	- Strategic Insights (e.g., Predictive analytics outcomes, Scenario planning insights)
Customers	- Large Enterprises (e.g. multinational corporations with extensive ESG requirements)

Element	Description
	- Medium Enterprises (e.g., companies with growing ESG needs)
	- Industry-Specific Organizations (e.g., Manufacturing, Supply Chain, Technology sectors)
	- Regulatory Bodies (e.g. organizations that require compliance tracking and reporting)
	- Internal Stakeholders (e.g. Sustainability officers, Compliance officers, Risk managers)

Competitive Positioning

Porter's Five Forces

As I began to chart the course for developing an ESG application, I knew that understanding the competitive landscape was crucial. The ESG management and reporting software market is dynamic, with new players emerging and established vendors continuously evolving. To navigate this terrain, I turned to Porter's Five Forces—a strategic framework that reveals the pressures and opportunities within any industry. When applied thoughtfully, it's a tool that can guide the development of a product that survives and thrives in a competitive market.

1. Rivalry Among Competitors: The Battle for ESG Supremacy

The first force that caught my attention was the rivalry among competitors. The world of ESG software is crowded, with giants and niche players vying for dominance. From EcoPlan's robust, customizable solutions to SecureGuard Technologies' risk management prowess, each competitor brings something unique. GreenSuite, for example, is a powerhouse with extensive global framework support, catering to large enterprises that need comprehensive digital systems. However, its complexity often makes it a daunting choice for smaller organizations.

In this competitive environment, the key to success lies in differentiation. Understanding that the market is saturated with feature-rich platforms, I realized that our ESG application must offer something beyond the norm. It's not just about matching the features of existing players but about identifying gaps and innovating where others fall short. For instance, while GreenSuite excels in process-level management, there's an opportunity to enhance data integration capabilities and introduce predictive analytics—features that could give our application a competitive edge.

2. Bargaining Power of Suppliers: The Backbone of ESG Data Integration

Next, I considered suppliers' bargaining power, which, in the context of ESG software, often translates to the data providers and integration partners that fuel the application's functionality. Platforms like SustainCloud have set the bar high with strong API capabilities and extensive data integration features. However, the complexity of integrating multiple data sources can be a challenge, especially for newer players in the market.

To mitigate the risks posed by supplier power, our ESG application must prioritize flexible and scalable data integration capabilities. The ability to seamlessly connect with various data sources—whether through REST APIs or more advanced methods—will be critical. By centralizing data and offering robust integration options, we can reduce dependency on any single supplier, ensuring that our application remains resilient and adaptable as the market evolves.

3. Bargaining Power of Customers: Meeting the Demands of the ESG-Conscious Consumer

The bargaining power of customers is a force that cannot be underestimated. In the ESG space, customers—whether they are large enterprises or SMEs—are increasingly demanding solutions that are not only comprehensive but also user-friendly and adaptable. InsightAI, with its customizable dashboards and strong data health check capabilities, is an example of how companies cater to their client's specific needs. Yet, its primary focus on large enterprises could be a drawback, particularly if smaller organizations feel underserved.

Our ESG application must be designed with customer empowerment in mind. This means offering a range of customization options and ensuring the application is accessible to businesses of all sizes. We can position our product as a flexible, intelligent solution that meets the market's diverse needs by providing features like enhanced reporting customization and AI-driven insights. Additionally, integrating real-time compliance monitoring could be a game-changer, offering customers the peace of mind that they are always ahead of regulatory requirements.

4. Threat of Market Entrants: Building Barriers Through Innovation

The threat of new market entrants is a reality in the rapidly growing ESG software market. While established players like GreenSuite and EcoFlow have built strong reputations, the barriers to entry are manageable. High investment demands, economies of scale, and brand loyalty are initial deterrents, but these can be overcome with the right strategy.

To safeguard our position, our ESG application must meet current industry standards and push the boundaries of what is possible. For example, incorporating advanced technologies like AI and machine learning can help differentiate our product. Integrating real-time data tracking and scenario planning tools will further enhance our offering, making it difficult for new entrants to replicate our success without significant investment. We can build and maintain high entry barriers by continuously innovating and securing our place in the market.

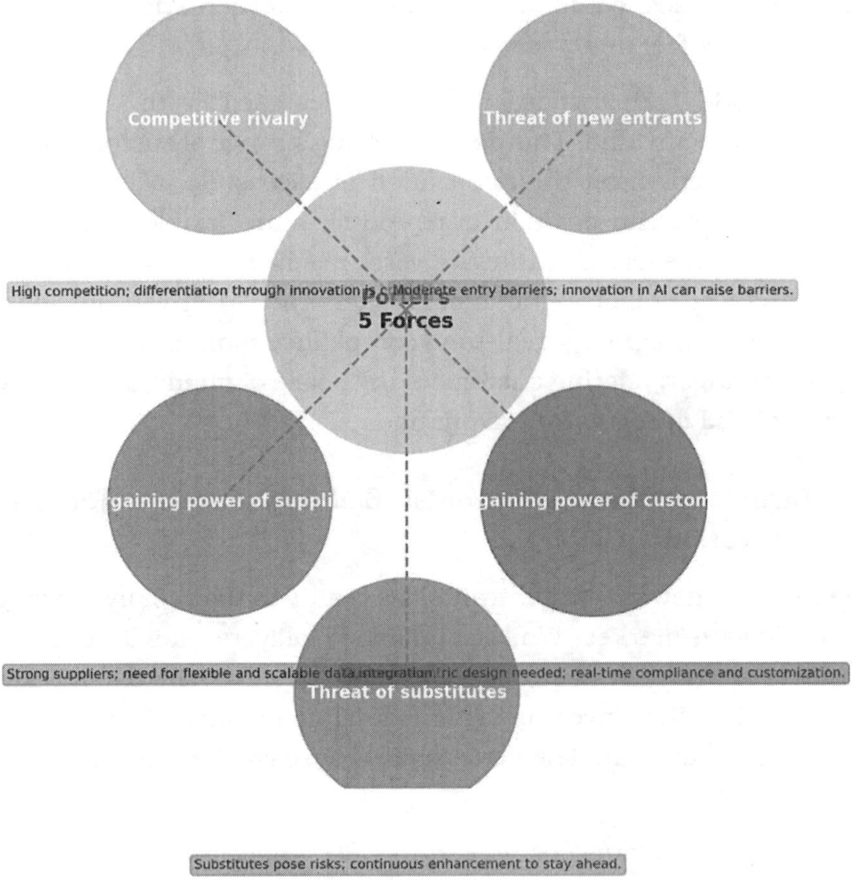

Figure 4.5 Porter's Five Forces analysis

5. Threat of Substitutes: Staying Ahead in the ESG Game

Finally, there's the threat of substitutes—alternative products or services that could lure customers away. In the ESG space, the availability of substitutes can significantly weaken a company's position, especially if they offer similar capabilities at a lower cost or with greater ease of use. For instance, platforms like ReportWise and EnviroHub offer robust compliance and reporting solutions, but their primary focus on specific regions or enterprise sizes could leave gaps in the market.

Our strategy must involve staying ahead of these substitutes by continuously enhancing our product's value proposition. This could mean developing better collaborative analytics tools, improving data management features, and integrating advanced AI-driven compliance tracking. By offering a more comprehensive, user-friendly, and forward-thinking solution, we can ensure that our ESG application remains the preferred choice, even in the face of viable alternatives.

Navigating the ESG Software Market: A Strategic Approach

Applying Porter's Five Forces to developing an ESG application revealed challenges and opportunities. The competitive landscape is intense, but we can carve out a niche for our product by understanding and strategically addressing each force. It's more than surviving in this market; it's about thriving by offering something unique.

By focusing on innovative data integration, customer-centric customization, and cutting-edge technologies, we can build an ESG application that competes with the existing giants and sets new industry standards. The journey ahead is challenging, but our ESG application can become a leader in this dynamic and evolving market with a clear strategy and a commitment to excellence.

Product Differentiation and Innovation Using Blue Ocean Strategy Canvas

Imagine steering a ship, navigating through familiar waters where every other captain battles over the same territory and resources. That's your market—the familiar competitive landscape where every move and countermove is predictable. But you've heard whispers of uncharted waters, where few have ventured, and the potential for discovery is enormous. Inspired, you chart a course into this new territory to find your Blue Ocean.

As you begin your journey, you gather your crew – the leadership team and key stakeholders of your ESG management tool. Together, you review the map of current market conditions. We plot each feature, pricing strategy, and customer service element your competitors offer on this map. This exercise reveals where you are and where everyone else is putting their efforts.

Amidst the discussion, someone points out a recurring pattern: many competitors focus intensely on advanced features, perhaps neglecting an area critically underserved—user simplicity and proactive compliance guidance. This observation sparks an idea. What if you simplify the user experience and integrate predictive compliance features that help customers foresee potential challenges instead of adding more complex features? Exploring this uncharted territory could set us apart from others.

With the idea taking shape, you sketch a new value curve – a strategic profile that diverges markedly from your rivals. Instead of fighting over the same features, you reduce the complexity and enhance elements that deliver real value but others currently overlook. The excitement grows as you visualize a product that doesn't just compete but changes the game's rules.

But you're cautious. To ensure this isn't just a siren's call, you conduct a small, targeted survey and a prototype test with a select group of customers. The feedback is invigorating—there's genuine interest and potential in your new approach. With confidence swelling, you ready your crew for full-scale implementation. Aligning your development team, adjusting marketing messages, and preparing customer support for the new focus are all involved in this process.

As the product launches, you communicate this bold new direction through stories that resonate with your customers – stories of ease, foresight, and empowerment. Internally, your team feels renewed purpose, understanding that they are not just selling a product but pioneering a new approach.

Months into the journey, you know your gamble has paid off as more customers come aboard and are delighted by what they find. You've not only discovered a Blue Ocean, but you've claimed it as your own. Your competitors are far behind, still battling over the same shrinking territories, while you sail ahead in clear, open waters, charting a course you can follow.

This journey isn't just about escaping competition; it's about creating a new market space where your product defines the standards, offering unique value that turns potential users into loyal advocates. Based on the market research document, I've conducted a value gap analysis using the Blue Ocean strategy framework. This strategy helps identify areas to eliminate, raise, create, and reduce (ERRC) to carve out a unique market position for the proposed ESG management software.

1. Eliminate

Complex, Non-User-Friendly Interfaces

- Current Situation: Many existing ESG management solutions have complex interfaces that require extensive training and can be challenging to navigate.
- Action: Eliminate complex interfaces and replace them with a more intuitive, user-friendly design that requires minimal training.

Redundant Features

- Current Situation: Some features are rarely used or overlap with other functionalities.
- Action: Eliminate redundant features to streamline the software and improve usability.

2. Raise

Integration Capabilities

- Current Situation: While some solutions offer integration with external systems, many fail to provide seamless and comprehensive integration.

- Action: Raise integration capabilities by supporting more systems and ensuring smooth data exchange. This process includes integrating ERP, CRM, HR, and other enterprise systems.

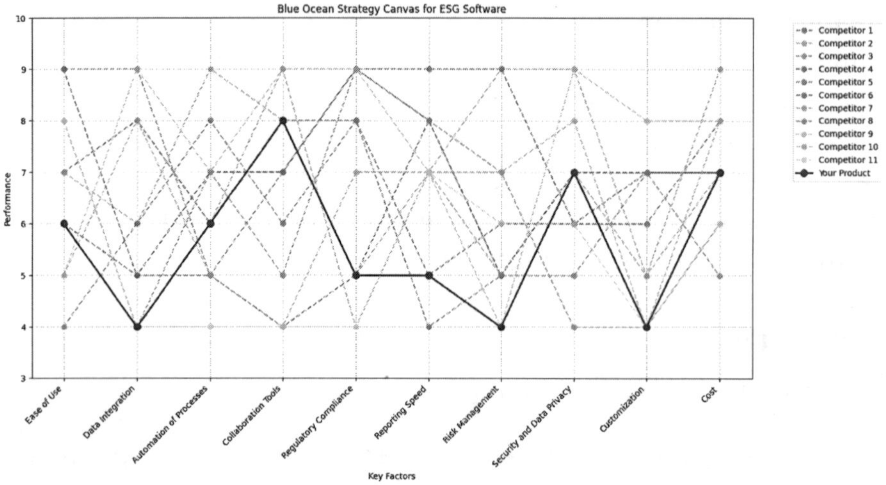

Figure 4.6 Blue Ocean Strategy Canvas for ESG Management Software

Checklist: Key Factors for ESG Software Market Using Blue Ocean Strategy Canvas

1. Ease of Use
    - Is the software user-friendly for ESG managers?
    - Does it minimize the learning curve?
2. Data Integration
    - Can the software integrate with various systems (e.g., ERP, SCM, carbon calculators)?
    - Does it provide a comprehensive and cohesive data set?
3. Automation of Processes
    - Does the software automate scheduling, data collection, and reporting?
    - How effectively does it reduce manual effort?

4. Collaboration Tools
    - Does the software include features like virtual workshops, real-time collaboration, and document sharing?
    - How well does it facilitate teamwork and communication?
5. Regulatory Compliance
    - Can the software handle complex regulatory requirements (e.g., GRI, CDP, SASB)?
    - Does it keep companies compliant with ease?
6. Reporting Speed
    - How quickly can the software generate audit-ready reports?
    - Does it provide accurate and timely reporting?
7. Risk Management
    - Does the software offer robust tools for identifying and managing ESG risks?
    - How proactive is it in helping companies mitigate risks?
8. Security and Data Privacy
    - Are the software's security features robust?
    - Does it comply with data privacy regulations?
    - How well does it protect sensitive information?
9. Customization
    - Can the software be tailored to meet specific organizational needs?
    - How flexible is it in adapting to different user requirements?
10. Cost
    - Is the software competitively priced?

  - Does the value provided justify the cost, including licensing, implementation, and ongoing maintenance?

- Current Situation: Basic reporting and analytics are common, but advanced predictive and real-time reporting are often lacking.
- Action: Incorporate advanced AI-driven predictive analytics and real-time reporting capabilities to raise the standard of analytics and reporting.

3. Create

Mobile Access and Remote Management

- Current Situation: Few solutions offer robust mobile access or remote management capabilities.
- Action: Create a mobile application and remote management features to allow users to access and manage ESG data anywhere.

Scenario Planning and Forecasting Tools

- Current Situation: Limited scenario planning and forecasting tools are critical for strategic decision-making.
- Action: Create comprehensive scenario planning and forecasting tools to help organizations plan and prepare for future ESG scenarios.

4. Reduce

Manual Data Entry

- Current Situation: Manual data entry is time-consuming and prone to errors, yet it's still prevalent in many solutions.
- Action: Reduce the reliance on manual data entry by automating data collection and validation processes.

Implementation Complexity

- Current Situation: High complexity in the implementation process can deter adoption and increase costs.
- Action: Reduce implementation complexity by providing more out-of-the-box solutions and streamlined setup processes.

Market Opportunities for ESG Solutions

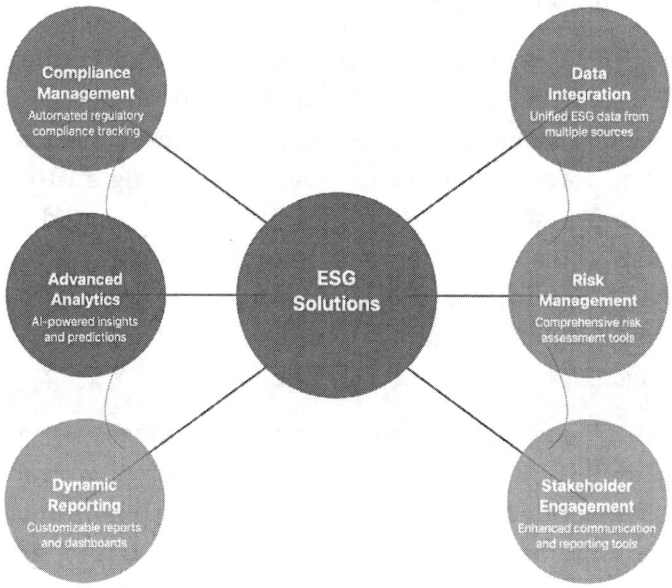

Market Opportunity Areas:

Each bubble represents a key market opportunity with significant growth potential in the ESG solutions space.
Connected lines show interdependencies and potential for integrated solutions.

What it meant for my ESG Management Software

During my deep dive into ESG software, I uncovered some fascinating insights. The market was buzzing with potential, but there were clear areas where we could make a splash. So, here's the exciting part: planning our roadmap to create something truly exceptional.

First, flexibility and customization emerged as significant needs. Imagine the thrill of giving users the power to tweak dashboards and indicators to their exact specifications. Our software had to be adaptable, allowing for high levels of customization to meet diverse needs. Next, I discovered that integration and user experience were game-changers. No one wants to struggle with a clunky system. I envisioned our software seamlessly blending with existing tools while being incredibly user-friendly. The goal was clear: make it intuitive and powerful simultaneously.

Another big revelation was the importance of comprehensive ESG coverage. Businesses don't just focus on one aspect – they care about environmental, social, and governance issues equally. I realized our software had to be holistic, covering all these bases without compromising. Geographical diversity and industry specificity also stood out. Whether a company operates in bustling New York or vibrant New Delhi, our software must cater to different markets. Plus, it had to adapt to various industry needs, providing a competitive edge regardless of location.

Scalability and accessibility were non-negotiables, too. I envisioned our software supporting both massive enterprises and smaller organizations. It had to scale effortlessly, ensuring everyone could harness its full potential. Automation and data management were the cherry on top. Automating data collection and offering robust data handling capabilities would save users countless hours. Our software needed to make life easier and more efficient.

With all these insights, I planned the roadmap. The journey was exhilarating as I turned market discoveries into actionable plans. I couldn't wait to see how our software would transform the ESG landscape, meeting real needs and setting new standards.

Recommendations for Proposed ESG Software

1. Develop Customizable Dashboards and Indicators. This will Allow users to tailor the software to their needs, ensuring flexibility and personalization.
2. Ensure Seamless Integration: Provide robust API capabilities and integration with major systems to enhance user experience and streamline data management.
3. Offer Comprehensive ESG Coverage: Ensure the software covers all aspects of ESG equally and can specialize in critical areas, like regulatory compliance or supply chain sustainability.
4. Expand Global Reach: Focus on making the software applicable to diverse geographical markets and supporting various regulatory frameworks and industry standards.
5. Prioritize User-Friendly Design: Balance powerful features with an intuitive, easy-to-use interface to accommodate both large and small enterprises.
6. Leverage Automation: Incorporate automated data collection and management features to enhance efficiency and data accuracy.
7. Build Scalability: Design the software to be scalable, supporting the needs of large and small to medium enterprises and ensuring broad market appeal.
8. Integrate Industry-Specific Solutions: Offer tailored solutions for different industries, addressing specific needs and regulatory requirements.

This analysis and these recommendations became the foundation for my journey to develop an ESG software solution. Armed with these insights, I was ready to create a product that would compete in this dynamic market and lead to innovation and user satisfaction. The road ahead was challenging, but with a clear understanding of the landscape and a strategic plan, I felt confident in my ability to significantly impact ESG management and reporting.

Chapter 5

Growth Planning and Strategic Options

Selecting the right strategy is akin to setting the compass on a ship before a long voyage. It's a decision that determines not just the destination but the journey itself—the challenges you will face, the resources you will need, and the opportunities you might seize along the way. In the complex and ever-evolving world of Environmental, Social, and Governance (ESG) management, making these strategic choices is even more crucial. The stakes are higher, the landscape is more uncertain, and the expectations—from stakeholders, regulators, and society—are relentlessly demanding.

As I embarked on developing our ESG application, the question of strategy selection loomed large. It wasn't just about picking a path that looked promising on paper; it was about choosing a strategy aligned with our core values, capabilities, and market realities. Through rigorous analysis and introspection, I found that strategy selection is not a one-size-fits-all process. Instead, it is a nuanced, multi-dimensional decision-making exercise that requires analytical rigor and creative foresight.

In this chapter, I will guide you through the intricate strategy selection process, drawing from our journey and the strategic frameworks that have shaped our path. We will explore how Mintzberg's 5P Model offers a multi-faceted lens through which to view strategy—not just as a plan, but as a ploy, a pattern, a position, and a perspective. This model helped us understand the different dimensions of strategy and how they interact, providing a comprehensive foundation for our decision-making.

Ansoff Matrix Analysis

As I embarked on the journey to develop our ESG application, I knew that growth wouldn't just happen by chance – it would require a deliberate strategy carefully crafted and tailored to our unique challenges and opportunities. That's where the Ansoff matrix comes into play. This strategic planning tool, developed by Harry Igor Ansoff, is a robust framework that helps chart a course through potential growth opportunities by considering two key factors: our products and the markets we serve.

The Ansoff matrix offers four strategies: Market Penetration, Product Development, Market Development, and Diversification. Each quadrant presents a different path and way of thinking about growing our business. Let me explain how I've been using this framework to guide our ESG application's growth strategy.

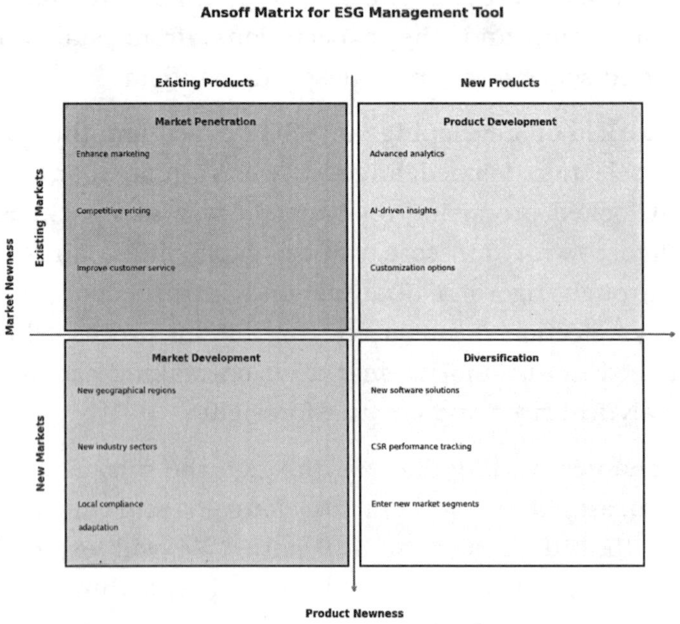

Figure 5.1 Ansoff Matrix for ESG Management Tool

1. Market Penetration: Deepening Our Roots in Familiar Soil

In the early stages of developing our ESG application, I realized that one of the most straightforward ways to grow was to focus on our existing market. Market Penetration is about deepening our roots and solidifying our position by increasing our market share. It's not just about reaching more customers; it's about convincing the ones we already have to engage more deeply with our product.

Since we are a new entrant, our first challenge is building brand recognition and trust. I knew we had to be aggressive with our marketing, using every opportunity to showcase the deep expertise that sets us apart. We crafted content that spoke directly to our audience's pain points, demonstrating that we understood their challenges and that our application was uniquely equipped to solve them.

But marketing isn't just about attracting new customers; it's also about keeping the ones you have. That's why we focused on optimizing our application, continuously improving it based on user feedback. By ensuring that our product is functional and delightful, we could encourage our existing customers to engage more frequently and rely on our solution for an ever-wider range of ESG needs.

2. Product Development: Innovating to Meet Market Demands

As we gained traction, it became clear that the market's needs were evolving, and so too must our product. This is where product development comes into play, creating new features and improvements that add value to our existing market.

We leveraged our industry knowledge to identify the features that would make a difference. Advanced predictive analytics, real-time compliance monitoring, and enhanced data integration were just some of the developments that could set us apart from the competition. We knew that our users needed more than just a one-size-fits-all solution; they needed a product that could evolve with their needs.

But product development isn't just about adding bells and whistles. It's about enhancing the core of our offer, ensuring that every new feature aligns with our users' goals and improves their experience. These innovations will keep our application relevant and indispensable in a crowded market.

3. Market Development: Expanding Our Horizons

Once we had a solid product that resonated with our initial audience, it was time to think bigger. Market Development is about taking what we've built and finding new audiences who need it—whether that means expanding into new geographic regions, targeting different industry sectors, or exploring new distribution channels.

For us, this meant looking at markets where ESG regulations were tightening—places like the European Union, where businesses are under increasing pressure to comply with stringent sustainability standards. We saw an opportunity to tailor our application to meet these specific regulatory requirements, positioning ourselves as the go-to solution for companies navigating these complex waters.

But entering new markets isn't just about translating our product into different languages or currencies. It requires a deep understanding of the local context, the competitive landscape, and the specific needs of new customer segments. We invested in market research and developed targeted marketing strategies to ensure that, when we expanded, we did so thoughtfully and impactfully.

4. Diversification: Venturing into New Frontiers

Finally, there's diversification—perhaps the most ambitious and challenging growth strategy. Diversification involves entering new markets with new products, a bold move that can help us reduce our reliance on a single market or product.

Given our financial constraints, this is a strategy we approach with caution. However, expanding our offerings beyond the core ESG application is intriguing. For example, horizontal diversification could involve developing new tools that complement our existing application, such as an ESG reporting tool that integrates seamlessly with other enterprise systems.

Or we might explore vertical diversification, taking control of more of the value chain by developing proprietary ESG data sources. This would enhance our product's capabilities and reduce our dependency on external data providers.

On the other hand, lateral diversification would involve venturing into entirely new markets—perhaps leveraging our expertise to offer consulting services or create educational content for businesses looking to improve their ESG practices. While this is a longer-term play, it could significantly broaden our impact and open new revenue streams.

The BCG Analysis

As I was diving deep into strategic management for our ESG application, I came across a tool that has stood the test of time: the BCG Matrix. Developed by the Boston Consulting Group in the 1970s, the BCG Matrix, or the product portfolio matrix, is a robust framework that helps businesses decide where to focus their resources and energy.

Imagine the matrix as a grid with two axes: the vertical axis represents the market growth rate, and the horizontal axis represents the relative market share. Where a product or service falls on this grid can tell us a lot about how we should approach its future – whether to invest heavily, maintain, or even consider divesting.

1. Cash Cows: The Steady Earners

In the BCG Matrix, 'Cash Cows' are products or services with a high market share in a mature, stable market. They're a business's workhorses—reliable, steady earners who don't require a lot of additional investment because the market isn't growing significantly.

Instead, they generate substantial cash flow, which can be used to fund other, more growth-oriented initiatives.

For our ESG application, we might still need to get a Cash Cow, but we could aspire to create one. Perhaps, one day, a specific module or feature within our platform will become the industry standard—so ubiquitous that nearly every business adopts it. Once that happens, we could reduce our investment in its development and shift those funds to more dynamic parts of our portfolio.

2. Stars: The Bright Opportunities

'Stars' in the BCG Matrix are those products with a high market share in a rapidly growing market. These rising stars are brimming with potential but also demand significant investment to maintain their position and capture growth opportunities.

Our ESG application itself is a potential star. The market for ESG solutions is increasing as businesses increasingly recognize the importance of environmental, social, and governance factors. But to capitalize on this, we must invest heavily in innovation—whether developing advanced analytics, enhancing our real-time compliance monitoring, or expanding our market reach. The goal is to ensure that our application maintains and grows its market share as the ESG market expands.

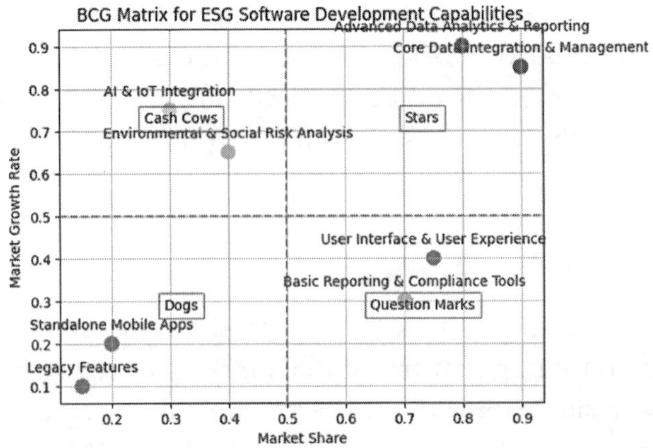

Figure 5.2 BCG Matrix Analysis for ESG Application Development

3. Question Marks: The Uncertain Potentials

'Question Marks' are products with low market share in a high-growth market. They're the wild cards of a portfolio—potentially promising but uncertain. These are the products that need careful consideration. Do we invest more to turn them into stars or cut our losses?

Certain new features or modules for our ESG application fall into this category. Perhaps a particular feature, like a specialized compliance tool, hasn't yet gained traction, even though the market demand is there. We must ask ourselves whether the potential reward justifies the investment required to boost its market share. This is where thorough market research and competitive analysis come into play. Investing in these question marks could be the key to our future growth if we see a clear path to success.

4. Dogs: The Low Performers

Finally, we have the 'Dogs' – products with low market share in a low-growth market. These are the underperformers that might be draining resources without much return. In many cases, the best course of action is to divest or phase out these products, freeing up resources to focus on more promising areas.

As much as we hope that all parts of our ESG application will thrive, some features or modules might not perform as expected. Perhaps they were built for a market that never materialized or didn't resonate with our customers. Identifying these dogs early allows us to make tough decisions, cutting back where necessary to ensure we're not spreading ourselves too thin.

The BCG Matrix will be invaluable as we continue developing and refining our ESG application. It helps us make informed decisions about where to allocate our resources, ensuring that we're not just reacting to market changes but strategically positioning ourselves for the future.

Whether we're nurturing a star, deciding the fate of a Question Mark, or optimizing a Cash Cow, this framework gives us the clarity we need to navigate the complex landscape of ESG management confidently.

Organizational Alignment and Implementation

McKinsey 7S Model

As I embarked on developing our ESG application, I quickly realized that building a successful product wasn't just about having the right features or understanding the market. It was about creating a cohesive, well-aligned organization where every part worked together seamlessly toward a common goal. That's where the McKinsey 7-S Model comes in – a framework that offers a holistic view of an organization by breaking it down into seven interdependent components: Strategy, Structure, Systems, Shared Values, Skills, Staff, and Style.

1. Strategy: The Roadmap to Success

Strategy is at the heart of everything we do. For our ESG application, the strategy represents our plan of action to achieve long-term goals—becoming a leading solution provider in the rapidly growing ESG market. Our approach is built on the foundation of our deep industry knowledge and the urgent market need for practical ESG management tools. We've decided to focus on developing features that meet today's regulatory requirements and anticipate future trends, like real-time compliance monitoring and advanced data analytics.

But strategy is more than just a plan; it's our guiding star. It helps us decide where to allocate resources, which markets to enter, and how to differentiate ourselves from the competition. As a new entrant with limited resources, our strategy also involves careful prioritization, focusing on the most impactful features and markets where we have a competitive edge.

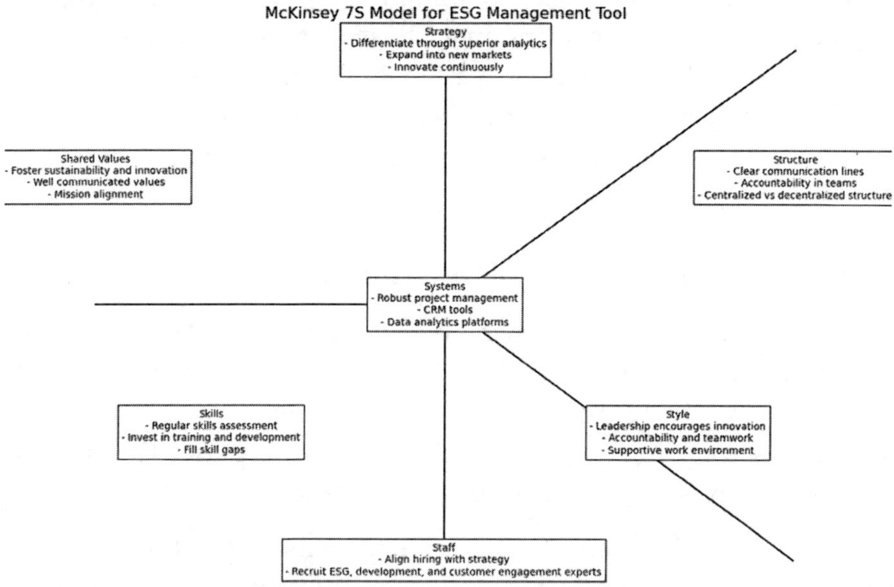

Figure 5.3 McKinsey 7S model for ESG management Tool

2. Structure: The Backbone of Our Operations

Our organization's structure is how we turn our strategy into action. It involves defining roles, responsibilities, and reporting lines. Given our startup nature, we've opted for a lean and flexible structure that allows us to be agile and responsive to market changes.

Our structure supports our strategy by facilitating rapid decision-making and efficient communication. For instance, we've kept our teams small but cross-functional, ensuring that developers, marketers, and customer support work closely together. This structure enables us to adapt quickly to feedback, iterate on our product, and focus intensely on our strategic goals.

3. Systems: The Processes That Keep Us Running

Systems refer to the formal processes, procedures, and routines that guide our daily operations. For our ESG application, these include our development methodologies, performance measurement systems, and customer feedback loops.

We've implemented agile development processes, allowing us to refine our product continuously based on user feedback. Our performance measurement systems help us track progress against key milestones, ensuring we stay on course. Our customer feedback systems are designed to capture insights that inform our product development and strategic decisions.

4. Shared Values: The Core of Our Culture

Shared values are the underlying beliefs and principles that shape our corporate culture. Our team's values are centered around sustainability, integrity, and innovation. By embedding these values into everything we do, we can create a product that meets market demands and contributes positively to society.

These shared values guide our decisions, from the features we prioritize to how we interact with our customers and partners. They are the glue that holds our organization together, ensuring everyone is aligned with our mission and vision.

5. Skills: The Capabilities That Drive Our Success

Skills refer to the competencies and capabilities of our team members. In the context of our ESG application, this means having the right mix of technical expertise, industry knowledge, and soft skills, like leadership and problem-solving.

Given our focus on ESG, we've prioritized building a team with deep expertise in environmental, social, and governance issues. However, we also recognize the importance of technical skills, especially as we integrate advanced features like AI-driven analytics. We invest in ongoing training and development to ensure we have the right skills, keeping our team at the cutting-edge of technology and industry trends.

6. Staff: The People Who Make It Happen

Our staff—our people—are the lifeblood of our organization. Recruiting, developing, and retaining talent is crucial to our success. We've focused on building a diverse team that brings a range of perspectives and experiences to the table, believing that this diversity will drive innovation and better decision-making.

But it's not just about hiring the right people; it's about placing them in roles where they can thrive and contribute to our strategic goals. We've worked hard to create a supportive environment where our team feels valued and motivated to do their best work.

7. Style: The Leadership That Sets the Tone

Style refers to the leadership style and behaviors exhibited by senior management. This means leading by example and fostering a culture of transparency, collaboration, and continuous improvement. Our leadership style aligns with our shared values, creating a work environment where innovation can flourish.

By setting the right tone at the top, we can inspire our team to take ownership of their work, think creatively, and push the boundaries of what's possible with our ESG application.

What It Meant for My ESG Management Software

During my deep dive into ESG software, I uncovered some fascinating insights. The market was buzzing with potential, but there were clear areas where we could make a splash. So, here's the exciting part: planning our roadmap to create something truly exceptional.

First, flexibility and customization emerged as significant needs. Imagine the thrill of giving users the power to tweak dashboards and indicators to their exact specifications. Our software had to be adaptable, allowing for high levels of customization to meet diverse needs. Next, I discovered that integration and user experience were game-changers. No one wants to struggle with a clunky system. I envisioned our software seamlessly blending with existing tools while being incredibly user-friendly. The goal was clear: make it intuitive and powerful simultaneously.

Another big revelation was the importance of comprehensive ESG coverage. Businesses don't just focus on one aspect – they care about environmental, social, and governance issues equally. I realized our software had to be holistic, covering all these bases without compromising. Geographical diversity and industry specificity also stood out. Whether a company operates in bustling New York or vibrant New Delhi, our software must cater to different markets. Plus, it had to adapt to various industry needs, providing a competitive edge regardless of location.

Scalability and accessibility were non-negotiables, too. I envisioned our software supporting both massive enterprises and smaller organizations. It had to scale effortlessly, ensuring everyone could harness its full potential. Automation and data management were the cherry on top. Automating data collection and offering robust data handling capabilities would save users countless hours. Our software needed to make life easier and more efficient.

With all these insights, I planned the roadmap. The journey was exhilarating as I turned market discoveries into actionable plans. I couldn't wait to see how our software would transform the ESG landscape, meeting real needs and setting new standards.

Recommendations for Proposed ESG Software

1. Develop Customizable Dashboards and Indicators. This will Allow users to tailor the software to their needs, ensuring flexibility and personalization.
2. Ensure Seamless Integration: Provide robust API capabilities and integration with major systems to enhance user experience and streamline data management.
3. Offer Comprehensive ESG Coverage: Ensure the software covers all aspects of ESG equally and can specialize in critical areas, like regulatory compliance or supply chain sustainability.
4. Expand Global Reach: Focus on making the software applicable to diverse geographical markets, supporting various regulatory frameworks and industry standards.

5. Prioritize User-Friendly Design: Balance powerful features with an intuitive, easy-to-use interface to accommodate both large and small enterprises.
6. Leverage Automation: Incorporate automated data collection and management features to enhance efficiency and data accuracy.
7. Build Scalability: Design the software to be scalable, supporting the needs of large and small to medium enterprises and ensuring broad market appeal.
8. Integrate Industry-Specific Solutions: Offer tailored solutions for different industries, addressing specific needs and regulatory requirements.

This analysis and these recommendations became the foundation for my journey to develop an ESG software solution. Armed with these insights, I was ready to create a product that would compete in this dynamic market and lead to innovation and user satisfaction. The road ahead was challenging, but with a clear understanding of the landscape and a strategic plan, I felt confident in my ability to impact ESG management and reporting significantly. Here's a detailed roadmap for developing software to meet ESG and sustainability requirements, broken down into near-term, mid-term, and long-term phases. Each phase prioritizes essential features and capabilities based on the typical evolution of product development.

Near-Term (0-6 Months)

Objective: Establish a solid foundation with essential features that quickly address immediate needs and demonstrate value.

1. **Core Data Integration and Management:**
    - Integrate with key data sources (e.g., IoT sensors, financial systems, HR, EHS, Social, governance, and supply chain data).

Develop a robust data management system to handle various data types and ensure data quality.

- **Regulations:** Organizations aiming to meet sustainability benchmarks must comply with initial data reporting standards, such as the Global Reporting Initiative (GRI) and the Sustainability Accounting Standards Board (SASB).
- **How It Helps:** By integrating key data sources and ensuring data quality, organizations can meet basic reporting requirements and provide transparent, accurate data to stakeholders.

2. **Basic Reporting and Compliance:**
    - Implement basic reporting capabilities to generate standard ESG reports.
    - Build initial compliance tracking features for major regulations (e.g., GRI, SASB).
    - **Regulations:** Immediate compliance with mandatory ESG reporting requirements from local rules, such as the E.U. Non-Financial Reporting Directive (NFRD) or the UK Modern Slavery Act.
    - **How It Helps:** Early reporting capabilities allow organizations to generate necessary reports quickly, demonstrating compliance and transparency and enhancing reputation and stakeholder trust.
3. **User Interface and Experience:**
    - Design and develop a user-friendly interface with intuitive dashboards.
    - Ensure ease of use for basic data entry, visualization, and reporting tasks.
    - **Regulations:** User-friendly interfaces help ensure compliance, making it easier for employees to input and manage ESG data accurately.

- **How It Helps:** Simplifies data entry and report generation, reducing the risk of errors and non-compliance.

4. **Stakeholder Management:**
   - Create tools for essential stakeholder engagement and communication.
   - Include features for sharing reports and updates with key stakeholders.
   - **Regulations:** Compliance with stakeholder engagement requirements from standards like the International Integrated Reporting Council (IIRC) is critical for organizations to communicate their sustainability efforts effectively.
   - **How It Helps:** Enables effective communication with stakeholders, keeping them informed and engaged, which is crucial for regulatory compliance and building trust.

5. **Project Management and Collaboration:**
   - Integrate simple project management tools to track ESG initiatives.
   - Enable collaboration features for team communication and task assignments.
   - **Regulations:** Supports compliance with project-specific ESG initiatives, ensuring they meet regulatory standards.
   - **How It Helps:** Facilitates the organization and tracking of ESG projects, ensuring they align with regulatory requirements and internal goals.

Mid-Term (6-18 Months)

Objective: Enhance functionality, improve user experience, and expand capabilities to cover broader requirements.

1. **Advanced Analytics and Insights:**

   Develop advanced analytics tools for deeper data analysis and trend identification.

- Implement predictive modeling and scenario analysis features.
- **Regulations:** Compliance with more advanced regulatory requirements, such as the E.U. Taxonomy Regulation, necessitates in-depth data analysis.
- **How It Helps:** Provides deeper insights into ESG performance, enabling organizations to meet more stringent reporting standards and make data-driven decisions.

2. **Comprehensive Reporting and Customization:**

   Expand reporting capabilities to support customizable reports for different stakeholders.

   - Include detailed metrics and KPIs relevant to various ESG aspects.
   - **Regulations:** The ability to customize reports for compliance with diverse regulations, such as the Task Force on Climate-related Financial Disclosures (TCFD) and the upcoming Corporate Sustainability Reporting Directive (CSRD), is essential for organizations to meet regulatory requirements.
   - **How It Helps:** It offers tailored reporting to meet various regulatory requirements, helping organizations stay compliant across jurisdictions.

3. **Enhanced Compliance and Audit Trails:**

   - Add comprehensive compliance tracking for a broader range of regulations.
   - Implement audit trails and version control for better accountability.
   - **Regulations:** Supports audit and compliance tracking for regulations requiring detailed accountability, such as the Sarbanes-Oxley Act (SOX) for financial disclosures.

- **How It Helps:** Provides robust audit trails and compliance tracking, ensuring organizations can demonstrate adherence to regulations during audits and reviews.

4. **Supply Chain Transparency and Monitoring:**

   Develop tools for detailed supply chain tracking and transparency.

   - Include features to monitor and report on supply chain ethics and sustainability.
   - **Regulations:** Compliance with supply chain transparency requirements, such as those mandated by the California Transparency in Supply Chains Act, is crucial for companies to ensure ethical practices and legal adherence.
   - **How It Helps:** It enhances visibility into supply chains and ensures compliance with regulations that mandate ethical sourcing and transparency.

5. **Carbon Footprint Calculation and Management:**

   - Build precise carbon footprint calculation tools.
   - Integrate with relevant data sources to automate carbon tracking and reporting.
   - **Regulations:** Compliance with carbon reporting regulations, like the Greenhouse Gas Protocol and the Climate Disclosure Standards Board (CDSB), is essential for organizations to accurately report and manage their carbon emissions.
   - **How It Helps:** Enables accurate tracking and reporting of carbon emissions, ensuring organizations meet regulatory requirements and improve their environmental performance.

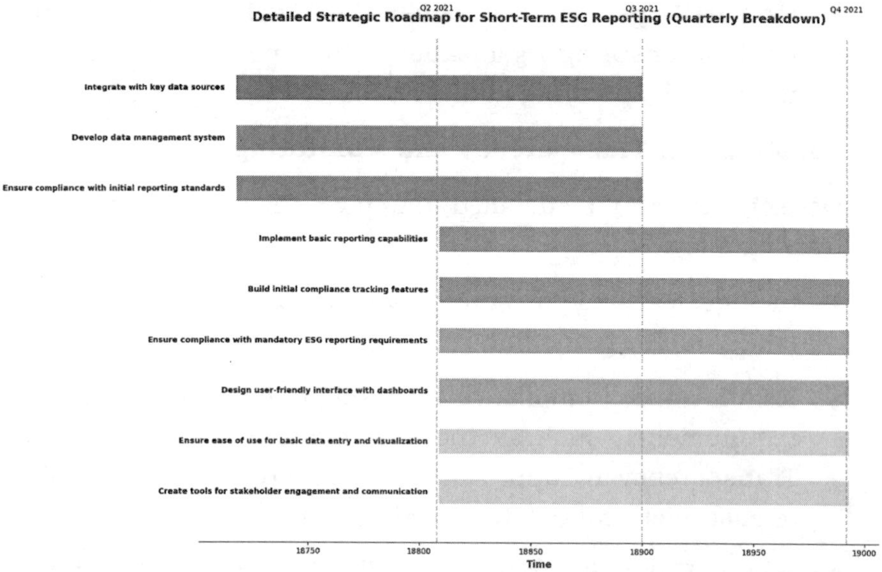

Figure 5.4 3-Year Strategic Roadmap of ESG Reporting and Data Management

Long-Term (18+ Months)

Objective: Future-proof the software, explore innovative features, and ensure scalability and adaptability.

1. **Scalable Architecture and Performance Optimization:**
    - Optimize software architecture for scalability to handle large data volumes and users.
    - Improve performance to ensure fast processing and real-time analytics.
    - **Regulations:** Preparedness for future regulations that may increase data volume and complexity requirements, such as enhanced disclosure standards under the CSRD.
    - **How It Helps:** Ensures the software can handle larger datasets and more complex analyses, keeping the organization compliant as regulatory requirements evolve.

2. **Modular and Customizable Capabilities:**
   - Our development team can create modular features that users can add or remove based on their needs.
   - Enable extensive customization options for different industries and use cases.
   - **Regulations:** Flexibility to adapt to new and changing rules without major overhauls, supporting compliance with evolving standards.
   - **How It Helps:** Allows organizations to easily add new modules or customize existing ones to meet new regulatory requirements, ensuring ongoing compliance.
3. **Scenario Planning and Strategic Insights:**
   - Implement scenario planning tools for strategic ESG decision-making.
   - Develop features that provide strategic insights and recommendations based on data analysis.
   - **Regulations:** Anticipate and prepare for upcoming regulations and standards related to climate risk and resilience.
   - **How It Helps:** Provides strategic planning and scenario analysis tools, helping organizations proactively manage regulatory risks and opportunities.
4. **AI and Machine Learning Integration:**
   - Explore AI and machine learning to enhance data analysis, predictive modeling and automation.
   - Implement features like intelligent reporting, anomaly detection, and recommendation systems.
   - **Regulations:** Enhance compliance with rules that require advanced analytics, such as those governing climate risk assessments and sustainability reporting.

- **How It Helps:** Leverages AI and machine learning to improve data accuracy, predictive capabilities, and compliance with complex regulatory requirements.

5. **Global and Industry-Specific Compliance:**
   - Expand compliance tracking to cover global regulations and industry-specific standards.
   - Develop features for automatic updates and alerts on regulatory changes.
   - **Regulations:** Comprehensive compliance with global and industry-specific regulations, such as the UN Sustainable Development Goals (SDGs) and industry-specific standards.
   - **How It Helps:** It ensures that the software supports a wide range of regulatory requirements, enabling organizations to comply with global and industry-specific standards.

6. **Continuous Improvement and User Feedback:**
   - Establish a continuous improvement process based on user feedback and market trends.
   - Regularly update and enhance features to stay ahead of evolving ESG requirements and user needs.
   - **Regulations:** Stay compliant with evolving regulations through regular updates and improvements based on user feedback and regulatory changes.
   - **How It Helps:** Maintains up-to-date compliance capabilities, ensuring that the software evolves in line with regulatory developments and user needs.

<table>
<tr><td colspan="4">The Potential Offer</td><td rowspan="4">Implement continuous improvement.
Personalized consulting services.
Integration with emerging technologies, like Generative AI/ChatGPT,
AI-Driven insights
Create custom reporting templates.
Library of industry-specific templates,
Advanced tools for interactive stakeholder engagement.</td></tr>
<tr><td colspan="3">The Augmented Offer</td><td>Integrated advanced analytics.
Predictive analytics,
Expand compliance features to cover a broader range of global regulations.
Provide automatic updates</td></tr>
<tr><td colspan="2">The Expected Offer</td><td rowspan="2">User-friendly interface,
Basic data entry
Tools for Stakeholder Engagement</td><td rowspan="2"></td></tr>
<tr><td>The Basic Offer</td><td>Integrated Data Sources
Data management
Basic reporting
Compliance tracking</td></tr>
</table>

Competitive Differentiation of ESG Reporting and Data Management

Additional Risk Management capabilities

- Holistic Risk and Opportunity Assessment:

  Implement sector-specific and company-specific risk analysis tools to assess internal and external ESG risks.

  Develop comprehensive risk mapping features to visualize risks and opportunities across the company's operations, supply chain, and business model.

  How it helps: Identify and prioritize ESG risks and opportunities unique to the company, enabling management to focus on the most critical areas.

- Environment and Social Risk Analysis:

  Build data collection systems to gather relevant environmental and social metrics, such as emissions, resource use, and labor practices.

  Develop tools for assessing external environmental factors and the company's relationships with business partners.

  How it helps: Enables comprehensive analysis of environmental and social risks, facilitating more informed risk management and mitigation strategies.

Integration with Global Information Databases:

Develop APIs to integrate the software with global databases for real-time access to relevant information, such as sanctions lists and court records.

Implement automated systems for continuous data updates and risk alerts.

How it helps: Keep ESG risk assessments up-to-date with the latest information, reducing the risk of unforeseen issues.

It became clear that staying ahead required not just awareness but proactive adaptation. We needed to leverage these insights to position our ESG management software strategically. The next chapter discusses the outcome we draw. Inspired by the 'Blue Ocean Strategy' principles, we identified our unique value proposition.

By focusing on the specific needs of SMEs and financial institutions, we could create solutions that were not only affordable and user-friendly but also robust and comprehensive. This approach allowed us to tap into underserved segments and develop new markets. Drawing from 'Playing to Win,' we set our strategic focus on becoming the leading ESG management solution for these segments. This focus guided our product development, marketing, and sales efforts, ensuring we remained aligned with our target market's needs and the broader trends shaping the ESG landscape.

Customer Experience and Feature Prioritization

How do we decide which features are essential and which might be fluff? First, let's talk about the Must-Haves (basic needs). These are the features that your customers cannot do without. In our ESG application, these were the core functionalities like compliance tracking and reporting. If we included these features, our customers would be delighted. However, having them didn't make our product extraordinary; customers expected them.

Then, we moved on to the Performance Needs (One-Dimensional). These features have a direct correlation with customer satisfaction. The better we executed them, the happier our customers would be. For our application, this meant things like data integration and user-friendly dashboards. The more efficient and intuitive these features were, the more our customers appreciated the product.

Here's where things got interesting – the Delighters (Attractive Needs). These are the features that customers don't necessarily expect, but when they find them, they are pleasantly surprised. For example, we added a feature that allowed users to generate visual sustainability reports with just a few clicks. Our customers loved it! They didn't anticipate this capability, which significantly boosted their satisfaction with our product.

On the other hand, there were indifferent needs. These features didn't significantly impact customer satisfaction, whether they were present or not. We initially considered including a feature for customizing the dashboard's color scheme, but through our research, we found that users needed to care about it. So, we decided to focus our efforts elsewhere.

Lastly, we had to be cautious about the Reverse Needs. If they are present, these features can actually cause dissatisfaction. For instance, we initially considered including an automated pop-up tutorial to guide new users. However, feedback from our user testing revealed that customers found it intrusive and preferred exploring the application at their own pace, so we scrapped that idea.

Using the Kano model to assess our product features was a game-changer. It provided a clear roadmap of what to prioritize, enhance, and avoid. This experience taught me that not all features are created equal, and understanding the different types of customer needs is crucial in developing a successful product.

By focusing on Must-Haves to ensure our application was reliable, optimizing Performance Needs to enhance user satisfaction, delighting our customers with unexpected bonuses, ignoring the indifferent, and avoiding the reverse, we created a product that resonated with our users. And that, my friends, is the magic of the Kano model. With the gathered insights, I began categorizing the features of my ESG management software:

- Must-Haves (Basic Needs): Regulatory Compliance Reporting: Ensures the software meets all regulatory requirements across different regions.
- Data Security and Privacy: Robust security measures to protect sensitive ESG data.

- User-Friendly Interface: Intuitive interface that makes it easy for users to navigate and use the software.

Performance Needs (One-Dimensional):

- Advanced Data Analytics: Provides deep insights and analytics capabilities for comprehensive ESG data analysis.
- Customizable Dashboards: Allows users to tailor dashboards to their specific needs.
- Automated Data Collection: Reduces manual effort and improves data accuracy through automated data collection from various sources.

Delighters (Attractive Needs):

- Predictive Analytics and Forecasting: Uses AI to predict future trends and provide actionable insights.
- Integration with External Systems: Seamless integration with enterprise systems, such as ERP, CRM, and HR software.

Mobile Access: Enables users to access and manage ESG data from mobile devices.

Indifferent Needs:

- Custom Themes and Colors: While some users might appreciate them, it doesn't significantly impact overall satisfaction.
- Detailed User Manuals: Users often prefer intuitive interfaces over detailed manuals.

Reverse Needs:

- Excessive Notifications: Too many alerts and notifications can overwhelm users and cause dissatisfaction.

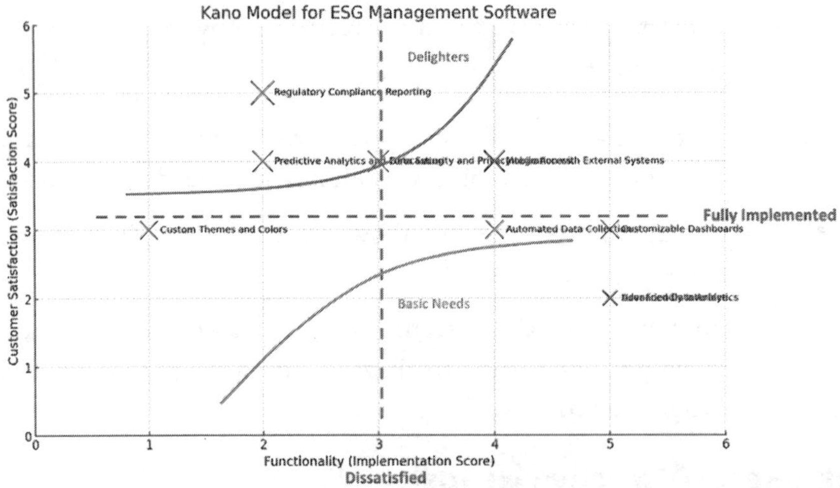

Figure 5.5 Kano model for ESG management software

Using the Kano Model

The Kano model provided a clear roadmap for prioritizing features:

1. Focus on Must-Haves: To avoid customer dissatisfaction, meet all basic needs. Our efforts included developing robust regulatory compliance reporting, ensuring data security, and creating a user-friendly interface.

2. Enhance Performance Needs: Improve advanced data analytics, customizable dashboards, and automated data collection to increase customer satisfaction.

3. Incorporate Delighters: Introduce features like predictive analytics, integration capabilities, and mobile access to delight customers and differentiate the product.

4. Minimize Indifferent and Reverse Needs: Avoid investing heavily in features that don't impact satisfaction or cause dissatisfaction.

Path Forward

Armed with the Kano model, I had a clear path forward:

1. Development Focus: Prioritize developing and refining must-have and performance features while gradually introducing delighters.
2. Customer Feedback Loop: Continuously gather customer feedback to reassess and update the Kano model, ensuring the software evolves with market needs.
3. Marketing and Positioning: Use the insights from the Kano model to craft compelling marketing messages highlighting the software's key features and benefits.
4. Differentiation Strategy: Focus on unique delighters to differentiate the software in a crowded market, positioning it as an innovative and comprehensive ESG management solution. By following these recommendations, I was confident that my ESG software would compete effectively and lead the market in driving sustainability and compliance for organizations worldwide. The journey was challenging, but with a clear strategy and focused execution, success was within reach.

Chapter 6
Market Assessment and Positioning

Navigating the complex terrain of strategic planning, especially when developing our ESG application, requires a well-thought-out sequence of tools, techniques, and methodologies. This is like having a roadmap that guides us through each phase, ensuring that nothing is overlooked and every decision is intentional. As I delved deeper into the strategic planning process, I realized that the order in which we apply these tools could significantly influence the outcome.

We began by defining our vision and mission. This wasn't just a formality; it was essential to clarify what we stand for and where we're headed. It's like setting the compass that guides every decision, ensuring we stay true to our core purpose and the impact we aspire to create in the market and society.

Once our direction was clear, we focused on understanding the external environment through a PESTLE analysis. This step was about seeing the bigger picture—recognizing the political, economic, social, technological, legal, and environmental factors that could influence our strategy. It was crucial to grasp these forces to know what we were against.

With the external landscape understood, we looked inward using a SWOT analysis. We looked at our strengths, weaknesses, opportunities, and threats here. It was a moment of honesty, acknowledging where we shine and where we need to improve. This introspection gave us a realistic view of our position and what we needed to focus on moving forward.

Armed with this understanding, we moved to market segmentation. We carefully identified and categorized our potential customers by industry, company size, geographic region, function, and user type. This step was all about understanding the distinct needs of each segment so that we could tailor our approach accordingly.

This is where the Kano model came into play. We used it to understand our customers' needs and preferences. It helped us categorize features into must-haves, performance drivers, and delight factors, ensuring that our product would meet and exceed customer expectations. It was about fine-tuning our ESG application to align perfectly with market demands.

With a clear picture of our customers' needs, we focused on positioning ourselves within the competitive landscape using Porter's Five Forces and the Blue Ocean Strategy. These tools helped us analyze the competition and identify areas where we could differentiate ourselves. It was about carving out a unique space in the market where our ESG application could thrive without getting caught in fierce competition.

Next, we used the Ansoff matrix to explore how to grow our business. This tool helped us decide whether to focus on market penetration, product development, or diversification. We were looking for the sweet spot where our product perfectly fits market demand.

The BCG Matrix helped us manage our product portfolio as we refined our strategy. It allowed us to identify which aspects of our ESG application were stars, cash cows, question marks, or dogs. This insight was crucial for allocating resources effectively and focusing on the areas with the highest potential.

To ensure that our internal capabilities were aligned with our strategic goals, we turned to the McKinsey 7S Framework. This tool helped us align our strategy, structure, systems, shared values, skills, style, and staff. It was about ensuring that every part of our organization worked harmoniously toward our goals.

Identifying and understanding our stakeholders was another critical step. We used stakeholder mapping and management to engage effectively with those who had a vested interest in our success. Building solid relationships with these stakeholders was vital to ensuring our ESG application resonated with those who mattered most.

A strategy is only complete if it considers the risks involved. So, we used a Risk Matrix and Scenario Planning to assess potential risks and develop mitigation strategies. This proactive approach helped us prepare for uncertainties and handle challenges.

Finally, we finalized our strategy using the Strategic Options Development and Analysis (SODA) approach after all the analysis and assessments. In this approach, we developed and evaluated different strategic options, choosing the path that best aligned with our vision and offered the highest potential for success.

Once our strategy was in place, we created a detailed implementation plan using the Balanced Scorecard. This tool allowed us to translate our strategy into actionable objectives, ensuring that every part of the organization knew what needed to be done. It also provided a framework for tracking our progress across financial, customer, internal process, and learning and growth perspectives.

Lastly, we used continuous feedback loops and the Balanced Scorecard to monitor our progress and make necessary adjustments. This final stage ensured that our strategy remained relevant and practical, allowing us to make data-driven decisions and continuously improve our ESG application.

By following this carefully thought-out sequence, we could confidently navigate the complexities of strategic planning for our ESG application. Each tool and technique built on the previous one, creating a comprehensive approach that ensured we were meeting the market's needs and aligning with our core values and strengths. This thoughtful, deliberate process positioned us for long-term success, allowing us to deliver meaningful value to our customers and stakeholders.

Our Vision and Mission for ESG Application

To truly understand the importance of core values, I turned to Simon Sinek's Golden Circle, a robust framework emphasizing the significance of starting with 'Why.' Starting with 'Why' helps create an emotional connection and a sense of belonging, setting a solid foundation for the company's mission, vision, and core values.

Simon Sinek's Golden Circle: The Power of Why

Simon Sinek's Golden Circle has three layers: Why, How, and What. This model is a blueprint for inspirational leadership and impactful business strategies.

1. Why - This is the core belief or purpose behind the company's existence. It's not about making money; it's about why we do what we do. The 'Why' inspires and motivates both the team and the customers.
2. How - This represents the process or values that guide how we achieve our purpose. This refers to the method or distinctive manner in which we implement our 'why.'
3. What - This is the result of our actions, the tangible products or services we offer. It's what we do and what the world sees.

Drawing inspiration from Sinek's Golden Circle, we established our core values by defining our 'Why.' Our purpose was clear: to empower organizations to achieve sustainable growth through effective ESG management.

Our Core Values:

1. Integrity: We uphold the highest standards of integrity in all our actions.

2. Innovation: We are committed to continuous innovation to drive progress.
3. Sustainability: We strive for environmental stewardship and sustainable practices.
4. Customer-Centricity: We prioritize our customers and aim to exceed their expectations.
5. Collaboration: We believe in teamwork and open communication.

As we developed our ESG management software, it became evident that having a clear and compelling mission statement was also crucial. The mission statement acts as the North Star, guiding the company's strategic direction and aligning everyone toward a common goal. It articulates a company's purpose and primary objectives and answers the question: Why do we exist? A well-crafted mission statement inspires and motivates the team, attracts customers, and guides decision-making processes.

Additionally, the mission drives a user-centric design approach. Product managers ensure that products meet the needs and expectations of users, always keeping the user in mind. To top it all off, they define success metrics to measure how well the product fulfills the mission, using these metrics to guide continuous improvement. It's a dynamic process where the mission is at the core of everything, from initial ideas to the final product and beyond.

Our Mission Statement for ESG Management Software

For our ESG management software, we crafted a mission statement that encapsulated our core purpose: 'Empower organizations to achieve sustainable growth through innovative and effective ESG management.'

Turning Our Mission into a Product

With our mission statement in place, we focused on translating it into our product strategy:

1. Empowerment through Innovation: We prioritized features that offered innovative solutions to ESG challenges, such as real-time data analytics and predictive modeling.

2. Effective Management: We designed our platform to be user-friendly and comprehensive, ensuring it provides all the tools necessary for effective ESG management.

3. Sustainable Growth: Our product roadmap included features that helped companies comply with ESG regulations and drove sustainable business practices.

A mission statement is more than just words; it embodies a company's purpose and aspirations. We set the foundation for our ESG management software's success by crafting a clear and compelling mission statement. Product managers are crucial in turning a company's mission into tangible products. They start by deeply understanding the company's mission and ensuring it's reflected in every product decision. It's like they carry the mission with them in everything they do. They then set clear objectives that align with this mission, ensuring every project contributes to the broader goal. When deciding which features to focus on, they prioritize based on how well these features support the mission, choosing those that deliver the most value.

Importance of Aligning Market Choices with Company Strengths and Capabilities

After establishing our Vision and Mission statements, aligning market choices with our company's strengths and capabilities was essential. This alignment ensured that we could effectively meet the needs of the target market segments, leveraging our unique strengths to create a competitive advantage. For instance, if our company excelled in data analytics and automation, targeting segments with high data complexity and needing automation would be ideal. This strategic alignment maximized our chances of success and allowed us to deliver superior value to our customers.

Value Proposition Development

As we refined our product vision and strategy, we focused on an equally crucial aspect of our journey: defining our business model. A well-crafted business model is the foundation for a successful product. To structure our approach, we utilized the business model canvas, a strategic tool that provides a comprehensive view of our business and its interdependencies.

The Business Model Canvas: Key Elements

The business model canvas is divided into several key components, each interconnected and impacting the bottom line. Here's how we defined each element for our ESG management application:

Key Partners

Identifying key partners was crucial for our success. We needed to collaborate with regulatory bodies, industry experts, and technology providers to ensure our platform was compliant, innovative, and valuable. Partnerships with data providers would enhance our analytics capabilities, while alliances with consulting firms could help us reach potential clients.

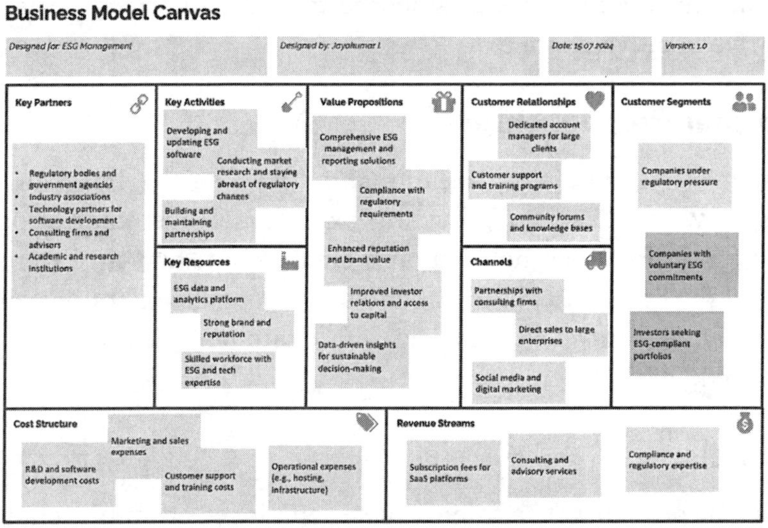

Figure 6.1 Business Model Canvas

Key Activities

Our key activities revolved around continuous product development, customer support, marketing, and compliance updates. Ensuring our platform remained cutting-edge and user-friendly required ongoing investment in technology and talent. Regular training sessions and webinars would help our customers stay informed and proficient in using our application.

Key Resources

Our essential resources included our development team, data scientists, compliance experts, and a robust IT infrastructure. These resources were crucial to building and maintaining our platform. Additionally, our partnerships and relationships with industry stakeholders were invaluable assets.

Value Propositions

Our value proposition was clear: We offer an intuitive, comprehensive platform that simplifies ESG management. This platform enables companies to meet compliance requirements and achieve sustainability goals. Providing actionable insights and robust reporting tools empowers businesses to make informed decisions and drive positive change.

Customer Relationships

Building strong customer relationships was at the heart of our strategy. We focused on providing exceptional customer support through multiple channels: phone, email, chat, and an extensive knowledge base. Regular updates, personalized onboarding, and proactive outreach ensured our customers felt valued and supported.

Channels

To reach our target audience, we employed a multi-channel approach. Our primary channels included our website, social media, industry conferences, webinars, and partnerships with industry organizations. These channels helped us build brand awareness, generate leads, and nurture customer relationships.

Customer Segments

We identified our primary customer segments as mid-sized enterprises needing help with ESG compliance and reporting. Within this segment, we further refined our focus to industries with stringent regulatory requirements, such as finance, manufacturing, and energy. Understanding our customer segments allowed us to tailor our messaging and solutions to their needs.

The Interconnectedness of the Business Model Canvas

Every decision in our strategy impacted the bottom part of the Business Model Canvas. For example, our choice of subscription and freemium models influenced our key activities (e.g., developing tiered features) and critical resources (e.g., support staff for free users). Similarly, our value proposition shaped our customer relationships and channels.

Understanding these interdependencies was critical. For instance, we needed strong key partners and robust, vital activities to deliver our value proposition effectively. Building customer relationships required us to invest resources like a dedicated support team. Each canvas element was interconnected, and any change in one area had ripple effects throughout the business.

Core Strategy Definition Using North Star Framework

I was intrigued and skeptical when I first encountered the North Star framework. Could one metric align my entire team and drive sustainable growth? I decided to give it a shot, and it turned out to be transformative. Let's talk about Leading KPIs first. These are like early signals from your ship's instruments, informing you if things are on track. Tracking new sign-ups and initial user interactions with new features was vital. These metrics acted like gentle nudges from a GPS, telling us if we needed to adjust our strategies to ensure we were on the right path.

Now, we have KPIs with varying levels of leading and lagging indicators. Your real-time feedback metrics sit somewhere between early signals and outcomes. For us, user engagement rates and repeat interaction frequencies were crucial. They provided a snapshot of our current trajectory, helping us refine our approach continuously, just like real-time traffic updates on a road trip.

Then there are the Lagging KPIs, which are more retrospective. They tell you the results of your past efforts – metrics like revenue growth, customer retention rates, and overall market share. These come too late to make immediate changes, but they validate whether our journey toward the North Star was successful. They're the final confirmation that we have reached our destination.

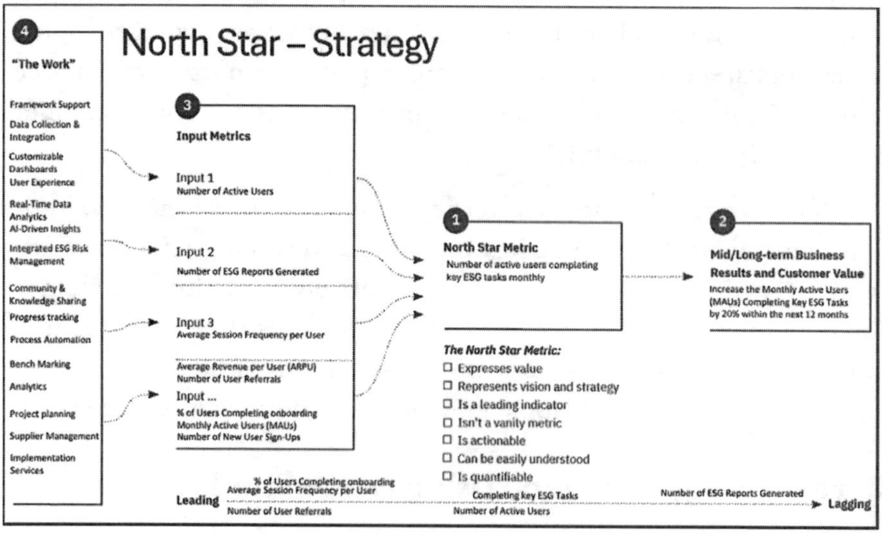

Figure 6.2 North Star Strategy

Market Expansion and Adjacency Exploration

Understanding the market landscape is crucial for any product manager aiming to position their product effectively. One powerful tool that I've found invaluable in this process is the petal diagram.

The petal diagram is a visual representation of intersecting markets that revolve around your core product, providing a holistic view of the ecosystem in which your product operates. This section will explore the significance of the petal diagram and illustrate how we can apply it to our ESG management solution.

The Petal Diagram: A Strategic Visualization Tool

The petal diagram is named for its resemblance to flower petals. Each petal represents a different market that intersects with your core product. By visualizing these intersections, product managers can identify key players, understand the competitive landscape, and uncover opportunities for collaboration and integration.

The petal diagram for our ESG management solution helps us see the broader ecosystem and identify how various markets contribute to the overall value proposition. Here's how we can visualize the petal diagram, focusing on critical intersecting markets: Data Providers, Analytics, Collaboration, Productivity, Value Chain Data Sources, Reporting, and Project Management.

Constructing the Petal Diagram for ESG Management Solution

1. Core Product: ESG Management Solution

   Our core product, the ESG management solution, is at the center of the petal diagram. This concept serves as the hub around which all intersecting markets revolve.

2. Petal 1: Data Providers

   ESG data is fundamental to our solution. Key players in this market provide the raw data necessary for comprehensive ESG reporting and analysis.

   - Companies: MSCI, Sustainalytics, Refinitiv, Bloomberg.

3. Petal 2: Analytics

   Advanced analytics transform raw data into actionable insights, enabling companies to make informed decisions about their ESG strategies.

- Companies: SAS, Tableau, Power BI, Alteryx.

4. Petal 3: Collaboration.

   Effective ESG management requires seamless stakeholder collaboration, including internal teams and external partners.

   - Companies: Slack, Microsoft Teams, Asana, Trello.

5. Petal 4: Productivity

   Productivity tools help streamline workflows and ensure efficient ESG-related tasks and project management.

   - Companies: Microsoft Office 365, Google Workspace, Notion, ClickUp.

6. Petal 5: Value Chain Data Sources

   Understanding the impact across the entire value chain is crucial for comprehensive ESG management. The data included comes from suppliers, distributors, and other partners.

   - Companies: SAP Ariba, IBM Sterling, Coupa, Kinaxis.

7. Petal 6: Reporting

   ESG reporting is critical to compliance and transparency. Reporting tools enable organizations to generate accurate and timely ESG reports.

   - Companies: Workiva, Diligent, Enablon, Figbytes.

8. Petal 7: Project Management

   Managing ESG initiatives effectively requires robust project management capabilities to track progress, allocate resources, and achieve objectives.

   - Companies: Jira, Monday.com, Smartsheet, Wrike.

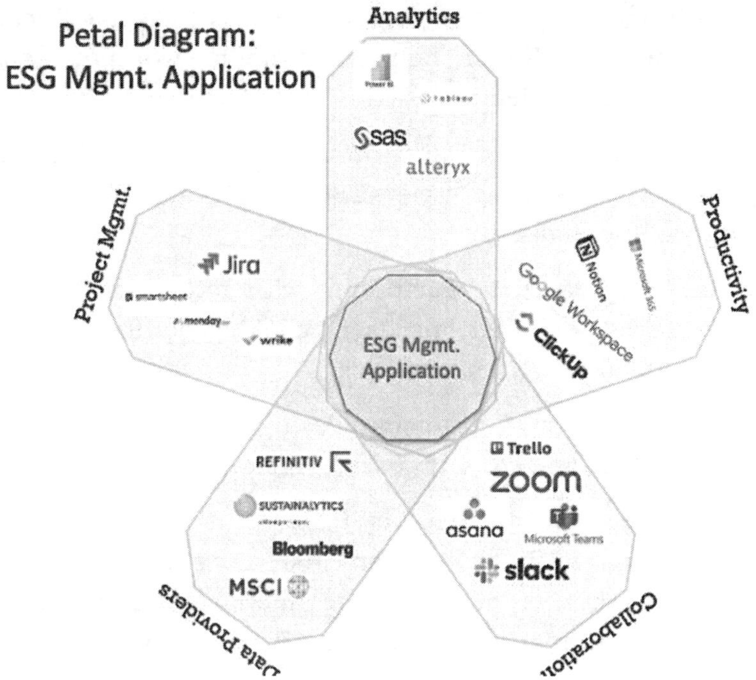

Figure 6.3 Petal Diagram for ESG Management Application

Applying the Petal Diagram in Practice

The petal diagram guided our strategic planning as we developed our ESG management solution. By understanding the intersecting markets and key players, we were able to:

- Integrate Data Providers: Partnering with leading data providers, such as MSCI and Sustainalytics, ensured our solution had access to high-quality ESG data.
- Enhance Analytics Capabilities: Incorporating advanced analytics tools like Tableau and Power BI allowed us to offer sophisticated data analysis features.
- Facilitate Collaboration: Integrating with collaboration platforms like Slack and Microsoft Teams improved user communication and coordination.

- Boost Productivity: Leveraging productivity tools like Google Workspace and Notion helped streamline workflows and enhance user efficiency.
- Leverage Value Chain Data: We utilized platforms like SAP Ariba and IBM Sterling to view ESG impacts across the value chain comprehensively.
- Streamline Reporting: Partnering with tools like Workiva and Enablon ensured our users could generate accurate and compliant ESG reports.
- Optimize Project Management: Using tools like Jira and Monday.com helped our users manage ESG initiatives effectively.

The petal diagram is more than just a visual tool; it's a strategic framework that helps product managers navigate the complexities of the market landscape. By understanding the intersecting markets and key players, we can create a product that meets current demands and anticipates future needs. The petal diagram was instrumental in shaping our strategic direction when developing the ESG management solution. It provided a clear roadmap for integrating various market elements, enhancing our value proposition, and positioning our product for success.

Risk Assessment of the Initiative

Risk management is critical for ESG (Environmental, Social, and Governance). We want to ensure our software is environmentally friendly, socially responsible, and ethically governed. By identifying risks early, we can avoid issues that might harm our reputation, finances, or compliance with regulations. For example, knowing how our software impacts the environment lets us take proactive steps to minimize our carbon footprint. Understanding social risks helps us create a better workplace for everyone.

Key Findings from Our Risk Assessment

After pouring much effort into developing our North Star, Vision, Mission, Strategy canvas, and Business model canvas, we focused on creating a solid Product Risk Management framework. Here's what we discovered:

Desirability Risks

1. Market Research Risk:
    - What's the risk? We might not fully understand what our customers need and want.
    - What can we do? We can conduct thorough market research, such as surveys, focus groups, and competitor analyses, to understand customer desires.
    - Impact: Medium.
    - Probability: High.
2. Customer Acceptance Risk:
    - What's the risk? Our product features might not appeal to our target audience.
    - What can we do? Get user feedback early on to make sure our product resonates with them.
    - Impact: High.
    - Probability: Medium.
3. Market Fit Risk:
    - What's the risk? The product might not address a significant pain point or fit well in the market.
    - What can we do? Keep an eye on market trends and adjust our product accordingly.
    - Impact: High.
    - Probability: Medium.

Usability Risks

1. User Experience Risk:
   - What's the risk? Users might find our software challenging to use.
   - What can we do? Conduct usability testing and incorporate feedback to improve the user interface.
   - Impact: High.
   - Probability: High.
2. Learning Curve Risk:
   - What's the risk? The software might be complex to learn.
   - What can we do? Provide comprehensive guides, tutorials, and customer support.
   - Impact: Medium.
   - Probability: Medium.
3. Accessibility Risk:
   - What's the risk? The software might not be accessible to all users, including those with disabilities.
   - What can we do? Ensure compliance with accessibility standards and test for accessibility.
   - Impact: Medium.
   - Probability: Medium.

Feasibility Risks

1. Technical Feasibility Risk:
   - What's the risk? There might be technical challenges that delay development.
   - What can we do? Conduct a feasibility study and ensure our team has the necessary skills and resources.

- Impact: High.
- Probability: Medium.

2. Resource Availability Risk:
    - What's the risk? We might not have enough resources (time, money, workforce).
    - What can we do? Secure funding, hire skilled personnel, and manage timelines effectively.
    - Impact: Medium.
    - Probability: Medium.
3. Cost Overrun Risk:
    - What's the risk? Development costs might exceed the budget.
    - What can we do? Implement strict budget controls and conduct regular financial reviews.
    - Impact: High.
    - Probability: Medium.

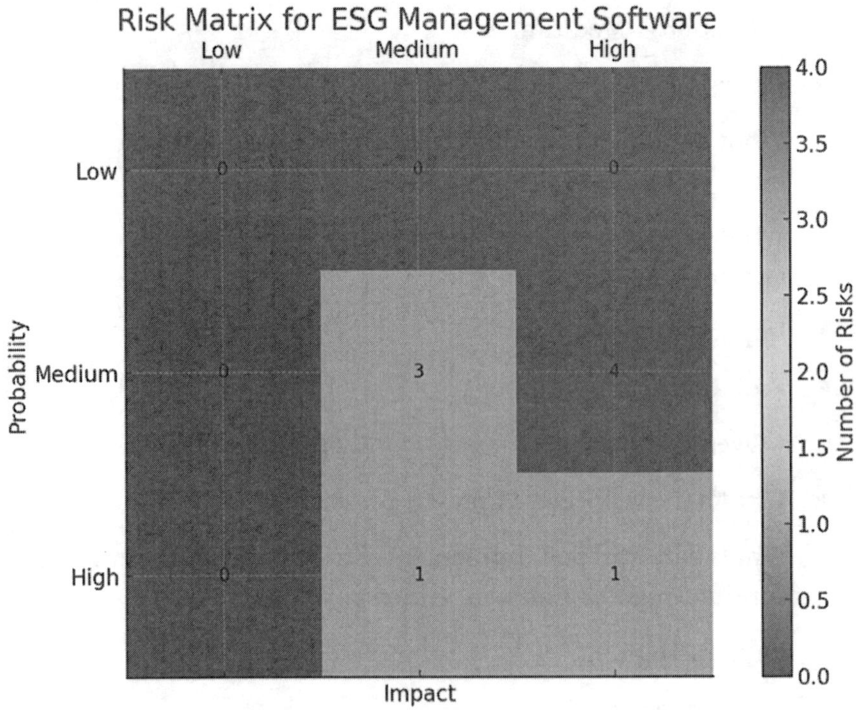

Figure 6.4 ESG Product Risk Assessment

Chapter 7
Customer Journey Map

One particularly enlightening experience was shadowing a compliance manager for a day. This hands-on approach provided insights that only a small amount of secondary research could. We observed their challenges: tracking ever-changing regulations and managing vast amounts of data from disparate sources. It became clear that their job was not just about ticking boxes but about ensuring the organization's operations aligned with complex regulatory landscapes, mitigating risks, and upholding the company's reputation. Let's step into the shoes of a manufacturing company navigating the complex world of ESG (Environmental, Social, Governance) and sustainability. Imagine you're at the helm of this company, tasked with ensuring that your operations are efficient but also sustainable and compliant with various regulations.

First Materiality Assessment

Imagine sitting at your desk, preparing to conduct a materiality assessment for your company. This isn't just another box to tick off; it's a critical process determining what ESG factors are most important to your business. But getting there is anything but straightforward.

First, you need to gather input from a wide range of stakeholders. This means coordinating schedules with busy executives, department heads, and external advisers. Everyone has different availability, and finding a standard time is like herding cats. You send several emails, draft agendas, and prepare materials for the upcoming workshops.

The workshops themselves constitute a significant challenge. You're facilitating discussions with people who often have conflicting priorities and perspectives. Finance might be focused on cost implications, while the operations team is concerned about compliance and efficiency. HR worries about employee welfare, and the sustainability team has environmental priorities. You must bring all these voices together to identify what truly matters.

During these sessions, you gather insights and try to build a consensus. This involves a lot of listening, meditating, and occasionally refereeing heated debates. You take detailed notes, capture key points, and ensure everyone's views are represented. It's like being a conductor of a very chaotic orchestra, trying to create harmony out of the racket.

Once the workshops are over, the real work begins. You sift through the notes and feedback to identify the key metrics material to your organization. This involves extensive analysis and often more follow-up with stakeholders to clarify points or resolve disagreements. It's a painstaking process, requiring meticulous attention to detail and a deep understanding of the various ESG aspects.

Even after identifying the material metrics, your task isn't over. You must ensure that these metrics align with regulatory requirements and industry standards. This means staying up-to-date with a constantly changing regulatory landscape, understanding complex guidelines, and ensuring your company's metrics meet these standards.

Throughout this process, you rely heavily on traditional tools like Excel for data tracking and Word for documentation. You're constantly updating spreadsheets, creating versions upon versions to capture the evolving consensus. The manual nature of this work makes it prone to errors and incredibly time-consuming.

And then there's the communication aspect. Keeping all stakeholders informed and engaged throughout the process would be best. This involves regular updates, meetings, and sometimes even more workshops. Keeping everyone on the same page is a monumental task in itself.

In summary, conducting a materiality assessment is like juggling flaming torches while riding a unicycle. It requires coordination, patience, and perseverance. But despite the challenges, it's a crucial step in ensuring your company's ESG strategy aligns with what truly matters.

This narrative captures the complexities and challenges of conducting a materiality assessment, highlighting the coordination, analysis, and communication efforts required to get it right.

Getting Data from Diverse Sources:

Imagine you've just finished the materiality assessment and are now gathering data from various sources. You're at your desk, thinking about the sheer scope of this next step. The data you need is scattered across different departments: finance, HR, operations, and sustainability—each with its way of managing information.

First, there's the financial data. Accessing this information is like navigating a labyrinth. It's tightly controlled and requires multiple layers of approval. You email the finance team to explain what you need and why. However, financial data is sensitive, and you encounter delays as your requests go through the necessary channels. Every step is monitored, and getting what you need feels like pulling teeth.

Next is the HR data. It's equally challenging, but for different reasons. HR handles a lot of personal and confidential information. You draft a carefully worded email, mindful of the sensitivities involved, and send it to the HR team. They respond cautiously, often requiring more explanations and assurances about how the data will be used. This back-and-forth takes time, and you need to be patient and persistent.

Environmental data comes from various sources. It's not just one department; you need data from operations, maintenance, and external vendors. Each source has its format and reporting method. Some send detailed logs, others provide summarized reports, and a few might even hand over handwritten notes. Collecting and standardizing this data is a monumental task. You send multiple emails, follow -up with phone calls, and sometimes even have face-to-face meetings to ensure you get the correct information.

Governance data is the toughest nut to crack. It's fragmented and often resides in outdated systems. The data is spread across different databases, and finding the right person who knows where everything is can be like searching for a needle in a haystack. You draft emails, make phone calls, and set up meetings, often chasing down leads to get a single piece of information.

Communication is vital throughout this process but also a significant hurdle. You must clearly explain what data you need, why, and how it will be used. Each department has priorities and concerns; you must tailor your communication accordingly. Sometimes, despite your best efforts, responses could be faster, and you must send multiple follow-ups. Keeping track of who has responded, who needs a reminder, and what data is missing becomes a task.

You rely heavily on email for this communication, and your inbox is a chaotic mess of requests, responses, and follow-ups. You use Excel to track who has sent what, creating multiple versions of spreadsheets to manage the influx of data. Each version is a snapshot in time, capturing the progress of your data collection. It's a manual, labor-intensive process, and keeping everything organized feels like an endless game of whack-a-mole.

And then there's the issue of data accuracy and consistency. The data you receive often has discrepancies, and departments might report the same metric differently. You spend hours cross-referencing and verifying the data, making corrections where needed. This involves more emails, clarifications, and adjustments.

Ensuring the data is reliable and consistent is a meticulous and time-consuming task.

In summary, gathering data from multiple sources is like being a detective, negotiator, and project manager all rolled into one. It requires clear communication, relentless follow-up, and meticulous organization. The challenges are immense, but getting it right is crucial for accurate ESG reporting.

Emails, Emails, and Emails

Start your day by opening your email inbox overflowing with messages. Emails from different departments, follow-ups, reminders, and new data requests flood your screen. As an ESG manager, you rely heavily on email to communicate your data needs and track responses, but it's far from a perfect system.

The first problem is the sheer volume of emails. You send initial requests for data to various departments—finance, HR, operations, and more. Each request must be clear and detailed, explaining precisely what data you need, why, and how it will be used. You tailor each message to the recipient, knowing that a one-size-fits-all approach won't work. But this means you're already juggling dozens of personalized emails from the get-go.

As replies start trickling in, you quickly realize how hard it is to keep track of everything. Some people respond promptly with the needed data, but others require multiple follow-ups. You send reminder emails, trying to be polite yet firm, as the clock ticks on your deadlines. Your inbox becomes a chaotic to-do list, with each thread representing a different task or follow-up.

The problem is compounded by the fact that each regulatory requirement demands specific data, often in different formats. You must ensure compliance with various regulations, and each data set must be meticulously organized and reported. One department's data might need to be formatted in multiple ways to satisfy different regulatory bodies. Managing these variations through email is cumbersome and prone to error.

Keeping track of who has sent what is a constant challenge. You create Excel spreadsheets to log responses, noting who has provided data and who hasn't. However, as the number of emails increases, so does the complexity of your tracking system. You end up with multiple versions of the same spreadsheet, each reflecting the status at different times. It's easy to lose track of the most current version, leading to confusion and potential mistakes.

Then there's the issue of data accuracy. The data you receive often contains discrepancies that need to be resolved. You spend countless hours cross-referencing figures, sending more emails to clarify numbers, and making corrections. Every clarification means more emails, adding to the growing pile in your inbox. The back-and-forth can be exhausting, and it's easy for important details to get lost in the shuffle.

If this weren't enough, you must also prepare for audits and respond to external stakeholders, like customers requesting ESG information. Each new request adds another layer of complexity. You need to gather specific data, ensure its accuracy, and present it in a way that meets the requester's needs. All of this is managed through email, which is far from efficient.

The manual nature of this process leaves you feeling overwhelmed. You spend more time managing emails and tracking responses than analyzing the data. Important tasks slip through the cracks, and deadlines loom large on the horizon. Maintaining everything organized and ensuring compliance with multiple regulatory requirements is relentless.

In summary, relying on email communication for data gathering and task management is a recipe for frustration. The sheer volume of messages, the need for constant follow-ups, and the difficulty of tracking everything make it a challenging and inefficient system. Yet, despite these shortcomings, you persevere, knowing that getting the data right is crucial for your company's ESG reporting.

Empathy Map: ESG Manager's Customer Journey

Says	- "I need to gather accurate data from multiple departments."
	- "The volume of emails is overwhelming."
	- "Coordinating with stakeholders is exhausting."
	- "We must comply with diverse regulations and reporting formats."
	- "Preparing for audits is stressful."
	- "We need to make leadership aware of ESG risks."
Thinks	- 'This process is critical for the company's reputation and compliance.'
	- 'Gathering data from different sources is like pulling teeth.'
	- 'Balancing conflicting priorities among stakeholders is a huge challenge.'
	- 'The manual data management processes are prone to errors.'
	- 'Convincing leadership to invest in ESG strategies requires a solid business case.'
	- 'Keeping track of everything is nearly impossible with so many moving parts.'
	- 'Sends numerous emails to request and follow-up on data from different departments.'
Does	- Facilitates workshops to align stakeholders on material ESG factors.
	- Analyses and cross-references data to ensure accuracy and compliance.
	- Creates presentations and reports to communicate findings and strategies to leadership.
	- Manages sensitive data with strict access controls, especially financial, HR, and governance data.
	- Tracks progress with Excel spreadsheets, creating multiple versions to capture evolving data and insights.
	- Prepares detailed documentation and audit trails to ensure regulatory compliance.
	- Educates and updates leadership on the importance of ESG risks and the need for proactive strategies.
Feels	- Overwhelmed: The sheer volume of tasks and the complexity of coordinating with various departments and stakeholders.

(*Contd.*)

	- Frustrated: The manual nature of data collection and the challenges of aligning different priorities.
	- Responsible for ensuring data accuracy, compliance, and the successful execution of ESG strategies.
	- Stressed: Due to tight deadlines, there is a need for precise documentation and high stakes of regulatory compliance.
	- Determined: To navigate the complexities, persuade leadership and ensure that the ESG strategies align with business goals and industry standards.

Diverse Regulations, Different Reporting Formats

After gathering all the necessary data through countless emails and follow-ups, your next monumental task is compiling this information into a comprehensive and audit-ready report. This is where the complexity and challenges of your job as an ESG manager become clear.

Firstly, the data you've collected is often in different formats and from various sources. You have Excel sheets from finance, PDFs from HR, handwritten notes from operations, and environmental data in multiple formats. Your first challenge is to standardize this data. You spend hours manually entering and correcting information, ensuring everything aligns correctly. This is a meticulous process, and the risk of human error is high. A single mistake can throw off your entire report, leading to inaccuracies that could be disastrous during an audit.

Next, you need to verify the accuracy and completeness of the data. This involves cross-referencing information from different departments to ensure consistency. You might find that the numbers from HR don't quite match up with those from finance or that the environmental data is incomplete. You send out more emails and make more phone calls to clarify and correct these discrepancies. This back-and-forth is time-consuming and frustrating, especially when deadlines are looming.

Once the data is standardized and verified, you move on to consolidation. This means creating Excel pivot tables, charts, and graphs to present the data clearly. Each piece of data needs to be precisely placed to ensure it tells the right story. This process is tedious and requires a high-level of attention to detail. You double and triple-check your work, knowing that any mistake could undermine the credibility of your report.

Compiling the report also involves ensuring compliance with multiple regulatory requirements. Each regulation has its own set of guidelines and formats that you must follow. You spend hours reading through regulatory documents, ensuring your report meets every requirement. This often means creating multiple versions of the same report, each tailored to a specific regulatory body. Keeping track of these versions and ensuring each one is accurate and up-to-date is a logistical nightmare.

Once the report is compiled, you need to make it audit-ready. Auditors require detailed records and proof of compliance, so you must ensure all data is backed up by documentation. This means compiling a vast amount of supporting evidence – emails, spreadsheets, notes, and more – and organizing it in a way that's easily accessible. You create detailed audit trails, documenting every step of the data collection and reporting process. This is another layer of meticulous work, and any gaps in your documentation can lead to questions and complications during the audit.

Preparing for an audit is stressful. You know that auditors will scrutinize every detail of your report, looking for inconsistencies or errors. The pressure is immense, and the stakes are high. Any mistakes can result in non-compliance, which can seriously affect your company. You spend sleepless nights reviewing your work, making sure everything is perfect.

In addition, you receive a request from a key customer who needs your company's ESG information for their assessment. This adds another layer of urgency and complexity to your already overwhelming workload. You must ensure your data is accurate, comprehensive, and aligned with the customer's requirements. This means creating another version of your report tailored to the customer's needs.

Despite all these challenges, you persevere. Your work is critical for your company's reputation and compliance. But the process is exhausting and leaves you constantly on edge, worrying about the next deadline, the next audit, and the subsequent request for information.

ESG Risk - Strategy

You've finally compiled your ESG data into a comprehensive report, and now it's time to present your findings to the leadership team. This step is crucial because their understanding and support are essential for implementing effective ESG strategies. However, making them aware of the risks and convincing them to act is no small feat.

First, there's the challenge of translating complex data into a compelling narrative that resonates with the leadership team. Executives often focus on immediate business outcomes like revenue, costs, and market share. ESG issues, while important, can seem abstract or secondary to these immediate concerns. Your task is demonstrating how ESG risks directly impact the company's bottom line and long-term sustainability.

You start by preparing a presentation. You must distill complex data into critical, easy-to-understand, compelling points. This involves creating clear visuals—charts, graphs, and infographics—highlighting the most essential ESG risks. Each slide must tell a story, showing how a particular risk can affect the company's operations, reputation, and financial performance.

Communicating the urgency of these risks is another challenge. Leadership teams are often inundated with information and requests, and it can take time to capture their attention. You must craft your message carefully, emphasizing the potential consequences of ignoring ESG risks. This might include legal penalties, financial losses, or damage to the company's reputation. However, it would be best to balance this with a positive outlook, showing how proactive ESG strategies can create opportunities for innovation, efficiency, and market differentiation.

Once you have their attention, the next step is proposing a clear strategy to control these risks. This involves presenting actionable steps that the company can take to mitigate each risk. But it's not just about listing actions; you must explain the rationale behind each step and how it aligns with the company's overall business strategy. This means tying ESG initiatives to business outcomes like cost savings, operational efficiencies, and brand enhancement.

One of the biggest challenges is getting buy-in for these strategies. Implementing ESG measures often requires investment in new technologies, processes, or training programs. Leadership might only allocate resources if they clearly understand the return on investment. You must build a solid business case, demonstrating how the initial investment will lead to long-term benefits. This might include cost savings from energy efficiency, risk reduction from better compliance, or revenue growth from sustainable products.

During your presentation, expect tough questions. Leadership will want to know why these risks are emerging now, how significant they are compared to other business risks, and what evidence supports your claims. They might challenge your data, ask for more detailed analysis, or request examples of how different companies handle similar issues. It would be best if you were prepared with thorough research, precise data, and compelling examples.

Engaging leadership isn't just about one presentation. It's an ongoing process of communication and education. You must keep them updated on ESG developments, showing progress and highlighting new risks as they arise. This means regular reports, follow-up meetings, and continuous advocacy. It would be best to build alliances and find champions in different departments to help push the ESG agenda forward.

In summary, making leadership aware of ESG risks and convincing them to act involves translating complex data into compelling narratives, demonstrating the business impact of ESG risks, proposing clear and actionable strategies, and building a solid business case for investment. Continuous communication, thorough preparation, and strategic thinking are required to align ESG initiatives with the company's goals.

Data Sensitiveness

Managing and sharing sensitive ESG data within an organization involves navigating a labyrinth of data sensitivity, authorizations, and internal controls. This adds another layer of complexity to your already demanding role as an ESG manager. Let's break down why this is such a daunting task.

You start your day by centralizing all ESG data on a SharePoint site for easier access and collaboration. This sounds simple enough, but the reality is far from straightforward. The first hurdle is data sensitivity. The information you're dealing with includes financial reports, HR records, environmental impact data, and governance documents. Each data type has its own set of confidentiality and privacy concerns.

Financial data, for example, is tightly controlled due to its critical nature. Access to this data is restricted to prevent unauthorized use and to protect against potential breaches. You need to ensure that only authorized personnel can view or edit these documents. This means setting up stringent access controls on your SharePoint site, specifying who can see what, and ensuring these controls are robust and foolproof.

HR data presents another set of challenges. This data includes sensitive personal information about employees, such as salaries, performance reviews, and personal details. Privacy regulations like GDPR require that this data be handled with the utmost care. You need to ensure that access is restricted within the organization and that any data sharing complies with these stringent regulations. Setting up these privacy controls on SharePoint involves meticulous planning and constant vigilance.

Environmental data might seem less sensitive, but it comes from diverse sources and often needs to be verified and cross-referenced with other data. This data is crucial for your sustainability reports and must be accurate and up-to-date. Ensuring this data is accessible while maintaining its integrity involves setting up workflows that track changes and approvals. You must ensure that any edits or updates are logged and can be audited if necessary.

Governance data is the most complex. It often includes policy documents, compliance reports, and audit trails. This data must be accessible and secure, requiring a delicate balance between openness and control. Setting up the correct permissions on SharePoint to allow necessary access while protecting sensitive information is a constant juggling act.

Once you've set up the initial access controls, the next challenge is managing authorizations. As projects evolve and team members change, you must constantly update who has access to what. This is not a one-time setup but a continuous monitoring and adjusting permissions process. Any lapse in this process can lead to unauthorized access or prevent crucial team members from accessing the necessary data.

Internal controls add another layer of complexity. Your organization likely has stringent policies on handling, sharing, and storing data. You need to ensure that your SharePoint site complies with these policies. This involves regular site audits, checking that all permissions are correctly set and data is used and shared according to company policies. Any discrepancies must be addressed immediately to avoid potential breaches or compliance issues.

In addition to setting up and maintaining these controls, you must educate and train your colleagues on using the SharePoint site correctly. This involves creating guidelines and best practices for data management and sharing. Ensuring everyone understands and follows these guidelines is crucial to maintaining the security and integrity of your ESG data.

Finally, despite all these efforts, there's always the human factor. Mistakes can happen, permissions can be accidentally altered, and sensitive data can be inadvertently shared. It would be best to have contingency plans for such scenarios, including quick response protocols and damage control measures.

In summary, managing and sharing sensitive ESG data on a SharePoint site involves navigating the complexities of data sensitivity, authorizations, and internal controls. It requires meticulous planning, continuous monitoring, and constant vigilance to ensure data is secure, accessible, and compliant with regulations and company policies. Despite these challenges, you persevere, knowing that getting this right is crucial for accurate and reliable ESG reporting.

Future State:

Picture this: You're about to dive into the ESG materiality assessment, but instead of bracing for a marathon of manual tasks, you're looking forward to it. Why? Because you've got this fantastic ESG management software that's about to make your life so much easier. Imagine you're gearing up for a materiality assessment, but instead of dreading the marathon of tasks, you're looking forward to it. Thanks to the new ESG management software, everything is streamlined and efficient.

Future State Empathy Map: ESG Manager with Advanced ESG Management Software

Quadrant	**Details**
Says	- "I can't believe how easy the materiality assessment is now."
	- "The software handles everything, from scheduling to data collection."
	- "Reporting is now accurate and instant, so there is no more stress over regulatory requirements."
	"Managing communications and follow-ups is seamless."
	- "Risk management and auditing are finally under control."
	- "This tool has transformed how I manage ESG."
Thinks	- 'This software is a game-changer for ESG management.'

Quadrant	**Details**
	- 'Automation has eliminated the most frustrating parts of my job.'
	- 'Integrating data from diverse sources is now straightforward and reliable.'
	- 'I have more time to focus on strategic initiatives rather than manual tasks.'
	- 'With everything centralized, tracking goals and adjusting strategies is so much easier.'
Does	It uses software to automate scheduling, data collection, and reporting tasks.
	- Leverages collaboration tools to facilitate stakeholder discussions and workshops.
	Generates audit-ready reports in minutes, ensuring compliance with various regulatory frameworks.
	- Monitors ESG risks using predictive analytics and adjusts strategies in real-time.
	Manages data sensitivity and security through the software's robust access controls.
Feels	Empowered: The software gives a sense of control over ESG processes.
	Relieved: No longer burdened by manual tasks and complex data management.
	Confident: Trusts the software to handle regulatory compliance and audit readiness.
	Focused: Able to dedicate more time to driving sustainability initiatives.
	- Optimistic: Sees a clear path to achieving ESG goals with the support of advanced technology.

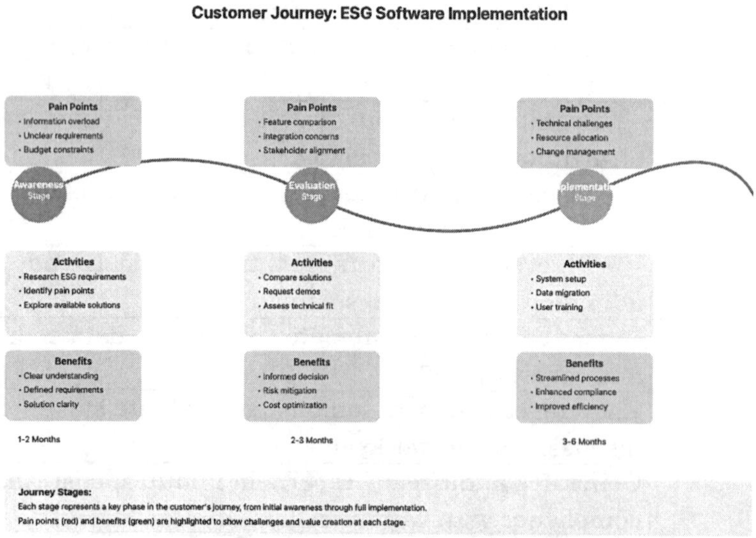

First is materiality assessment. This used to be a massive headache. Gathering input from stakeholders and trying to find a standard time for everyone to meet was like herding cats. Now, the software does all the heavy lifting. It automatically aligns everyone's schedules, sends reminders, and collects their input. You no longer have to chase after people or send endless emails. Everything is coordinated seamlessly, making the whole process a lot smoother.

Next is collecting data from diverse sources. Previously, collecting data took a lot of work. You had to pull information from various departments using different systems and formats. The software changes all that. It integrates with all your existing systems, from ERP to supply chain management and even carbon emission calculators. It pulls data from all these sources into one place, ensuring a comprehensive and cohesive dataset. There is no more manual data entry or reconciling different formats—it's all automated and standardized.

Managing Communications and Follow-Up was another big challenge. Facilitating discussions among stakeholders with different priorities and perspectives was tough. The software's collaboration tools make this so much easier. Virtual workshops with real-time collaboration features like digital whiteboards, instant polls, and document sharing mean everyone can contribute and collaborate effectively. All interactions are recorded and organized, so you don't miss a thing. Follow-ups are automated, too, with the software sending reminders and tracking responses, so you're always on top of things.

The software truly shines when it comes to Generating Reports for Diverse Regulatory Requirements. It's built to handle the complexities of ESG reporting. The software ensures compliance if you report in line with GRI, CDP, SASB, or any other framework. It automatically updates with the latest regulatory changes, generates audit-ready reports, and even helps you with the intricate details of each framework. Reports that took weeks to compile are now ready in minutes, accurate, and compliant.

Strategy Management used to require juggling multiple tools and spreadsheets to track goals and progress. Now, the software centralizes all this. You can set targets, track performance, and adjust real-time strategies. It provides dashboards that visualize your progress and highlight areas needing attention so you're always on top of your sustainability goals.

Risk management and auditing were other areas fraught with challenges. Identifying risks, managing audits, and ensuring everything was in order could be overwhelming. The software simplifies this with built-in risk management tools. It identifies potential risks through predictive analytics, helps you manage audits with comprehensive tracking and documentation features, and ensures everything is audit-ready. Auditors can access the necessary data directly, streamlining the entire process and making it more efficient.

Lastly, Data Sensitivity. Ensuring data privacy and security is paramount. The software is designed with robust security features to protect sensitive information. It complies with data privacy regulations and offers granular access controls, ensuring that only authorized personnel can access specific data. This protects sensitive information and builds trust among stakeholders that their data is secure.

Manual tasks and complex processes no longer slow you down in this future state. The software handles scheduling, data collection, communication, reporting, strategy management, risk management, and data security. Thus, you can focus on driving sustainable business practices and making a positive impact, knowing you have a powerful tool to support you every step. This is the new way of managing ESG—intelligent, seamless, and stress-free.

Value Proposition Canvas for ESG Streamline

As we've seen in earlier sections, we have explored Customer Jobs, Pains, and our vision for the future state of our software. Now, let's generate a detailed customer profile and discuss our observations.

We started by identifying the key jobs our customers are trying to accomplish. These include collecting, verifying, and standardizing ESG data from multiple sources—a demanding and meticulous task. They must also ensure this data complies with various and ever-changing regulatory requirements. Preparing comprehensive, audit-ready reports is another critical job. Beyond data management, they engage with stakeholders and conduct materiality assessments. They manage data security, access control, and authorizations while analyzing ESG data for strategic decision-making, rounding out their extensive list of responsibilities.

Next, we considered the pains they face. Manual data collection and entry are time-consuming and prone to errors. The data they pull from various sources often needs more consistency. Keeping up with the rapidly changing regulations can be like trying to hit a moving target. Given the extensive documentation required, preparing for audits brings its stress. Engaging stakeholders and ensuring their input is considered adds another layer of complexity. Securing sensitive data and managing access controls are constant concerns. Lastly, they need more real-time insights and predictive analytics, which are crucial for efficient decision-making.

We then focused on their desired gains. They want streamlined and automated data collection and verification processes, consistent, accurate, standardized ESG data, and simplified compliance through automated reporting templates. Anything that eases audit preparation, like comprehensive audit trails, is a significant gain. Effective stakeholder engagement and streamlined materiality assessments are critical. Robust data security and access controls are also top priorities.

This assessment showed that our customers face immense complexity and pressure. They need a solution that manages the technical aspects of data and compliance, reduces their manual workload, and provides real-time insights. Our future state software vision aims to address these needs comprehensively.

Automating data collection and verification saves them time and minimizes errors. Standardizing ESG data and ensuring compliance helps them stay ahead of regulatory demands. Our automated reporting templates and comprehensive audit trails simplify the audit process, reducing stress. Advanced security features ensure their data is protected. Stakeholder engagement becomes more efficient with our streamlined tools, providing all inputs are considered without the hassle of endless meetings and follow-ups. Predictive analytics offer the real-time insights they need for confident, strategic decision-making.

Our software is designed to transform their workflow, making complex tasks manageable and efficient, allowing them to focus on driving sustainability and compliance within their organizations. This understanding guides us in continually enhancing our software to meet their evolving needs, significantly benefiting their daily operations.

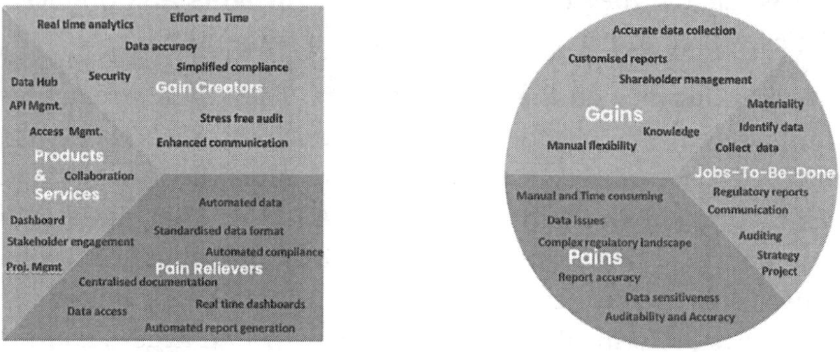

Figure 7.1 Value Proposition Canvas for ESG Management

Summary of Customer Profile

Let's talk about who we're helping with our ESG Streamline software. Picture this: medium to large enterprises spread across various industries, all with a global reach. These companies are primarily focused in regions where ESG regulations are pretty stringent. We're talking about ESG managers, sustainability officers, compliance officers, data analysts, and other key stakeholders within these organizations.

Their day-to-day involves a lot of heavy lifting. They tackle materiality assessments, data collection, reporting, auditing, and strategic planning tasks. Imagine the work it takes to keep everything running smoothly in these areas.

Now, let's explore their pain points. These folks spend much of their day dealing with time-consuming manual processes. They constantly fight data inconsistencies and face challenges with regulatory compliance. Preparing for audits is a massive stressor because of the extensive documentation required. They must also manage a mountain of communications and worry about data security. On top of all that, they work with limited real-time insights, which makes decision-making even harder.

But here's where we come in. Our software aims to bring them some serious gains. We're talking about boosting efficiency and ensuring data accuracy. We make regulatory compliance a breeze and take the stress out of audit preparation with streamlined processes. Communication becomes smoother and more effective, and our robust data security measures keep everything safe. Plus, our advanced analytics provide real-time insights that these professionals desperately need.

This comprehensive profile helps us understand our target users and align our software's features and value proposition to meet their needs. By effectively addressing these challenges, we're offering a tool and a solution to transform their work and make their lives significantly more straightforward.

Identifying Which Opportunities to Chase

Using the value proposition canvas from Osterwalder's book, we started by mapping out their jobs, pains, and gains. This approach helped us get into the heads of our customers. First, we identified the jobs they're trying to get done: the nitty-gritty of ESG management. Then, we honed in on their pain points. Time-consuming manual processes, data inconsistencies, regulatory compliance challenges, and the stress of audit preparation bog down these folks. They also have to manage a flood of communications and worry about data security, all while lacking real-time insights crucial for decision-making.

Next, we looked at the gains they're seeking. They need efficiency, data accuracy, simplified compliance, stress-free audit preparation, enhanced communication, robust data security, and real-time insights. By mapping these out, we could see where our software could make the most significant impact. Significantly comes into play, and this is where Osterwalder's framework shines. We can't tackle everything at once, so we prioritize based on the significance of each pain point and gain. For instance, manual data entry and collection being so labor-intensive is a top pain point, so automating this process is a high-priority. Ensuring data accuracy and consistency is another critical area, so solutions that standardize data formats are prioritized next. Each feature we develop aligns directly with a top pain or desired gain from our customer profile.

Focusing on these high-impact areas first means delivering the most value right out of the gate. This approach not only makes our development process more efficient but also ensures that our customers see immediate improvements in their workflow. The significance of this prioritization can't be overstated—it's the difference between creating a product that's just good and genuinely transformative.

Our value proposition is about turning these complex, stressful tasks into streamlined, manageable processes. We're not just building software; we're providing solutions that transform how these professionals work, making their lives significantly more accessible and their organizations more efficient. This is how we ensure that our ESG Streamline software effectively meets their needs and delivers real, tangible benefits.

Let's dive into how we prioritized the opportunities for our ESG Streamline software using Alexander Osterwalder's value proposition framework. This framework helped us systematically evaluate and rank each opportunity based on the significance of the gains, pains, and jobs involved.

First, we needed to understand the gains our customers are looking for. We measured these gains from 'nice to have' to 'really essential.' Essential gains directly impact the efficiency and effectiveness of the customers' work, such as accurate data collection and real-time insights. On the other hand, gains that are nice to have might improve the user experience but aren't critical for day-to-day operations.

Next, we rated the pains our customers experience from 'moderate' to 'really extreme.' Extreme pains cause significant stress and inefficiency, such as manual data entry and keeping up with changing regulations. While still substantial, moderate pains are less disruptive to the customers' workflow.

Finally, we evaluated the jobs our customers need to perform and ranked them on a scale from 'not important' to 'important.' Critical jobs include data collection, regulatory compliance, and audit preparation. Less important jobs might still need to be done, but they don't directly affect compliance or strategic decision-making.

Using these scales, we classified and prioritized our opportunities as follows:

1. Automate Data Collection and Entry:
   - Gains: Essential (significant time savings and error reduction)
   - Pains: Extreme (time-consuming, manual processes, and error-prone)
   - Jobs: Important (the core task of data collection)
   - Priority: High
   - Reason: This directly addresses a critical pain and provides essential gains, making it a top priority
2. Enhance Data Accuracy and Consistency:
   - Gains: Essential (reliable and usable data)
   - Pains: Extreme (inconsistent and error-prone data)
   - Jobs: Important (data verification and standardization)
   - Priority: High
   - Reason: Ensuring data accuracy is foundational for all other processes, making it an urgent priority
3. Simplify Regulatory Compliance:
   - Gains: Essential (simplified compliance and reduced risk)
   - Pains: Extreme (difficulty keeping up with regulations)
   - Jobs: Important (ensuring regulatory compliance)

- Priority: High
- Reason: Compliance is critical for avoiding penalties and ensuring smooth operations

4. Streamline Audit Preparation:
    - Gains: High (stress-free audit preparation)
    - Pains: High (stress of preparing for audits)
    - Jobs: Important (audit preparation)
    - Priority: Medium-High
    - Reason: While audits are crucial, they are periodic. Streamlining them provides significant benefits but after foundational tasks.
5. Improve Stakeholder Engagement:
    - Gains: Medium (effective communication)
    - Pains: Moderate (complexity in engaging stakeholders)
    - Jobs: Important (stakeholder engagement)
    - Priority: Medium
    - Reason: Effective communication is essential, but it follows after ensuring data accuracy and compliance.
6. Provide Real-Time Insights and Advanced Analytics:
    - Gains: High (strategic decision-making)
    - Pains: Medium (lack of real-time insights)
    - Jobs: Important (data analysis and strategic planning)
    - Priority: Medium
    - Reason: While beneficial, advanced analytics are built on accurate and consistent data, making this a secondary priority.
7. Ensure Robust Data Security and Access Controls:
    - Gains: Essential (data protection)

- Pains: High (managing sensitive data securely)
- Jobs: Important (data security management)
- Priority: Medium
- Reason: Security is always a priority, but basic measures can be implemented initially, with advanced controls developed alongside other features.

Prioritization

Categorizing Gains, Pains, and Jobs

Gains: From 'Nice to Have' to 'Really Essential'

1. Nice to Have
   - Enhanced Communication: Improve communication with stakeholders.
   - Comprehensive Training and Support: Provide comprehensive training resources and dedicated support.
2. Moderately Important
   - Real-Time Insights and Analytics: Provide real-time data insights and analytics.
   - Simplified Compliance: Simplify compliance reporting and stay up-to-date with regulatory changes.
3. Essential
   - Efficiency and Time Savings: Automate data collection and entry, reducing follow-up time.
   - Data Accuracy and Consistency: Improve data accuracy and ensure consistent data formats.
   - Robust Data Security: Enhance data security with advanced access controls and secure data storage.
   - Stress-Free Audit Preparation: Simplify audit preparation with comprehensive audit trails and centralized documentation.

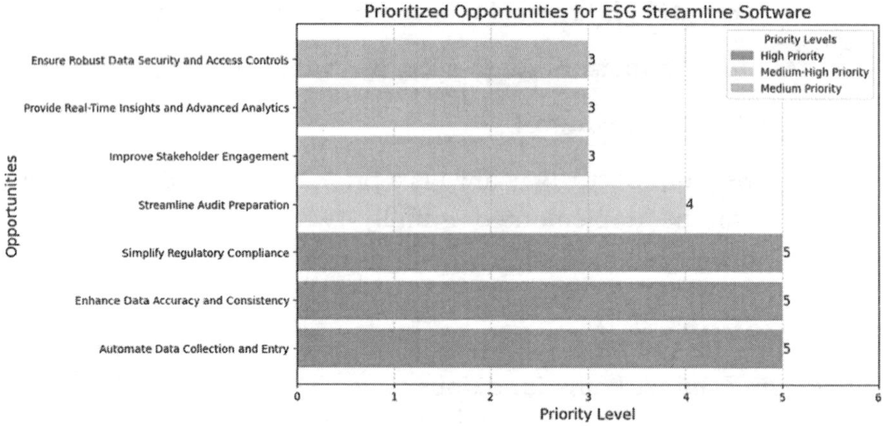

Figure 7.2 Prioritized Opportunities

Pains: From 'Moderate' to 'Really Extreme'

1. Moderate
    - Communication Overload: Managing countless emails and follow-ups is overwhelming.
    - Limited Real-Time Insights: Difficulty in getting real-time data for timely decision-making.
2. Severe
    - Data Inconsistency and Errors: There is a high-risk of errors during manual data entry and consolidation.
    - Complex Regulatory Compliance: Keeping up with ever-changing regulations is challenging.
3. Extreme
    - Time-Consuming Processes: Manual data collection and entry are labor-intensive.
    - Audit Preparation Stress: Gathering and organizing extensive audit documentation is stressful.
    - Data Security and Access Control: Ensuring sensitive data is securely stored and accessed only by authorized personnel.

Jobs: From 'Not Important' to 'Really Important'

1. Not Important
   - (No significant job falls into this category, as all listed jobs are crucial for ESG management.)
2. Moderately Important
   - Conducting Materiality Assessment: Organizing workshops and meetings with stakeholders, facilitating discussions, and gathering insights.
   - Reaching out to Data Owners: Sending initial data requests to various departments and following up with stakeholders to ensure data is provided.
3. Important
   - Identifying Data Sources: Mapping out necessary data points across departments, understanding where data resides and how it is stored.
   - Getting Data and Doing Follow-Ups: Collecting data in different formats from multiple sources, verifying data accuracy, and resolving discrepancies.
   - Creating Reports: Standardizing and consolidating data into a unified format, creating pivot tables, charts, and graphs.
   - Sharing with Leadership: Preparing presentations, translating complex data into critical insights, and regularly updating leadership on ESG metrics and risks.
   - Conducting Audits: Compiling audit-ready documentation, ensuring all data and processes comply with regulatory standards.
   - Developing Strategy: Analyzing data to identify risks and opportunities, formulating strategies to mitigate risks, and capitalizing on opportunities.

We systematically prioritized the opportunities by applying Osterwalder's framework and these scales. This process ensured that we focused on the areas that would first deliver the most significant benefits to our customers. It's all about addressing the most pressing pains and providing the most essential gains, making our software valuable and indispensable for our users. This structured prioritization helps us stay aligned with our customer's needs and create a genuinely impactful product.

Opportunity Solution Tree

Now, let's discuss how we can streamline ESG management and make it more efficient, accurate, and compliant. We've identified high-level opportunities and developed solutions addressing common pain points.

First up, Automate Data Collection and Entry. Imagine reducing those tedious, time-consuming manual processes. Right now, manually collecting and entering data is a labor-intensive task. What if we could implement automated data collection from various sources via secure API integrations? This would save so much time and significantly reduce errors. Plus, think about how much easier life would be without the need for continuous follow-ups. Using AI to send automated reminders and track responses, we can free up time to focus on more strategic tasks.

Next, we can enhance Data Accuracy and Consistency. One big issue is that data from different sources often comes in varying formats, which is a headache to standardize manually. By implementing solutions that automatically standardize data formats, we can ensure that the data is consistent and accurate across the board. No more juggling multiple formats and risking inconsistencies.

Simplifying Regulatory Compliance is another significant opportunity. Keeping up with changing regulations is tough, but with the right tools, it doesn't have to be. Automated compliance checks can ensure that all data aligns with the latest regulations, reducing the risk of non-compliance and the stress that comes with it.

Now, let's talk about streamlining audit preparation. Preparing for audits involves extensive documentation and can be incredibly stressful. Imagine having comprehensive audit trails that are automatically generated and updated. This means being audit-ready at all times with minimal effort, making the whole process much less daunting.

We also see a big win in improving stakeholder engagement. Engaging stakeholders and ensuring their input is considered can be complex and time-consuming. With streamlined engagement tools, we can facilitate better communication and collaboration, ensuring everyone's voice is heard without the hassle of endless meetings and follow-ups.

Another exciting opportunity is to provide Real-Time Insights and Advanced Analytics. Currently, more real-time insights are needed to improve effective decision-making. By leveraging advanced analytics, we can offer predictive insights that help make informed strategic decisions. This means being proactive rather than reactive, which is a game-changer.

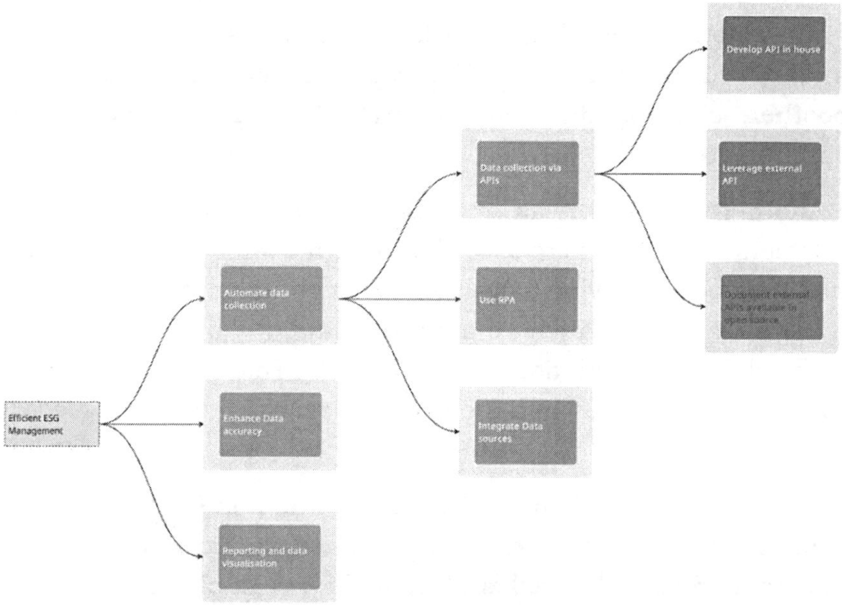

Figure 7.3 Opportunity Solution Tree - Sample\

Lastly, ensuring Robust Data Security and Access Controls is non-negotiable. Managing sensitive data securely is a significant challenge. Implementing robust security measures and access controls can protect this data, ensuring only authorized personnel have access and reducing the risk of data breaches.

By addressing these opportunities, we can transform how ESG management is handled. Automation, standardization, and advanced analytics will save time, reduce errors, and provide insights that drive strategic decisions. Enhanced security measures will protect sensitive data, building trust and compliance. This is how we envision the future of ESG management—efficient, accurate, and incredibly effective. We started with the idea that automating data collection and entry could significantly streamline our processes. This would save time and reduce human errors, which is crucial for maintaining high data quality. From there, we explored a few critical solutions.

First, we investigated automated data collection via APIs. The concept is straightforward: using APIs, we can connect different systems and automatically pull data from various sources without manual intervention. We realized the importance of having a standardized API framework. This would make integration much smoother, allowing different platforms to connect quickly and communicate consistently.

Another big win was real-time data synchronization. By implementing this, we ensured that all our systems had the latest data. Imagine not having to wait for overnight batch processes—the data is instantly updated. To maintain data quality, we integrated advanced data validation mechanisms. This way, errors or anomalies are caught when the data comes in, keeping our records clean and accurate.

Next, we explored Robotic Process Automation (RPA). RPAs can handle repetitive tasks like data entry, which frees our team to focus on more complex tasks. We aimed for scalable RPA solutions that can grow with our needs. The RPA can handle more without a complete overhaul as our data volume increases. By integrating AI and machine learning, our RPA can do more than follow scripts – it can make decisions based on patterns it recognizes in the data. For example, it could flag unusual data entries that might indicate a problem. Of course, monitoring these processes is crucial to ensure they're running efficiently. A centralized dashboard helps us keep track of all RPA activities and adjust as needed.

Lastly, we considered integrating these automated processes with our existing data management systems. Middleware solutions help bridge the gap between different systems, enabling smooth data flow and ensuring everything works together seamlessly. Establishing standards for how different systems communicate ensures they can work together without issues. It's like setting standard rules that everyone follows. We use continuous integration and deployment (CI/CD) pipelines to keep everything running smoothly. Any new integration or update is automatically tested and deployed, reducing downtime and keeping the systems up-to-date.

By implementing these solutions, we've created a robust automated data collection and entry system. The primary outcomes are pretty exciting. We've significantly reduced the time spent on manual data entry, allowing our team to focus on more strategic tasks. Automated validation and real-time synchronization mean our data is more accurate and up-to-date. The solutions we've put in place can grow with us, handling larger volumes of data as needed. With advanced validation and monitoring, we ensure that our data is secure and that any issues are quickly addressed.

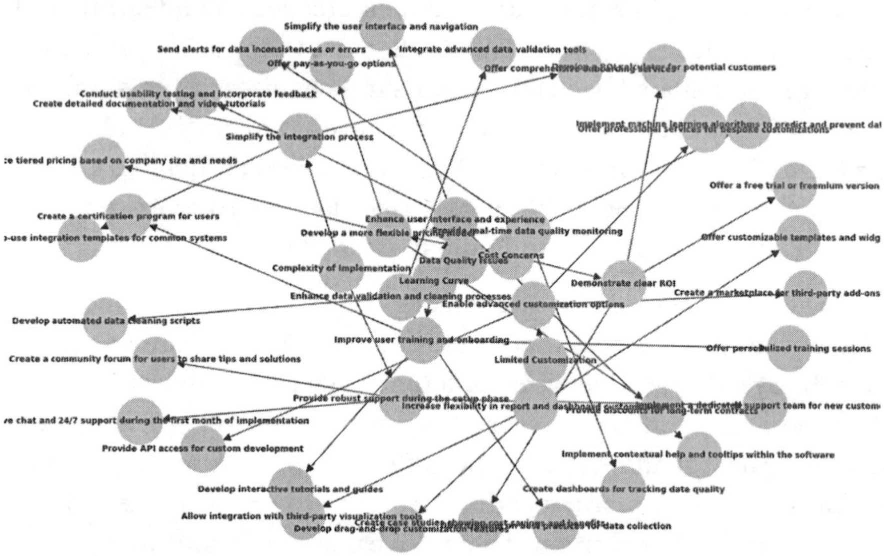

Figure 7.4 Opportunity solution tree for a subset of opportunities

I've been examining some fascinating insights into how to enhance our product's value proposition. It's all about understanding what our users genuinely need and crafting solutions that meet those needs and exceed their expectations. Let's explore some exciting opportunities and how we can tackle them.

Imagine using a new software, and everything makes sense from the start. The navigation is smooth, and the interface is intuitive. That's precisely what simplifying the user interface and navigation aims to achieve. It's like walking into a beautifully organized store where you can find everything easily. Now, add some contextual help and tooltips, and it's like having a friendly guide by your side, ready to help whenever you're stuck. This enhancement can make the entire experience much more enjoyable and less frustrating.

Data quality is another biggie. Picture a robust system that monitors real-time data quality, sending alerts if something seems off. It's like having a vigilant guard ensuring everything is in top shape. Integrating advanced data validation tools can act as this guard, preventing insufficient data from creeping in. And those alerts? They're like little nudges, letting you know something needs your attention before it becomes a significant issue.

Now, let's talk about customization and flexibility. People love having options. Offering customizable templates and widgets allows users to tailor the software to their liking. It's like customizing your car, picking the features that matter most to you. Imagine being able to rearrange your workspace with a simple drag-and-drop. It's all about making the experience as seamless and adaptable as possible.

Support and training are crucial, too. Imagine starting with a new tool and having a thorough onboarding process that guides you every step of the way. It's like having a personal coach who's there to ensure your success. Personalized training sessions and interactive tutorials can be beneficial, making the learning curve less steep. And robust support during the setup phase? That's like having a safety net—knowing someone's got your back if you run into trouble.

Building a community can enhance user engagement. Imagine a platform where users share tips, solutions, and success stories. It's like being part of a club where everyone is eager to help each other. This kind of collaborative environment can be a goldmine of knowledge and support.

Another critical area is simplifying integration. Imagine effortlessly connecting the pieces of a puzzle. Providing easy-to-use integration templates for standard systems can make this process much smoother. Allowing integration with third-party visualization tools is like giving users a toolkit to create their masterpieces. Implementing machine learning algorithms to predict and prevent data issues is like having a crystal ball, offering proactive solutions to potential problems.

Finally, demonstrating clear ROI is essential. People want to see the value they're getting. Creating a marketplace for third-party add-ons can add versatility and appeal to the product. Offering a free trial or freemium version is like giving users a taste test—they experience the benefits first-hand before committing fully. Long-term support contracts provide that extra assurance, making users feel secure in their investments.

We can craft a value proposition that meets and surpasses user expectations by addressing these opportunities with thoughtful solutions. It's all about making their journey with our product as smooth, enjoyable, and valuable as possible.

Solution Ideation

We will brainstorm possible solutions for each high-level opportunity and then prioritize them based on feasibility and potential impact.

1. Automate Data Collection and Entry

   Solutions:

   - API Integrations: Develop APIs to integrate with familiar data sources, such as ERP systems, HR databases, and environmental sensors.
   - AI-Powered Data Extraction: Use AI to extract and standardize unstructured data from emails and PDFs.
   - • Automated Reminders: Implement an AI-driven system to send reminders and follow-ups for data collection.

2. Enhance Data Accuracy and Consistency

   Solutions:

   - AI Validation Tools: Implement AI tools to cross-check and validate data entries for consistency.
   - Real-Time Data Standardization: Machine learning algorithms standardize data formats as they are collected in real time.

3. Simplify Regulatory Compliance

   Solutions:

   - Dynamic Compliance Templates: Create templates that automatically update based on the latest regulatory requirements.

- Regulatory Monitoring: Develop a system to monitor regulatory changes and update compliance requirements in real time.

4. Streamline Audit Preparation

   Solutions:

   - Comprehensive Audit Trails: Automatically generate detailed audit trails for all data entries and modifications.
   - Centralized Documentation: Provide a central repository for all audit-related documents, with easy access and search capabilities.

5. Improve Stakeholder Engagement

   Solutions:

   - Virtual Workshop Tools: Develop tools for virtual workshops and surveys to gather stakeholder input.
   - Centralized Communication Platform: Create a platform that centralizes stakeholder communication, providing clear and consistent messaging.

6. Provide Real-Time Insights and Advanced Analytics

   Solutions:

   - Real-Time Dashboards: Implement dashboards that provide real-time data insights and analytics.
   - AI-Driven Insights: Use AI to analyze data trends and provide predictive insights.

7. Ensure Robust Data Security and Access Controls

   Solutions:

   - Advanced Access Controls: Develop granular access controls and encryption to ensure data security.
   - Centralized Data Hub: Provide a secure hub for all ESG data.

Identifying Experiments to Run

Let's discuss how we've developed these experiments to test our solutions for the ESG Streamline software. We took a page from Alexander Osterwalder's value proposition book to ensure we met our customers' needs. First, we focused on automating data collection and entry. We brainstormed different ways to tackle this and thought, 'Why not test them all?' One experiment involves integrating with a single external data source using APIs to see how much time we save compared to doing it manually. We'll also pilot this with multiple data sources to test the robustness of these API integrations. Another idea is to use RPA, so we'll set up RPA for repetitive tasks and measure how much time and error reduction we achieve. And, of course, we'll integrate with existing data management systems to pull data directly and stress test this under high data loads.

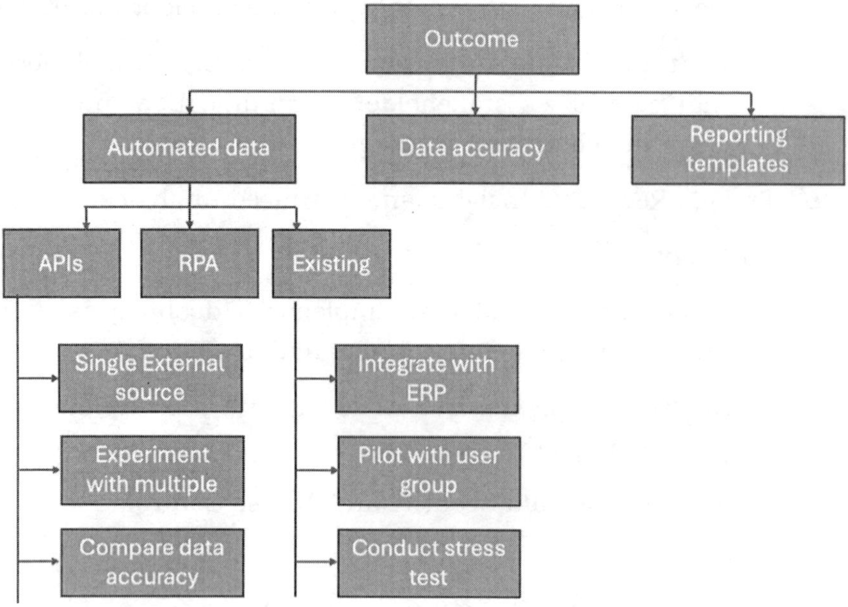

Figure 7.5 Opportunity Solution Tree with Experiments

Next, we tackled enhancing data accuracy and consistency. Here, we're thinking about automatically standardizing data formats and validating them right when entered. To test this, we'll compare the tool's validation results against manual processes. We're also considering machine learning for real-time inconsistency correction, so we'll train a model on historical data and see how well it performs. For blockchain, we'll implement a ledger for a subset of data entries and evaluate security and integrity.

Another big one is simplifying regulatory compliance. We'll test automated compliance checks with one regulation first to see if they reduce errors, and then we'll expand them to multiple rules. Another experiment is a compliance management module that tracks and notifies users of regulatory changes. We're considering integrating compliance consulting services, so we'll trial this to see the uptake and satisfaction levels.

We're looking at automatically generating detailed audit trails to streamline audit preparation. We'll measure how much this reduces preparation time and conduct a mock audit to check reliability. Another experiment involves using an AI-powered document management system for audit-related documents and comparing it with manual methods. We'll also provide templates and checklists for audit prep to see how well they guide users.

Improving stakeholder engagement involves several different tools. We'll implement real-time collaboration tools for a project and measure participation rates. We'll also create a stakeholder portal, track engagement metrics, and develop a mobile app to see if it boosts on-the-go engagement.

For real-time insights and advanced analytics, we're implementing AI-driven predictive analytics and will evaluate prediction accuracy. We'll also develop interactive dashboards and measure how much they improve data exploration and usage. Of course, advanced visualization tools are on the list, so we'll test these to see how they enhance data understanding.

Finally, it is crucial to ensure robust data security and access controls. We'll start by implementing advanced encryption and multi-factor authentication for a subset of data and conducting penetration testing to find vulnerabilities. We'll also develop a role-based access control system and measure the reduction of unauthorized access incidents. End-to-end encryption will be implemented and audited to ensure effectiveness.

By generating these experiments, we're following Osterwalder's framework to test and validate our solutions. This approach helps us ensure that the features we develop meet our customer's needs and provide the most value. It's all about creating a value proposition that resonates profoundly and effectively addresses our users' real challenges.

Ideas and experiments.

Summary of Experiments

To validate these solutions, we will design experiments to gather feedback and iterate on the solutions. Each experiment will involve creating a prototype or MVP (minimum viable product) and testing it with a small group of users.

Experiment 1: API Integrations and AI-Powered Data Extraction.

Objective: Test the effectiveness of automated data collection and standardization.

Prototype: Develop an essential API integration and an AI-powered data extraction tool.

Testing: Select a few familiar data sources and test the integration and extraction with a group of users.

Metrics: Measure the reduction in manual data entry time and the accuracy of the standardized data.

Feedback: Gather user feedback on ease of use and effectiveness.

Experiment 2: AI Validation and Real-Time Data Standardization

Objective: Validate the accuracy and consistency of AI-validated and standardized data.

Prototype: Create a simple AI validation tool and a real-time data standardization module.

Testing: Use historical data to test the validation and standardization process.

Metrics: Measure the error rate and consistency improvements.

Feedback: Get user feedback on the accuracy and reliability of the AI tools.

Experiment 3: Dynamic Compliance Templates and Regulatory Monitoring

Objective: Test the usability and effectiveness of dynamic compliance templates and real-time regulatory updates.

Prototype: Develop a basic dynamic compliance template and a regulatory monitoring system.

Testing: Use current regulatory requirements and simulate changes to test updates.

Metrics: Measure the time saved in creating compliance reports and the accuracy of the updated templates.

Feedback: Collect feedback on the compliance tools' ease of use and reliability.

Experiment 4: Comprehensive Audit Trails and Centralized Documentation

Objective: Validate the usefulness of automated audit trails and centralized documentation.

Prototype: Build a simple audit trail generator and a centralized documentation repository.

Testing: Conduct a mock audit using the tools and gather user feedback.

Metrics: Measure the time taken to prepare for the audit and the completeness of the documentation.

Feedback: Obtain feedback on the usability and thoroughness of the audit preparation tools.

Experiment 5: Virtual Workshop Tools and Centralized Communication Platform

Objective: Test the effectiveness of stakeholder engagement tools.

Prototype: Develop an essential virtual workshop tool and a centralized communication platform.

Testing: Conduct virtual workshops and centralize stakeholder communications.

Metrics: Measure engagement levels and the clarity of communication.

Feedback: Gather user feedback on the tool's effectiveness in improving stakeholder engagement.

Experiment 6: Real-Time Dashboards and AI-Driven Insights

Objective: Validate the value of real-time dashboards and AI-driven insights.

Prototype: Create a simple, real-time dashboard and an AI analytics module.

Testing: Use live data to populate the dashboard and generate AI insights.

Metrics: Measure the accuracy and usefulness of the insights provided.

Feedback: Collect feedback on the clarity and actionability of the dashboards and insights.

Experiment 7: Advanced Access Controls and Centralized Data Hub

Objective: Test the robustness of data security and access controls.

Prototype: Develop a primary access control system and a centralized data hub.

Testing: Implement the system in a controlled environment and test with users.

Metrics: Measure security incidents and user satisfaction with data access.

Feedback: Gather feedback on the ease of managing access controls and data security.

Mapping Different Segments

We will organize the proposed solutions into the Customer Jobs, Pains, and Gains categories to create a comprehensive view.

Stacked Solutions: Jobs, Pains, and Gains.

Let's discuss how we're using Alexander Osterwalder's value proposition framework to develop solutions for our customers' jobs in ESG management. This framework helps us focus on what matters to our customers by tailoring solutions that address their jobs, pains, and gains.

First up, Conducting Materiality Assessments. We know this can be a real challenge, especially when getting input from all stakeholders. So, we're introducing virtual workshop tools. These tools will easily facilitate stakeholder input and provide a seamless way to conduct virtual workshops and surveys. Imagine having everything you need right at your fingertips, making the whole process much more efficient and less stressful.

Next, let's discuss Identifying Data Sources. Manually gathering data from various sources can be a huge time sink. That's why we're implementing API integrations. Secure API integrations allow us to automate data collection from multiple sources. It's all about making data collection as easy and reliable as possible, freeing time for more critical tasks.

Following up with data owners can take time. To solve this, we're using automated reminders. AI will handle sending out reminders and follow-ups for data collection, ensuring nothing slips through the cracks. This means fewer manual tasks and more focus on analyzing the data.

We've developed a two-pronged approach to collecting data and conducting follow-ups. First, AI-powered data extraction will extract and standardize data from unstructured sources. This ensures that we're getting clean, usable data without manual intervention. Second, we're doubling down on automated reminders, providing timely and efficient follow-ups.

Another primary task is creating reports. To streamline this, we're introducing real-time data standardization, which will standardize data formats in real time. Additionally, we're offering dynamic compliance templates that automatically update based on regulatory requirements. This makes reporting quicker and ensures it's always up-to-date and compliant.

Having clear and insightful data is critical when it's time to share with leadership. That's why we're rolling out real-time dashboards. These dashboards provide real-time data insights and analytics, making it easier to present actionable information. Moreover, AI-driven insights will analyze data trends and provide predictive insights, while a centralized communication platform will streamline communication with stakeholders.

Finally, Conducting Audits can be daunting. We're making this easier with comprehensive audit trails. These trails generate detailed records for all data entries and modifications, ensuring transparency and traceability. This means audits can be conducted smoothly, with all necessary information readily available.

Stacking these solutions based on the value proposition framework ensures that every aspect of our customer's jobs, pains, and gains is addressed. It's all about making their work more efficient, accurate, and less stressful. This structured approach ensures that the software meets the practical requirements of ESG managers, alleviates their pain points, and delivers significant value through enhanced efficiency, accuracy, compliance, and strategic insights.

Conclusion

We've made some significant progress. After identifying our high-priority opportunities and devising solid solutions and experiments, it's time to take the next big step. We plan to automate data collection, enhance data accuracy, and bolster data security, among other things. These solutions are designed to tackle our users' most pressing needs head-on.

The next crucial task on our journey is building our minimum viable product (MVP). The MVP is the initial version of our software that includes the essential features needed to address our customers' core problems and deliver immediate value. Think of it as a prototype that we can use to gather feedback and iterate quickly.

In the next chapter, I'll explain how I identified and developed our MVP. We'll explorc which features made the cut, how I prioritized them, and the best strategies I found for getting the MVP into users' hands as swiftly as possible. This is where the rubber meets the road, and it's fascinating to see all our hard work start to come to life.

Stay with me because next, I'll outline the roadmap for creating an MVP that genuinely delivers. We'll focus on making intelligent choices, staying agile, and keeping our eye on providing value every step of the way. It's a thrilling part of the process, and I can't wait to share how it all comes together to meet and exceed our users' expectations.

Chapter 8
From Prototyping and Prioritizing

Imagine you're standing at the edge of a breakthrough, ready to transform bold ideas into tangible solutions that can change the game. This is where it all gets real, friends. Developing an MVP is like embarking on a daring expedition. It's about pushing boundaries, testing our mettle, and refining our product based on the invaluable feedback we gather from the real world. Our mission? To align the value map with the customer map perfectly. We must ensure that every gain creator we design matches the customer gains, every pain reliever effectively tackles customer pains, and our products are laser-focused on solving the customers' jobs.

Let me share how we navigated this thrilling terrain, moving from raw experiments to a polished, validated MVP. The first step was identifying the high-risk hypotheses—those critical assumptions that could make-or-break our success. This was like pinpointing the hidden pitfalls in our path. We needed to validate these early on to ensure we were on solid ground.

Then came the designing of small, focused experiments. Picture this: each experiment is a strategic move, a calculated step that lets us test our hypotheses quickly and efficiently without risking too much at once. It's like sending scouts ahead to survey the land. Next up was the exhilarating part – building prototypes. These weren't just prototypes; our vision was brought to life, albeit in a basic form. These prototypes incorporated the essential features we identified, and while they weren't perfect, they were good enough to be put in the hands of real users.

Testing with users was a rollercoaster ride of insights. We handed over our prototypes and eagerly awaited feedback. This step was a goldmine, revealing what worked brilliantly and what needed tweaking. We iterated, adjusted, and improved with this treasure trove of insights. It was a relentless cycle of testing, learning, and refining. Finally, after several rounds of rigorous iteration and refinement, we developed our MVP. This wasn't just any MVP; it was a version of our product that we were confident would deliver significant value and solve our users' most pressing problems.

MVP Development and Validation Process

The MVP development and validation process consists of identifying high-risk hypotheses, designing focused experiments, building prototypes, testing prototypes, and iterating based on user feedback.

Step 1: Identify High-Risk Hypotheses

The first big step in our journey is pinpointing the highest-risk hypotheses tied to our top priority opportunities. These hypotheses are our educated guesses about our solutions. If we get these wrong, it could throw a wrench in our plans for the MVP. Let's break it down with a few examples:

Hypothesis for Automated Regulatory Updates: Compliance managers will save a lot of time and make fewer errors if we provide automated regulatory updates. Imagine how much smoother their workflow could be with this feature!

Hypothesis for Data Integration Tool: We bet automated data integration will significantly boost data accuracy and make operations more efficient. Imagine all the headaches we could eliminate by making the data flow seamlessly.

Hypothesis for Simplified Interfaces: We're convinced that a simplified, user-centric interface will skyrocket user satisfaction and adoption rates. If it's easy and intuitive to use, people will love it and stick with it.

Hypothesis for Real-Time Dashboard: Real-time insights will be a game-changer for decision-making and sustainability performance. Imagine having all the crucial data at your fingertips, updated in real-time—it's a manager's dream come true.

These hypotheses are our compass, guiding us toward building a successful MVP. Now, let's dive into how we test these hypotheses to ensure we're on the right track.

Step 2: Design Small, Focused Experiments

Now, let's get into the nitty-gritty of testing our hypotheses. This is where things get interesting! We will design experiments to test these hypotheses in the slightest, fastest, and cheapest way possible. Here's how we're going to do it.

Experiment for Automated Regulatory Updates:

First, we have the experiment for automated regulatory updates. We observed that compliance managers spend too much time tracking regulatory changes. So, our big question is: Will automating updates reduce this time and improve accuracy?

- Observation: Compliance managers spend excessive time tracking regulatory changes.
- Question: Will automated updates reduce this time and improve accuracy?
- Hypothesis: Automated updates will save time and reduce errors.
- Prediction: Compliance managers using the feature will report a 50% reduction in time spent on manual tracking and a 30% reduction in errors.
- Test: Implement a basic version of the automated update feature for a small group of users and collect feedback over one month.

Experiment for Data Integration Tool:

Next, we have the experiment for the data integration tool. We've noticed that manual data entry often leads to frequent errors. So, our question is, can automated data integration reduce these errors and improve efficiency?

- Observation: Manual data entry leads to frequent errors.
- Question: Will automated data integration reduce errors and improve efficiency?
- Hypothesis: Automated integration will decrease data entry errors by 40%.
- Prediction: Users will report fewer errors and spend less time on data entry.
- Test: Deploy an initial version of the data integration tool in one department and measure error rates and time spent on data entry.

Experiment with a Simplified Interface

Then, there's the experiment for Simplified Interfaces. We've seen that complex interfaces frustrate users, so we're wondering, will a simplified interface increase satisfaction and adoption?

- Observation: Complex interfaces frustrate users.
- Question: Will a simplified interface increase satisfaction and adoption?
- Hypothesis: A user-centric design will improve satisfaction and adoption rates.
- Prediction: Users will rate the new interface higher in usability tests and show increased engagement.
- Test: Conduct usability testing with a redesigned interface prototype and collect user feedback.

Experiment for Real-Time Dashboard:

Lastly, we have the experiment for the Real-Time Dashboard. We know that the need for real-time insights helps decision-making. So, our question is, will real-time insights improve decision-making and performance?

- Observation: Lack of real-time insights hinders decision-making.
- Question: Will real-time insights improve decision-making and performance?
- Hypothesis: Real-time dashboards will enhance decision-making.
- Prediction: Users will report better decision-making capabilities and improved performance metrics.
- Test: Launch a prototype of the real-time dashboard and gather user feedback over a few weeks.

We'll gather valuable data to validate our hypotheses and refine our MVP by running these experiments. It's all about testing, learning, and iterating based on real-world feedback. I'm excited to see where these experiments lead us and how they shape our final product!

Step 3: Build Prototypes

Now, we've reached the part where we bring our ideas to life by building prototypes. This is crucial because it allows us to test our hypotheses with something tangible. The key here is to develop prototypes that are functional enough to test our ideas but simple enough to build quickly and cost-effectively. Let's dive into the prototypes we're creating.

The first is the automated regulatory updates prototype. This essential feature is designed to fetch and display real-time regulatory updates. Think of it as a real-time news feed but for regulatory changes. It's all about giving compliance managers instant access to the latest updates without manually tracking everything.

Next, we have the data integration tool prototype. This one's a bit of a game-changer. It's a simplified tool that automates data collection and entry from critical sources. Imagine no more tedious manual data entry – this tool grabs the data you need from different sources and integrates it seamlessly.

Then, there's the Simplified Interface Prototype. With this one, we're focusing on usability and intuitive navigation. It's a redesigned interface aims to make the user experience smooth and frustration-free. Users should feel like they're navigating through a well-laid-out app without hassle.

Lastly, we're working on the real-time dashboard prototype. This is where we display critical metrics in real-time with interactive elements. Picture a dashboard that gives instant insights at your fingertips, helping you make informed decisions. It's interactive, real-time, and designed to be incredibly user-friendly.

Building these prototypes is crucial to validating our hypotheses. Each prototype is a mini-experiment, helping us gather valuable feedback and make informed decisions on the next steps. I'm excited about this part because it's where our ideas take shape, and we begin to see their actual impact.

Step 4: Test Prototypes with Users

Now comes one of the most exciting parts of our journey – testing the prototypes with actual users. This is where we gather real-world feedback and validate our hypotheses. It's all about getting our ideas into the hands of the people who will use them and seeing how they perform in the wild.

First, we've got the Automated Regulatory Updates Test. Here, we will measure how much time we save and how many errors we reduce for compliance managers. It's all about efficiency and accuracy – two critical factors in regulatory compliance.

Next is the data integration tool test. We'll track error rates and look for improvements in efficiency during the data entry process. The goal is to see if our tool makes data integration smoother and more reliable.

Then, we have the Simplified Interfaces Test. For this one, we'll collect usability scores and user engagement metrics. We want to know if our redesigned interface is as intuitive and user-friendly as we hoped. High usability scores and increased engagement will be the indicators of success.

Lastly, there's the real-time dashboard test. We'll gather feedback on how this dashboard improves decision-making and performance metrics. We aim to provide users with real-time insights that help them make better decisions faster.

By conducting these tests, we're validating our ideas and learning what works, what doesn't, and how we can improve. It's a crucial step in our journey to build an MVP that meets our users' needs. I can't wait to see the results and use this feedback to improve our product.

Step 5: Iterate Based on Feedback

Once we've gathered feedback and data from our tests, it's time to dive into the analysis. This is where we figure out what worked, what didn't, and, most importantly, why. It's a crucial step in refining our prototypes and hypotheses to ensure we're on the right track.

First, let's discuss Feedback Analysis. We need to review all user feedback to identify common issues and areas for improvement. This is like gathering all the puzzle pieces and seeing the bigger picture. What are the recurring problems? What features did users love or hate? Understanding these elements is critical to improving our product.

Then, it's all about iteration. Based on the feedback, we'll make the necessary adjustments to our prototypes and, if needed, re-test them. This iterative process is essential because it ensures continuous improvement and keeps us aligned with user needs.

It's like fine-tuning an engine – each tweak gets us closer to optimal performance. We're honing our MVP to meet and exceed user expectations by thoroughly analyzing feedback and iterating on our prototypes. This step is about learning and adapting, ensuring we're offering something precious and user-centric when we launch.

I'm excited to see how these iterations shape our product and bring us closer to a solution that works and delights our users. Let's keep pushing forward, learning, and improving every step of the way!

Step 6: Develop the MVP

Once we've validated our prototypes through repeated testing and iteration, it's time to consolidate the successful features into a cohesive MVP. This step is crucial because we must ensure that our MVP addresses the core jobs, pains, and gains identified in our customer profiling. This is where all our hard work comes together into something truly impactful. So, what does our MVP look like? Here are the key features we've decided to include:

Automated Regulatory Updates: This fully functional feature provides real-time updates and alerts. It's designed to save compliance managers significant time and reduce errors by automating the tracking of regulatory changes.

Data Integration Tool: This comprehensive tool integrates data from multiple sources with real-time validation. It aims to make data entry smoother and more accurate, reduce manual work, and increase operational efficiency.

Simplified Interface: We've designed a user-centric interface with customizable dashboards and intuitive navigation. By making the tool easy-to-use and navigate, we aim to enhance user satisfaction and adoption.

Real-Time Dashboard: This feature offers advanced analytics and visualization tools, providing real-time insights. It's designed to improve decision-making and performance metrics by giving users immediate access to crucial information.

By bringing these features together, we're creating an MVP that meets and exceeds user expectations. We're addressing their core needs and pain points while delivering significant value. Building and validating an MVP for an ESG management application is quite an adventure. It revolves around experiments designed to test high-risk hypotheses and refine our solutions based on user feedback. By following a structured approach—observing, questioning, hypothesizing, predicting, testing, and iterating—we can develop a robust MVP that aligns with customer needs and delivers real value. This iterative process is like a treasure hunt. Each experiment brings us closer to uncovering the best version of our product. By minimizing risks and ensuring our final product effectively addresses our target users' jobs, pains, and gains, we're paving the way for a successful product-market fit.

How Long to Prototype a First Version: Lessons from Rapid Prototyping and MVP Examples

Prototyping the first version of a product should be a fast and iterative process. It involves quickly testing assumptions and gathering feedback to determine what works and what doesn't. Tom Chi's case study of the rapid prototyping of Google Glass is an excellent example of this approach. His work offers some fantastic insights into how to achieve this rapid iteration.

But it doesn't stop there. Looking at famous MVP examples from giants like Facebook, Google, and Amazon can further deepen our understanding of the importance of launching early and iterating often. These companies have mastered quickly releasing products, learning from user feedback, and continuously improving.

Case Study: Tom Chi and Rapid Prototyping of Google Glass

Let's examine an inspiring example from Tom Chi, one of the co-founders of Google X, who led the rapid prototyping of Google Glass. The key to their approach was creating quick iterations to test core functionalities and gather immediate feedback. This fantastic story highlights the importance of speed over perfection and is incredibly relevant to our journey with the ESG management application.

Speed Over Perfection: The team created their prototype of Google Glass in just one day using simple materials like a coat hanger and a projector. Can you believe that? This quick approach allowed them to test the concept and get a tangible sense of the product early on. They didn't wait for a perfect model – they jumped right in. For our ESG management application, this means we don't need to wait until everything is flawless. We can start with a basic version that incorporates essential features and get it into the hands of users quickly to begin gathering feedback.

Iterative Process: They built multiple prototypes over the next few weeks, each improving on the previous version based on user feedback. This iterative cycle enabled them to refine the product rapidly. Each iteration brought them closer to a version that users loved. Applying this to our ESG management application, we can continuously refine our tool based on what users tell us. Each version gets better, more intuitive, and more aligned with our users' needs.

Learning from Failure: Early prototypes were imperfect, but each failure provided valuable insights. The team embraced the idea that if they weren't embarrassed by their first version, they had launched too late. This is a powerful lesson: Don't be afraid to fail early and learn quickly. This means embracing feedback, no matter how critical, and using it to strengthen our application. Each misstep is an opportunity to improve.

The rapid prototyping of Google Glass shows that the goal is to learn quickly and iterate. Speed and adaptability are crucial, and early versions don't need to be perfect. This approach is incredibly beneficial for our ESG management application because it allows us to be flexible, responsive, and user-focused.

Getting Your First Prototype: Embrace Imperfection

As Reid Hoffman, the founder of LinkedIn, famously said, "If you are not embarrassed by the first version of your product, you've launched too late." This quote perfectly captures the essence of rapid prototyping and the importance of launching early to learn from honest user feedback. Let's dive into how we can apply this wisdom to our ESG management application. Here are the key steps to prototype quickly and effectively:

Identify Core Features: Focus on the most critical features that address your users' primary job, pain, or gain. For our ESG management application, this means zeroing in on features like automated regulatory updates, data integration tools, simplified interfaces, and real-time dashboards. These features will immediately deliver the most value to our users.

Use Simple Materials: Don't wait for perfect materials or tools. Use what you have to create a functional prototype quickly. Like Tom Chi's team used a coat hanger and a projector for Google Glass, we can use essential tools and software to build our initial prototypes. The goal is to create something tangible that we can test, not something perfect.

Gather Feedback Early: Get your prototype into the hands of users as soon as possible to start collecting feedback. This step is crucial. The sooner we get our ESG management application in front of real users, the sooner we can learn what works and what doesn't. Early feedback is invaluable and can save us from costly mistakes.

Iterate Rapidly: Use the feedback to make improvements and create new versions quickly. This iterative process ensures we continuously refine our product based on real-world use. Each iteration brings us closer to a product that meets our users' needs and exceeds their expectations.

Following these steps allows us to develop our ESG management application efficiently and effectively. Rapid prototyping allows us to be agile, responsive, and user-focused. It's about getting our ideas out there, learning from real users, and iterating quickly to build a product that makes a difference.

Famous MVP Examples:

Look at some famous examples of rapid prototyping and MVPs from industry giants like Facebook, Google, and Amazon. These stories provide incredible insights into how launching early and iterating often can lead to massive success, and they offer valuable lessons we can apply to our ESG management application.

Facebook:

The first version of Facebook, initially called 'The Facebook,' was straightforward. It was a platform that allowed Harvard students to create profiles and connect. The interface was primary, and many of the features we see today were not included.

Lesson: Facebook launched early to a limited audience, gathered feedback, and rapidly iterated. This approach allowed them to refine the product based on fundamental user interactions. For us, this means we don't need to wait until our ESG management application is perfect. We can launch a basic version, get it in front of users, gather feedback, and improve from there.

Google:

Google's initial search engine, launched as 'Backrub,' was a minimalist web page with a simple search box. It focused on the core functionality of search without any of the additional features we see today.

Lesson: By focusing on its core value proposition—efficient and accurate search results—Google could launch quickly, gain traction, and improve the product based on user feedback. For our application, this means focusing on key features like real-time regulatory updates and data integration tools. By nailing these core functionalities, we can launch quickly and refine them based on feedback.

Amazon:

Amazon started as an online bookstore. The website was essential, with a simple interface for browsing and purchasing books. Jeff Bezos chose to begin with books due to their universal demand and ease of shipping.

Lesson: Amazon's MVP was focused on a specific niche, allowing them to validate their business model and grow organically. The initial simplicity enabled them to iterate and add features over time. Starting with a focused set of features for our ESG management application allows us to validate our core functionalities before expanding.

Validating Your MVP: The Iterative Process

Now, let's talk about how to use the scientific method to test our MVP. This approach is compelling to ensure we're on the right track with our ESG management application. It's a structured way to identify problems, test solutions, and iterate based on what we learn. Here's how it works:

Make an Observation: First, we must identify a market problem or need. For our ESG management application, compliance managers might need help keeping up with regulatory changes, or teams might need help integrating data from multiple sources.

Ask Questions: Next, we dig deeper to understand what our users struggle with or need. This is all about getting to the heart of the problem by asking the right questions. What are their pain points? What are the specific challenges they face?

Form a Hypothesis: Based on our observations and questions, we hypothesize how our product will solve the problem. For instance, we might hypothesize that automated regulatory updates will save compliance managers significant time and reduce errors.

Make Predictions: Then, the hypothesis is correct. We can predict the outcome; for example, in the fulfillment of automated updates, we expect a 50% reduction in time spent on manual tracking and a 30% reduction in errors.

Test the Prediction: This is where the rubber meets the road. We build a prototype and test it with real users. For our example, we could create a basic version of the automated updates feature and let a group of compliance managers use it for a month. We'll gather data on time saved and error reduction.

Iterate: Finally, we use the feedback and data to refine our product and repeat the process. Suppose our hypothesis is confirmed, great! We'll build on that success. If not, we'll tweak our approach and test again based on our learning.

Using the scientific method ensures that we're not just guessing but making informed decisions based on real-world testing and feedback. This approach helps us build a robust MVP that meets our users' needs and delivers real value.

Example Process for ESG Management Application:

1. Observation: Compliance managers are overwhelmed by manual regulatory updates.
2. Question: Will an automated update feature reduce their workload and improve compliance accuracy?
3. Hypothesis: An automated update feature will save time and reduce errors.
4. Prediction: Compliance managers will report a 50% reduction in time spent on manual updates.
5. Test: Implement a basic version of the automated update feature and pilot it with a small group.
6. Iterate: Collect feedback, make necessary improvements, and test again.

The goal of an MVP is to quickly validate your core hypotheses by putting a simplified version of your product into users' hands. Learning from Google Glass's rapid prototyping approach and the

MVP launches of Facebook, Google, and Amazon, you should aim to build and test your first version rapidly. Embrace imperfection, gather feedback, and iterate continuously. This process helps refine the product and ensures that you effectively address real customer needs.

Prototyping and Testing Your MVP: A Step-by-Step Guide

To successfully develop and validate your MVP, following a structured approach that leverages experimentation, prototyping, and iterative testing is crucial. This section outlines a process inspired by the rapid prototyping methods of some of the most innovative companies. It provides practical steps for creating and refining your MVP. Please think of this as our roadmap. By following these steps, we were able to turn our ideas into a tangible product that meets real user needs and delivers genuine value. This process isn't just about building something quickly; it's about building something meaningful and impactful.

Step 1: Experiment Work as a Blueprint for Your Prototype

First, we analyzed the experiment's results in-depth. Analyzing the data and feedback from these experiments was like uncovering hidden treasure. We could see exactly what worked and what didn't. This step was crucial because it helped us understand the strengths and weaknesses of our initial ideas based on fundamental user interactions.

Next, we defined the core features for our MVP. Based on the outcomes of our experiments, we listed the essential features. These elements provided the most value and directly addressed our users' primary jobs, pains, and gains. It was like distilling our grand vision into the most impactful components.

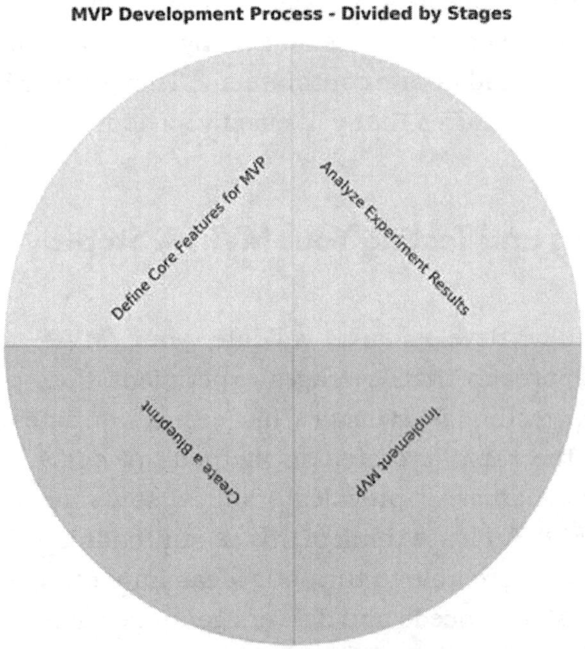

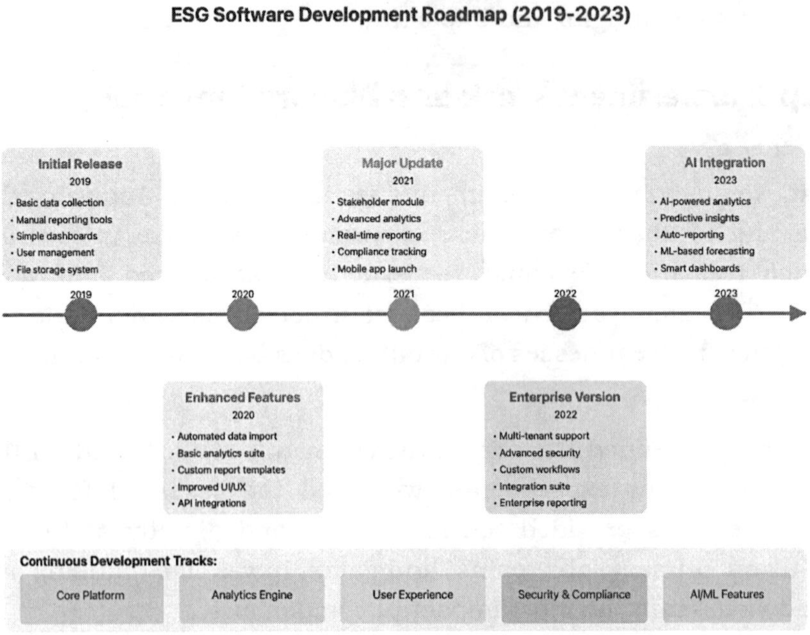

Figure 8.1 MVP development process – Divided by Stages

Then, we moved on to creating a blueprint. This was where we outlined the structure and flow of our MVP, focusing on how to implement these core features. Think of it as drawing up architectural plans before constructing a building. This blueprint gave us a clear direction and ensured everyone on the team was aligned.

For instance, one of our experiments showed that automated regulatory updates significantly reduced the workload for compliance managers. This insight was gold. It became clear that this feature had to be a core component of our blueprint. We knew it was a win because it directly addressed a significant pain point.

Step 2: Breadboarding to Map Out the Experience

First, we started by sketching the user journey. This involved creating a visual map outlining our product's user journey, highlighting fundamental interactions and touchpoints. It was like crafting a story where our users were the protagonists. We wanted to see exactly how they would navigate the application from when they logged in to when they generated compliance reports. Next, we identified the key screens and actions. We determined the essential screens that users would interact with and their actions during their journey. This step was crucial because it helped us focus on what mattered – the core interactions that would define the user experience.

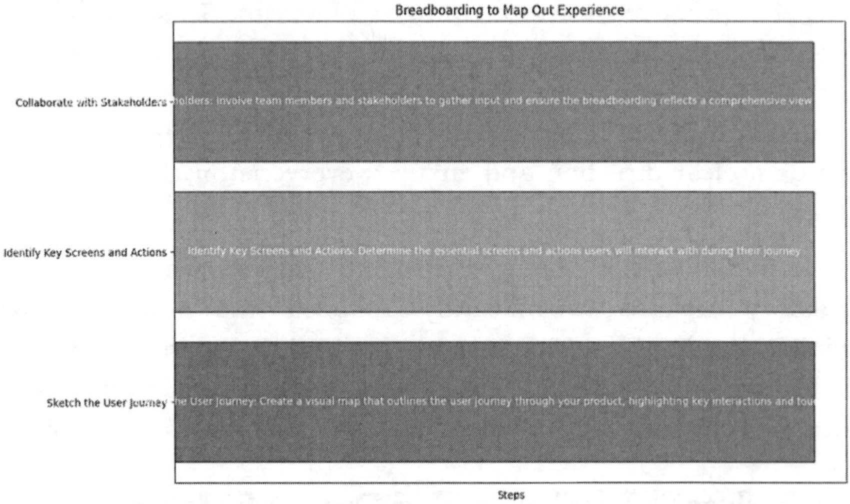

Figure 8.2 Breadboarding to map out experience

We collaborated closely with stakeholders to ensure we covered all the bases and didn't overlook any critical details. We involved team members and stakeholders to gather their input and ensure our storyboarding reflected a comprehensive view of the user experience. Their insights were invaluable.

For example, we sketched the journey of a compliance manager using our ESG management application. We mapped everything from logging in and receiving automated regulatory updates to generating detailed compliance reports. This exercise helped us see the product from the user's perspective and ensured we built something that met their needs. Storyboarding the user experience was like putting ourselves in the users' shoes and walking through their journey. It gave us a clear picture of how our application would be used in the real world and highlighted areas where we could improve the experience.

Step 3: Focus on Key Actions of an Experiment - Keep It Simple

As we moved forward in our journey, we realized the importance of focusing on the key actions of our experiments and keeping things simple. This approach was critical in validating our MVP hypotheses and ensuring we were on the right track without getting bogged down in unnecessary complexity.

The first step was to Prioritize Core Interactions. We honed in on the most critical interactions essential for validating our hypotheses. For our ESG management application, this meant focusing on the interactions demonstrating the value of automated regulatory updates and the generation of compliance reports. These were the core features that our users needed most.

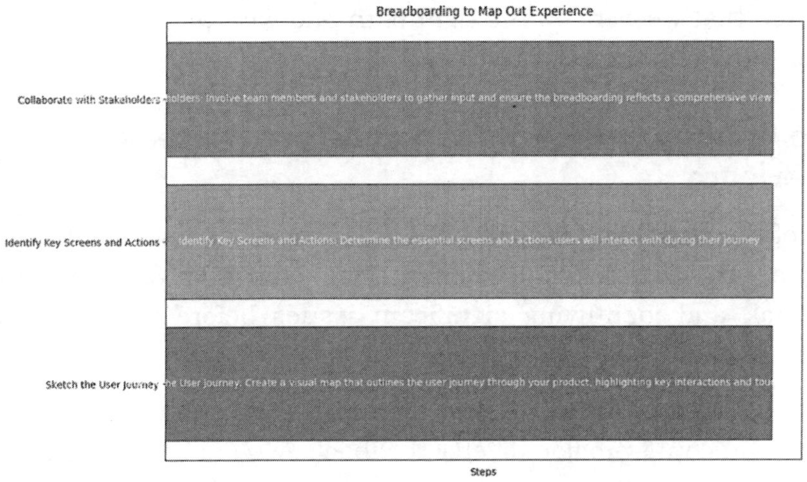

Figure 8.3 Focus on critical actions of an experiment

Next, we aimed to Simplify Features. Although incorporating every possible feature in our prototype was tempting, we knew simplicity was vital. We implemented only the features necessary to perform these key actions, avoiding unnecessary complexity. This way, we could ensure that our prototype was functional and user-friendly without being overloaded with extras.

Then, we set out to build a functional prototype. This version of our MVP allowed users to perform the prioritized interactions seamlessly. We ensured that the prototype enabled users to receive automated regulatory updates and generate compliance reports, even if other features were still in development. We aimed to validate our core hypotheses with a functional, straightforward product version.

For example, we ensured our ESG management application prototype allowed compliance managers to get automated regulatory updates and efficiently generate detailed compliance reports. Even if other features were still working, these fundamental interactions were fully functional and ready for testing.

By focusing on these critical actions and keeping our approach simple, we were able to validate our hypotheses effectively. It ensured that we were on the right path and gave us the confidence to continue refining our product.

Step 4: Jump to the Fat Market Before Polishing the Experience

One of the most exciting parts of our journey was testing our MVP with a larger, targeted audience. This step involved gathering feedback and identifying significant issues before polishing the experience.

Selecting Target Users: We first identified a larger group of target users who could provide diverse feedback. We aimed to find users from various industries who would use our ESG management application differently. This diversity was crucial for getting a well-rounded understanding of how our product performed in real-world scenarios.

Launching the MVP: After identifying our target users, we released our MVP to a broader group. This phase was nerve-racking but incredibly valuable. We focused on gathering feedback on the core features and overall usability. It was essential to see how the key functions—like automated regulatory updates and compliance report generation—held up under broader use.

Collecting and Analyzing Feedback: We gathered feedback through surveys, interviews, and analytics. This multi-faceted approach gave us a comprehensive view of user experiences. We paid close attention to both quantitative data and qualitative insights to understand how users interacted with the application and where improvements were needed.

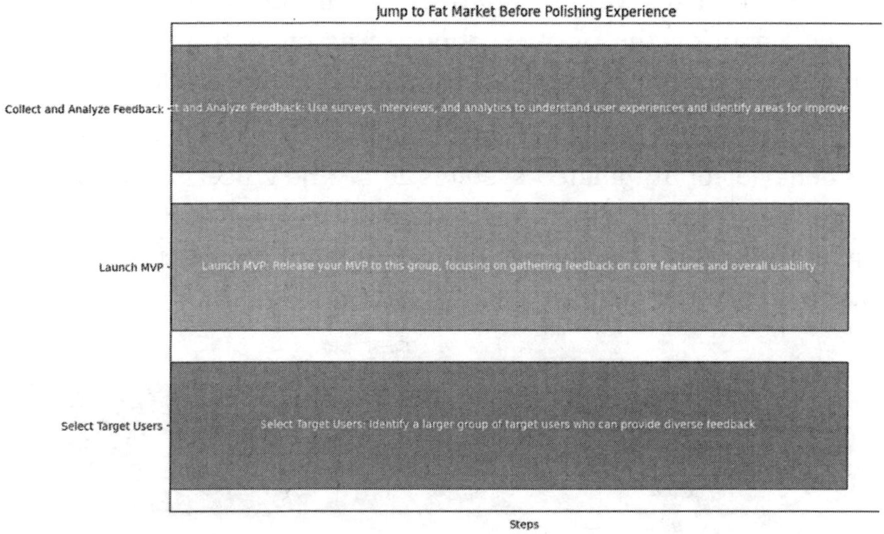

Figure 8.4 Jump to the fat market before publishing experience.

For example, we released the ESG management application to a broader group of compliance managers from various industries. We gathered detailed feedback on its usability and effectiveness, looking for joint pain points or areas where the application excelled. We gathered invaluable input from a larger audience by jumping to the market before polishing every detail. This feedback helped us identify significant issues and areas for improvement that we might have yet to catch with a smaller test group. It was a critical step in refining our product and ensuring it met the needs of a diverse user base.

Step 5: Concierge and Wizard Testing

One of the most insightful steps in developing our ESG management application was using concierge and Wizard of Oz testing. This approach allowed us to manually simulate complex or not-yet-automated features to validate their necessity and effectiveness.

Concierge Testing: This involved manually performing tasks behind the scenes that our product would eventually automate while the user interacted with the interface. It was like being the invisible helper, ensuring the user experience was smooth and collecting valuable data on how these tasks impacted their workflow.

Wizard of Oz Testing: In this method, we had a human simulate the behavior of automated systems to see how users reacted and interacted. Think of it as having a wizard behind the curtain, pulling the levers, and making things happen without the user knowing it wasn't fully automated.

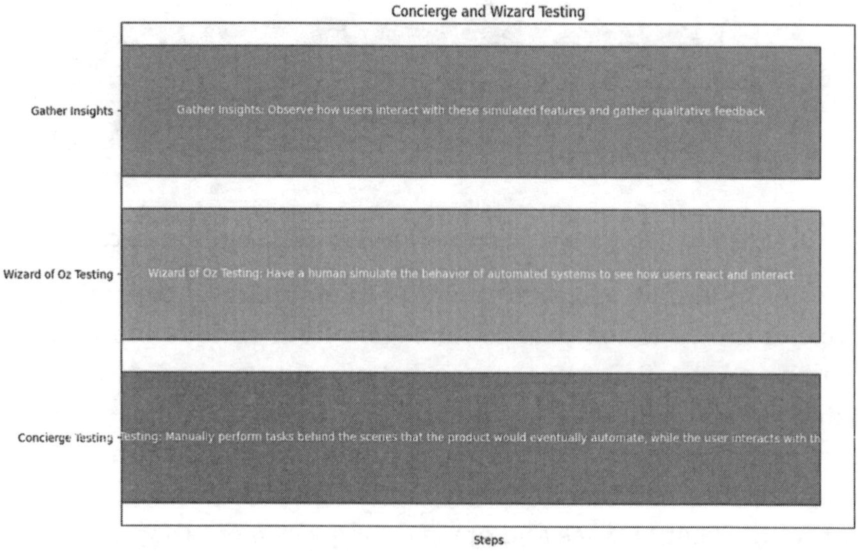

Figure 8.5 Concierge and Wizard testing

Gathering Insights: Throughout these tests, we carefully observed how users interacted with these simulated features and gathered qualitative feedback. This hands-on approach gave us deep insights into user needs and preferences that we might have yet to capture through automated systems alone.

For example, with our ESG management application, we manually provided compliance updates and insights to users while interacting with the prototype interface. This simulation of the automated features allowed us to see how users would react and what they valued most about these updates. Using concierge and Wizard of Oz testing was incredibly revealing. It showed us how critical certain features were and whether they worked as intended. This method also allowed us to adjust on the fly and immediately see the impact of those changes.

Step 6: Fidelity Testing

One critical phase in developing our ESG management application was increasing the fidelity of our prototypes. This process was about refining and polishing the user experience, gradually moving from simple to more complex and detailed versions of our product.

Low-Fidelity Prototypes: We started with simple, low-fidelity prototypes. These basic wireframes allowed us to test fundamental functionality and user interactions without getting bogged down in details. It was like sketching out the broad strokes of a painting, focusing on the overall composition rather than the finer details.

High-Fidelity Prototypes: As we gathered feedback from these initial tests, we gradually increased the fidelity of our prototypes. This meant incorporating more detailed design elements, richer interactions, and additional functionality. Each iteration brought us closer to the final product, allowing us to see how users would interact with a more polished version.

Iterate and Improve: Throughout this process, we continuously iterated on the prototype, incorporating user feedback and making improvements. This testing, learning, and refining cycle helped us enhance the overall user experience. Every round of feedback provided new insights that guided our next steps.

For instance, we began with a simple wireframe of the ESG management application. We moved to more detailed mockups and interactive prototypes as we collected feedback. Each version was more sophisticated than the last, reflecting the input we received and the improvements we made. This approach allowed us to ensure that every aspect of our application was user-friendly and met the needs of our target audience. By gradually increasing the fidelity, we could thoroughly test and refine each element before moving on to the next level of detail.

Following this structured approach, we efficiently developed and validated my MVP, ensuring it met user needs and expectations. Rapid prototyping, iterative testing, and incorporating user feedback at each stage were crucial to creating a successful product. We aimed to learn quickly, iterate often, and continuously improve the product based on real user insights.

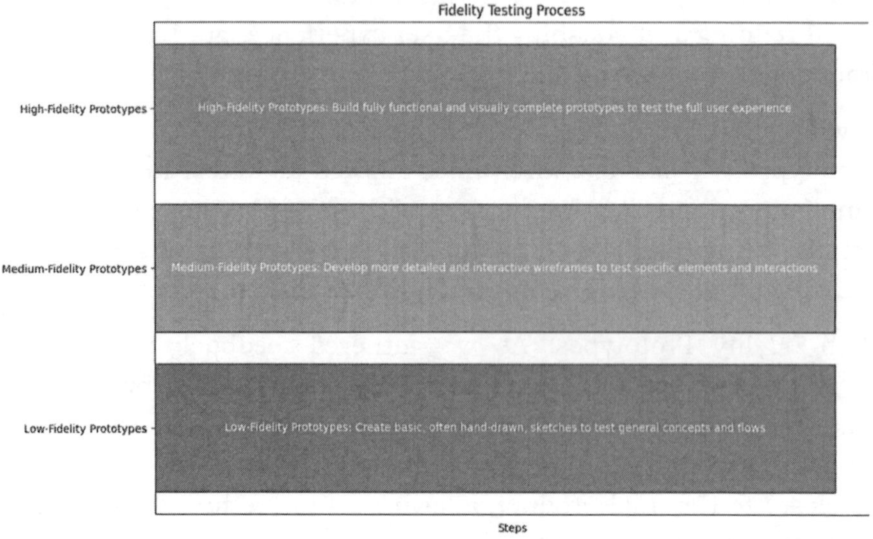

Figure 8.6 Fidelity testing process

With creativity and a disciplined approach, we turned our vision into a functional and valuable MVP. Agile, responsive, and user-focused are the fundamental principles. We built an ESG management application that meets and exceeds user expectations by embracing these principles.

In the end, the journey of developing an MVP is about more than just building a product. It's about understanding users, learning from them, and constantly striving to improve the product. With this mindset, we were able to create something truly impactful and valuable. So, keep iterating, keep learning, and stay committed to delivering value to your users. Your vision is well within reach!

Important Rules for Prototyping

Throughout my journey in product development, I've learned that prototyping is a crucial phase. It involves creating preliminary models of your product to test ideas and gather feedback. By following specific rules, I've found that the process can be efficient and effective, leading to valuable insights. Here are some key lessons I've learned along the way:

1. Focus on Solutions for the Highest Priorities and Opportunities

Prioritize: Concentrate on the most critical features that address the highest-priority opportunities identified through customer profiling and your Opportunity Solution Tree (OST). This focus ensures that you're working on the aspects of the product that will deliver the most value to your users.

Impact: Ensure that the solutions you prototype will significantly impact user satisfaction and product success. Focusing on high-impact features can drive meaningful improvements and achieve better user and product outcomes

2. Start with Small and Simple Solutions

Simplicity: Begin with simple, small-scale prototypes to validate basic concepts before adding complexity. Starting allows you to test fundamental ideas quickly and efficiently without getting bogged down by unnecessary details. This approach helps to ensure that your core concepts are sound before moving on to more elaborate features.

Incremental Development: Gradually build upon these small prototypes, adding more features and refining functionality as you gather feedback and learn from each iteration. This step-by-step approach enables you to continuously improve the product based on real user insights, ensuring that each new feature adds value and enhances the overall user experience.

3. Use Tools You're Comfortable With

Throughout my journey in product development, I've learned the value of using tools that my team and I are comfortable with. Here are some key lessons that have made a significant impact:

Familiarity: Choosing prototyping tools that you and your team are already familiar with is essential. This familiarity speeds up the process and reduces the learning curve, allowing us to focus more on the product's design and functionality rather than figuring out new software. For instance, sticking with tools we knew well meant we could dive right into creating and refining our prototypes without any delays.

Efficiency: Tools like Figma, Sketch, InVision, and even PowerPoint have proven incredibly effective for creating low-fidelity and high-fidelity prototypes. These tools offer a range of features that cater to different prototyping stages, from simple wireframes to detailed, interactive models. By leveraging these familiar tools, we could move quickly from initial concepts to functional prototypes, streamlining our workflow and enhancing productivity.

Using tools that we were comfortable with boosted our efficiency and allowed us to iterate rapidly based on user feedback. This approach ensured we could quickly adapt and make necessary improvements, ultimately leading to a product that met our users' needs and expectations.

4. Don't Reinvent the Wheel Where You Don't Have To

One of the most valuable lessons I've learned in product development is not reinventing the wheel when you don't have to. Here are some key insights that have guided my approach:

Leverage Existing Solutions: Utilizing existing design patterns, UI components, and libraries can save time and effort. We can maintain consistency and improve usability by leveraging these resources without building everything from scratch. This approach allows us to focus our energy on unique aspects of the product that genuinely add value.

Standards and Best Practices: Following established UX/UI standards and best practices ensure our prototypes are user-friendly and intuitive. Adhering to these guidelines helps create a seamless user experience and makes navigating and interacting with the product more accessible. It's about building on the industry's collective knowledge to deliver a polished and effective solution. By leveraging existing solutions and adhering to best practices, I was able to streamline the development process and create a more consistent, user-friendly product.

5. More Prototypes Mean More Learning

My product development journey taught me that more prototypes mean more learning. Here are the key lessons that have shaped my approach:

Iterate Frequently: The more prototypes you create and test, the more insights you'll gather. This iterative process is essential for refining your product and ensuring it aligns with user needs. Each prototype serves as a stepping stone, helping you uncover what works and what needs improvement. Frequent iterations allowed me to rapidly test ideas, gather feedback, and make necessary adjustments.

Feedback Loops: Use each prototype as an opportunity to collect feedback and improve the next iteration. Creating a feedback loop is crucial for continuous improvement. By actively seeking and incorporating user feedback, you can enhance the user experience and address any issues. This testing, learning, and iterating cycle ensures your product evolves based on user needs and preferences.

By embracing frequent iterations and establishing strong feedback loops, I was able to learn more about user needs and refine my MVP effectively. These lessons have been pivotal in developing a product that meets and exceeds user expectations. I navigated the prototyping phase efficiently and effectively by remembering these lessons, leading to a more refined and valuable MVP. Prototyping isn't just about building; it's about learning, iterating, and continuously improving. These lessons have been instrumental in my journey, and I hope they can be just as valuable for you.

Prototyping Process

From my experience developing our ESG management application, creating visual maps of different user interface (UI) and user experience (UX) designs was crucial. This approach helped me more effectively understand user flows and interactions. Here's how I went about it and the results I achieved.

Visualization: I created detailed visual maps for various aspects of our application. These maps helped illustrate the different UI and UX designs for each feature, making understanding how users would navigate and interact with the system easier. For example, I designed wireframes for the login screen, dashboard, regulatory updates, data integration, reporting, and audit trail. These sketches served as blueprints for our development process, ensuring that each screen was user-friendly and aligned with our goals.

Comparative Analysis: Once the visual maps were created, I conducted a comparative analysis to evaluate which designs best addressed the identified opportunities and user needs. By comparing these visual maps, I could determine which elements most effectively provided a seamless user experience. This analysis helped prioritize features and interactions that would deliver the highest value to our users.

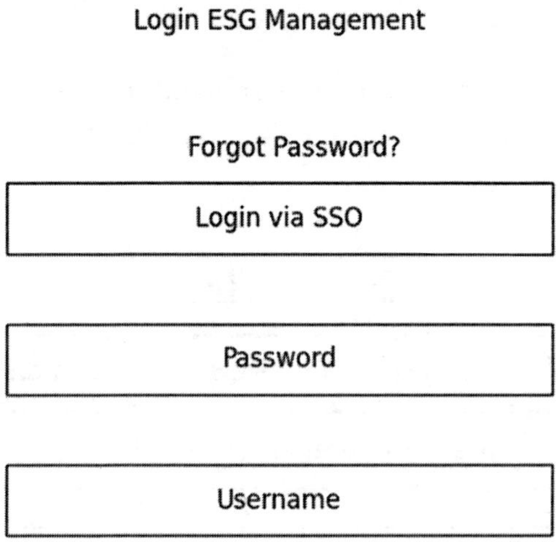

Log in Screen

The login screen was designed to be simple and secure, providing users straightforward access to their accounts.

Dashboard

The dashboard provided an overview of compliance status, alerts, and critical metrics. It included widgets for quick access to essential data and functions.

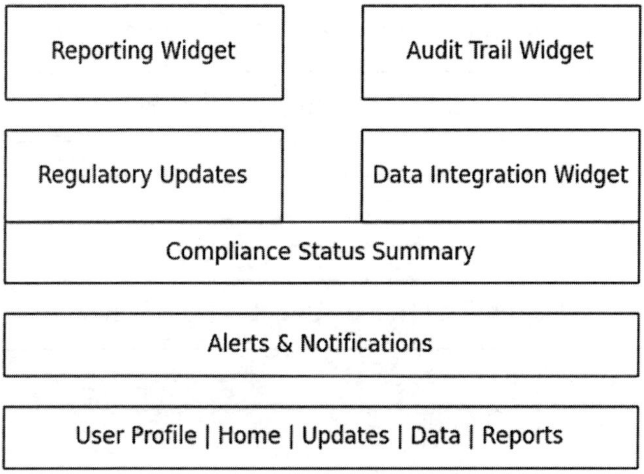

Regulatory Updates

The regulatory updates screen displayed real-time updates and alerts about regulatory changes. Users could filter updates by date, category, and relevance.

2023-07-20	HR	Updated policies for...
2023-08-01	Finance	New regulations on...
Date	Category	Description

Filter by: [Date] [Category] [Relevance]

User Profile | Home | Updates | Data | Reports

Data Integration

The data integration screen allowed users to connect and sync data sources with real-time sync status and logs for monitoring.

EHS	Inactive	2023-08-02 15:45
S4/HANA	Active	2023-08-03 10:00
Work Day	Status	Last Synced

[Add Source]

User Profile | Home | Updates | Data | Reports

Reporting

The reporting screen provided customizable templates for generating detailed compliance reports, making it easy for users to create and download reports.

Reporting

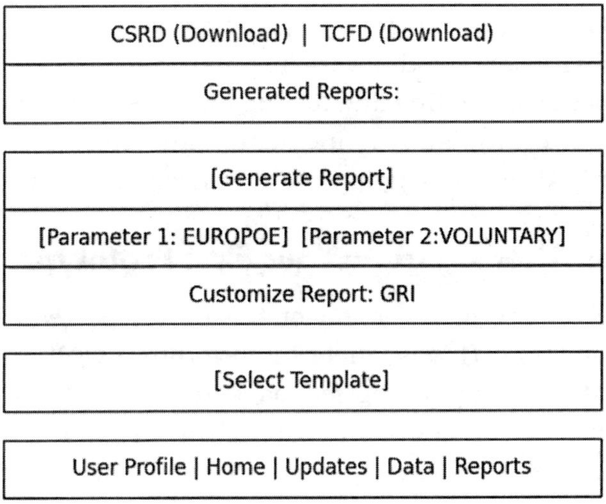

Audit Trail

The audit trail screen displayed a comprehensive activity log of all compliance activities, with options to export logs for external review.

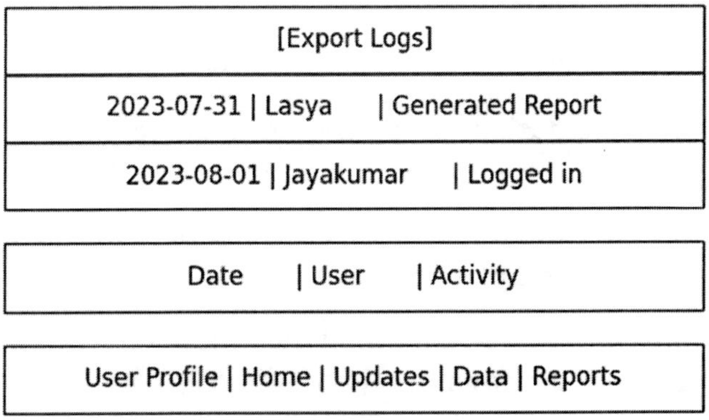

By mapping out these UI and UX designs and comparing them, I was able to refine our approach and ensure that our ESG management application met the needs of our users effectively. This process was instrumental in creating a product that was not only functional but also intuitive and user-friendly. Following these rules for prototyping helps ensure a focused, efficient, and iterative development process. You can quickly create prototypes that provide valuable insights by starting with simple solutions, using familiar tools, and leveraging existing components. The iterative process of creating and testing multiple prototypes enables continuous learning and refinement, ultimately leading to a well-validated MVP that aligns with user needs and expectations.

Next Steps After Creating Your First Prototype

So, once I had the first version of the prototype ready, the real fun began—testing. This is where I had to put myself in the user's shoes and dig into gathering feedback to shape the subsequent iterations. It's like stepping into a user's world and seeing things from their perspective. This phase involved all sorts of prototyping and research tasks. I started with concept validation to ensure our core ideas hit the mark. Then, I tested the navigation to ensure users could easily find their way around the application. Next up were the specific features, where I drilled down into the details to see how each part of the app performed. And let's not forget about the microcopy—those tiny bits of text that guide users through the interface.

Types of Prototyping and Research Tasks

1. Concept Validation: Ensuring that users understand the purpose of the product and find it valuable.
2. Navigation: Testing how easily users can navigate the product and complete tasks.
3. Specific Features: Focusing on the functionality and usability of particular features.

4. Microcopy: Evaluating the effectiveness and clarity of the text used within the product.

Critical Questions for Low-Fidelity Prototypes:

Before Users See the Prototype:

- What would they expect from this type of product?
- How would they expect it to look and function?

After Showing the Prototype:

- Do users understand what the product does?
- How does the prototype measure up to their expectations?
- What features do they think are missing?
- Does anything seem out of place or unnecessary?

How do users feel when using the prototype?

- If users could change anything about the product, what would it be?
- How likely are they to use this product once it's finished?

Testing and Iteration Process

Building, testing, and iterating involve continuously refining the prototype based on user feedback. This cycle of testing and iteration ensures that the product evolves to meet user needs and expectations better.

Methods for Testing Prototypes

When it came time to test our prototypes, we needed to gather real-world feedback. That's when we decided to set up a Usability Café. It's a super effective way to get diverse user input in a relaxed, casual setting—think coffee shop vibes, with plenty of snacks and comfy seating.

Setting up the Usability Café was all about creating an inviting environment. We wanted our participants to feel at ease, almost like they were hanging out rather than participating in a formal testing session. So, we filled the space with cozy chairs, ambient music, and endless coffee and cookies.

We invited a diverse group of users to join us, ensuring a mix of tech-savvy individuals and those who needed to become more familiar with digital tools. This variety was crucial because it gave us a broad perspective on how different types of users interacted with our prototypes.

We set up several testing stations around the room, each focusing on a different part of our ESG management application. Users might navigate the login and dashboard at one station, while at another, they might work through the data integration process. At each station, a team member was present to guide the users through specific tasks, observe their interactions, and take detailed notes.

As users moved through the stations, we encouraged them to think out loud. We wanted to know their immediate thoughts – what they found intuitive, what confused them, and what they liked or disliked. This real-time commentary was gold for us, providing insights we could never have gathered from surveys or second-hand feedback.

During these sessions, it became clear how well potential users understood our prototypes. For example, many users found the dashboard layout intuitive and appreciated the precise information organization. They quickly grasped how to navigate through different sections, which validated our design choices.

However, not all was smooth sailing. Some users needed help with data integration, mainly connecting new data sources. This highlighted a critical area for improvement. We realized we needed to simplify this process and provide more guidance to make it user-friendly.

After users had explored the prototypes, we interviewed them informally. We asked open-ended questions about their overall experience, what they found valuable, and any frustrations they encountered. These conversations were incredibly revealing and often sparked new ideas for improvements.

One critical insight we gained was that users highly valued real-time updates and notifications about regulatory changes. They found this feature not only helpful but essential for staying compliant. This feedback reassured us we were on the right track with our priorities. With all this feedback, we gathered as a team to analyze the data. We looked for common themes, identified pain points, and noted any features that received particularly positive reactions. This analysis guided us in making targeted adjustments to our prototypes.

For example, we decided to enhance the data integration interface, adding step-by-step instructions and tooltips to assist users. We also made the dashboard widgets more customizable, allowing users to tailor the information they see at a glance. The Usability Café was more than just a testing session; it was an opportunity to see our application through the eyes of our users. It allowed us to validate our concepts, refine our navigation, and ensure our features were precious. Plus, it was a great way to build a sense of community with our users – they felt heard and involved in the development process, which was incredibly rewarding for everyone involved.

Overall, the Usability Café was a huge success. It helped us fine-tune our prototypes and confidently move forward, knowing we were building something that genuinely met our users' needs. If you ever get the chance to run one, I highly recommend it—it's an invaluable part of the design and development journey.

Usability Test of Simple Spreadsheet Prototype (UX School)

When we started developing the reporting features for our ESG management application, we knew that nailing the reporting formats was crucial. Different regulations required different reporting formats, and we needed to ensure our tool could handle this variety seamlessly. So, to test our ideas quickly and efficiently, we decided to leverage a simple yet powerful tool: spreadsheets.

We created a prototype using a basic spreadsheet. The goal was to mimic the reporting functionality of our application in a familiar and flexible format. This approach allowed us to iterate rapidly and gather valuable feedback without getting bogged down in complex development work early on. Here's how we went about it:

Setting up the Spreadsheet Prototype:

We designed the spreadsheet to include various reporting templates corresponding to regulatory requirements. Each template was structured to capture the necessary data points and generate the required reports. We ensured the layout was clear and easy to navigate, reflecting how we envisioned the final application would function.

Inviting Participants:

We contacted compliance managers, sustainability officers, and other key stakeholders who would be the primary users of our reporting feature. Their insights were vital because they dealt with these regulations day in and out during the Testing Sessions:

During the usability testing sessions, we invited participants to sit with us in a relaxed setting, similar to our Usability Café. We then gave them the spreadsheet prototype and walked them through a few initial steps to familiarize them with the layout.

Guided Tasks:

We then gave them specific tasks to complete using the prototype. For example, we asked them to generate a compliance report for a particular regulation or to input data and see how it was formatted in the final report. As they worked through these tasks, we observed their interactions closely.

Gathering Feedback:

We encouraged participants to vocalize their thoughts and reactions as they used the prototype. What did they find straightforward? What confused them? Were there any features they wished the tool had? This real-time feedback was precious.

Insights Gained:

1. Clarity and Ease of Use: While the basic structure of our reporting templates was sound, users appreciated the clear labels and instructions embedded within them. This guided them in what data to input and where making the process smoother.
2. Customization Needs: Users expressed a need for more customizable templates. They wanted the ability to tweak the formats slightly better to fit their specific regulatory needs or internal reporting standards. This insight led us to prioritize flexibility in our final design.
3. Error-Handling: Another critical insight was the importance of error-handling. Users wanted prompts or warnings when data was missing or formatted incorrectly. This feedback guided us in building more robust validation features for the final application.
4. Time-Saving Features: Participants loved any feature that saved them time, such as auto-populating standard fields or carrying forward data from previous reports. These were noted as high-value features to include in our final product.

Iterating on Feedback:

We iterated on our spreadsheet prototype based on the feedback from these sessions. We made the labels more apparent, added instructions, and introduced customization elements. We also included basic validation rules to mimic error-handling.

Transitioning to the Final Application:

With a solid understanding of what worked and what needed improvement, we transitioned these insights into developing the final reporting feature within our ESG management application. The lessons learned from the spreadsheet prototype informed our design and functionality decisions, ensuring the final product was user-friendly and effectively met regulatory needs.

Validation and Confidence:

When we implemented these features in our application, we were confident they would resonate with users. We had iterated multiple times based on honest user feedback, and the spreadsheet prototype allowed us to do this quickly and efficiently.

In the end, leveraging a simple spreadsheet prototype for usability testing proved to be a game-changer. It enabled us to validate our ideas early, make informed design decisions, and ultimately create a reporting feature that met the diverse needs of our users. If you're developing a feature with complex requirements, I highly recommend starting with a low-fidelity prototype like this – it's an invaluable step in the development process.

Phase 4 in Design Sprint - Prototype Session (Interaction Design Foundation)

When we created the dashboard views for our ESG management application, we wanted to ensure that the design was user-friendly and efficient in delivering critical information at a glance. To achieve this, we turned to design sprints, a method the Interactive

Design Foundation championed that helps teams solve problems and prototype solutions quickly.

What are Design Sprints?

A design sprint is a five-day process for answering critical business questions through design, prototyping, and testing ideas with customers. It's a highly focused approach that brings together cross-functional teams to work on a specific challenge and rapidly develop a solution.

Setting Up the Design Sprint

1. Gathering the Team:

   We assembled a diverse team for the design sprint, including designers, developers, product managers, and stakeholders. This diversity ensured we had multiple perspectives and expertise contributing to the process.

2. Defining the Challenge:

   The specific challenge we aimed to tackle was creating effective and intuitive dashboard views for our ESG management application. We wanted these dashboards to provide users with real-time insights, compliance statuses, and key metrics, all in an easily digestible format.

The Five-Day Sprint Process

Day 1: Understand

We kicked off the sprint by diving deep into the problem. We discussed the dashboard's goals, identified the key metrics to display, and reviewed user feedback and existing data. This helped us build a shared understanding of the problem and set clear objectives for the sprint.

Day 2: Ideate

On the second day, we encouraged everyone to brainstorm and sketch as many ideas as possible. This was a no-judgment zone—wild ideas were welcome. We used techniques like Crazy 8s, where each person sketched eight ideas in eight minutes. By the end of the day, we had a wall of diverse concepts for our dashboard views.

Day 3: Decide

With many ideas, we moved on to the decision-making phase. We reviewed all the sketches, discussed the pros and cons of each, and then voted on the best ideas. This led us to create a storyboard, a step-by-step plan for our prototype, combining the most vital elements from the brainstormed ideas.

Day 4: Prototype

This was where the rubber met the road. Our design and development teams collaborated closely to turn the storyboard into a tangible prototype. Using tools like Figma and InVision, we created interactive mockups of the dashboard views. These prototypes were functional enough to give users a realistic sense of how the final product would look and behave.

Day 5: Test

The final day was all about validation. We brought real users—compliance managers, sustainability officers, and other stakeholders—to test the prototype. We observed their interactions, asked them to perform specific tasks, and gathered their feedback. This user testing was crucial in identifying what worked, what didn't, and what needed improvement.

Insights and Iterations

The design sprint provided us with a wealth of insights. Here are some key takeaways:

User Preferences:

We discovered that users preferred a clean, uncluttered interface with customizable widgets. They valued the ability to personalize their dashboards to display the most relevant information for their specific needs.

Navigation:

The testing highlighted the importance of intuitive navigation. Users wanted quick access to detailed reports and the ability to drill down into data without feeling overwhelmed.

Real-Time Updates:

Real-time updates and notifications were a hit. Users appreciated the immediate visibility of compliance statuses and regulatory changes, which helped them stay proactive rather than reactive.

Iterative Improvements:

Based on the feedback, we made several iterations to the prototype. We simplified the navigation, enhanced the customization options, and ensured the design was scalable to accommodate different data sets and user preferences.

The Power of Design Sprints

Leveraging design sprints for generating dashboard views was a game-changer. It allowed us to condense what could have been months of work into just five days. The rapid prototyping and user testing cycles enabled us to iterate quickly and effectively, ensuring that our final product was well-aligned with user needs and expectations.

By the end of the sprint, we had a validated prototype that met our objectives and delighted our users. The process was intense but incredibly rewarding. If you want to solve complex design challenges and need to move quickly, I can't recommend design sprints highly enough. They are a method that promotes clarity, creativity, and collaboration, driving innovation and delivering results.

Reflecting on our journey, it's incredible to see how each method we used played a crucial role in validating our ESG management application prototypes. Let's walk through how these methods contributed to refining our product and ensuring it met user needs.

Usability Café

First off, the ability Café was a game-changer. Setting up this relaxed, coffee-shop-like environment allowed us to gather genuine, real-time feedback from diverse users. Watching users navigate through our prototypes gave us invaluable insights. For instance, the login screen and dashboard received a thumbs-heir intuitive layout, but the data integration process needed simplification. This feedback guided us to make necessary adjustments early, ensuring a smoother user experience.

Spreadsheet Prototypes for Reporting Formats

Then came the usability testing with spreadsheet prototypes for our reporting features. This method was particularly effective because it allowed us to iterate quickly without diving deep into complex coding. Using a simple spreadsheet, we could mimic the reporting functionality and get immediate feedback from compliance managers and key stakeholders. They loved the clarity and ease of use but wanted more customization and error-handling features. This led us to build a robust, flexible reporting system that could effortlessly cater to various regulatory requirements.

Design Sprints for Dashboard Views

Finally, the design sprints were pivotal in shaping our dashboard views. Over five intense yet rewarding days, we brainstormed, prototyped, and tested different concepts. The rapid prototyping helped us experiment with various layouts and functionalities. Users appreciated the clean, customizable widgets and the real-time updates. The iterative nature of the design sprints meant we could incorporate feedback swiftly, refining our dashboard to deliver key metrics and insights in an engaging and accessible manner.

Bringing It All Together

Each of these methods helped us validate different aspects of our ESG management application:

- Usability Café: Validated the overall user experience and identified areas for improvement in navigation and interaction.
- Spreadsheet Prototypes: Ensured our reporting features were user-friendly, flexible, and aligned with regulatory needs.
- Design Sprints: Rapidly prototyped and refined our dashboard views, focusing on delivering real-time, customizable insights.

We developed a well-rounded, user-centric ESG management application by combining these approaches. Each step brought us closer to understanding our users' needs and preferences, ensuring the final product was functional and delightful. In conclusion, leveraging these methods allowed us to iterate quickly, gather deep insights, and validate our prototypes effectively. It's been a transformative journey, and I'm excited to see how these validated features will help our users manage their ESG compliance with greater ease and efficiency.

Prioritizing After Tests: Aligning with Your Value Map and Increasing the Value Gap

We've made significant progress in developing our ESG management application. We've tested prototypes, gathered invaluable user feedback, and iterated our designs. BNw, it's time to tackle the final step: prioritizing which MVP (minimum viable product) to focus on. This step is crucial because it determines where we direct our energy and resources to create our product's most impactful initial version.

We approached this prioritization methodically, ensuring every decision was backed by data and aligned with our overall vision. Our journey began with a thorough review and analysis of all the feedback gathered during our prototype testing phases. We wanted to ensure we fully understood the users' needs, preferences, and pain points.

Next, we aligned these insights with our value map for the ESG management application. This step ensured that our MVP delivered maximum value to our users. We aimed to create a product that not only met basic needs but also exceeded expectations, making a significant positive impact on our users' workflows. To make our MVP stand out, we focused on increasing the value gap – the difference between what users currently have and what they can achieve with our product. This involved identifying features and improvements that would provide the most significant benefits and drive adoption.

Then, we applied different prioritization techniques. We used a mix of frameworks and tools to evaluate potential MVP features based on criteria such as user impact, feasibility, and alignment with our strategic goals. This thorough analysis helped us make informed decisions and set clear priorities.

Finally, we created a prioritized MVP, a distilled version of our product that captures the most critical and high-impact features. This MVP will be our initial offering to users, designed to deliver immediate value and lay a solid foundation for future enhancements. In the next segment, we'll dive into the step-by-step activity of how we went through this prioritization process. From reviewing feedback to applying prioritization techniques, I'll walk you through how we made these crucial decisions and set the stage for our MVP's development.

1. Review and Analyze Feedback

Let's discuss the first step in our MVP prioritization journey: reviewing and analyzing the feedback we gathered from our prototypes. This phase was incredibly enlightening, giving us a clearer picture of how our ESG management application was shaping up in the eyes of our potential users.

We kicked things off by summarizing our findings. We collected a ton of feedback from our Usability Café sessions, spreadsheet prototypes, and design sprints. Organizing all this feedback was like putting together a puzzle—each piece helped us understand what users liked and needed improvement. We categorized the input based on different application features, such as the login process, dashboard views, data integration, and reporting functionalities. This categorization helped us see which areas were on point and which needed more tweaking.

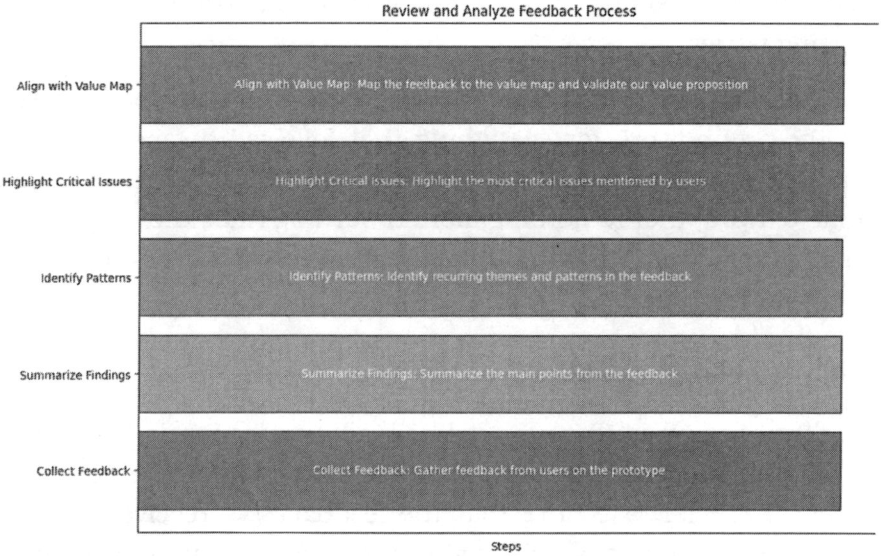

Figure 8.7 Review and analyze the feedback process.

Next, we delved into identifying patterns in user behavior. This part was fascinating. By analyzing how different users interacted with our prototypes, we started to see some clear trends. For example, many users found the dashboard intuitive and appreciated the real-time updates but needed help with the data integration process. These patterns showed us where our design was working and where there were consistent challenges.

Pinpointing these patterns also led us to identify critical issues. We focused on the pain points that users frequently mentioned. The complexity of connecting new data sources was a significant hurdle; users needed more guidance and a more straightforward interface. While users loved the customizable widgets on the dashboard, they wanted even more flexibility in tailoring these to their specific needs.

This analysis phase was crucial. It gave us a solid understanding of what users valued most and where they encountered the most significant challenges. With these insights, we were ready to move forward and align our findings with our value map for the ESG management application. This alignment would ensure that our MVP delivers maximum value and immediately addresses the most pressing issues.

Reviewing and analyzing the feedback from our prototypes laid the groundwork for everything that followed. It ensured our decisions were grounded in real user needs and experiences. And let me tell you, there's nothing more rewarding than knowing we're building something that genuinely resonates with users, even at this prototype stage.

2. Align with Your Value Map

So, after we reviewed and analyzed all the feedback from our prototypes, we needed to align these insights with our value map. This was crucial to ensure that the feedback we received would directly inform our customer value proposition canvas. The goal was to highlight any gaps in value and focus on significant gains, pains, and jobs that our users faced.

We started by mapping all the detailed feedback to our value map. This map visually represents the value we aim to deliver through our ESG management application. It includes vital components like what our users are trying to achieve (their jobs), the challenges they face (pains), and the benefits they seek (gains).

First, we examined feedback on users' primary jobs and what they tried to accomplish with our application. For instance, users needed to track regulatory updates, integrate various data sources, generate compliance reports, and monitor real-time ESG metrics. Understanding these jobs ensured that our application focused on effectively supporting these critical tasks.

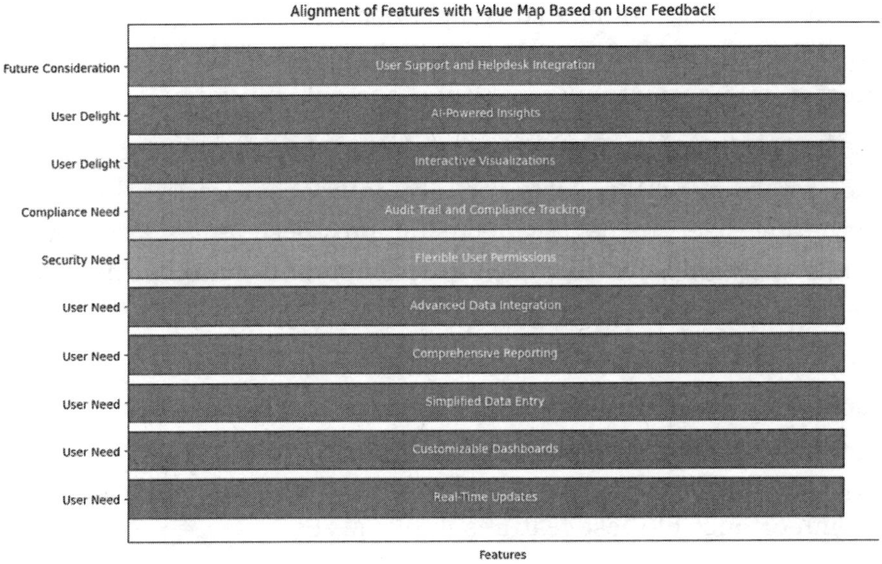

Figure 8.8 Alignment of features with value map based on user feedback

Then, we highlighted the pains users experienced. This part was incredibly enlightening. Users frequently mentioned the complexity of data integration, difficulty customizing reports, and difficulty staying updated with real-time regulatory changes. Addressing these pain points would make our application significantly more valuable to our users.

On the other hand, we also considered the gains users sought. They wanted a simplified interface, real-time updates, and customizable widgets on their dashboard. They also highly valued features that could save them time and reduce errors. Mapping these gains helped us see which features and functionalities would deliver the most significant benefits and enhance user satisfaction.

With this mapped feedback, we turned to our customer value proposition canvas. This canvas helps us articulate how our product solves user problems and delivers benefits. We could validate and refine our value proposition by aligning the feedback with the canvas.

We validated that features like real-time updates, customizable dashboards, and automated compliance reporting were significant gains for our users. Users repeatedly highlighted these aspects as substantial improvements over their current solutions.

The feedback also confirmed that simplifying data integration and providing clear, user-friendly interfaces were critical to alleviating user pains. By focusing on these areas, we could significantly improve the user experience and address the most pressing challenges our users faced.

Mapping the feedback also validated the essential jobs our application needed to support. Ensuring users could easily track regulatory updates, integrate data, and generate reports were key functionalities that our users relied on. This alignment reinforced the importance of these features in our MVP.

By aligning the feedback with our value map and validating it through the customer value proposition canvas, we could see the gaps in value—areas where our current prototype didn't fully meet user expectations. This process was crucial because it highlighted where we needed to focus our efforts to increase the value gap, making our application more appealing and valuable. We then prioritized features and improvements to bridge these gaps, ensuring our MVP delivered maximum value. This alignment process wasn't just about validating what we got right and understanding where to improve and innovate.

Aligning with our value map and customer value proposition canvas gave us a clear, user-centered direction for our development. It ensured that our efforts focused on creating an application that resonated with users, addressing their most significant pains, fulfilling their critical jobs, and delivering the gains they valued the most. So, this step was all about connecting the dots—taking user feedback, mapping it to our value goals, and validating that we were on the right track. Ensuring our MVP would hit the mark and deliver accurate, meaningful value to our users was essential.

3. Increase the Value Gap

After aligning our feedback with the value map, our next step was to increase the value gap. This meant focusing on features that would significantly enhance the value of our ESG management application. We knew that by doing this, we could create something that truly stood out and met our users' needs in a big way.

We started by deepening the feedback again, focusing on identifying high-value features. These are the features that users found most beneficial and were most excited about. We wanted to ensure we prioritized the correct elements that would have the most impact.

One of the standout high-value features was real-time updates. Users loved the idea of getting immediate notifications about regulatory changes. It saved them time and kept them proactive rather than reactive. Another high-value feature was the customizable dashboard. Users appreciated being able to tailor their dashboards to show the most relevant information for their specific needs, making their workflow more efficient and personalized.

Data integration also came up as a critical area. Users wanted a seamless, intuitive way to integrate various data sources. This feature was essential for simplifying their workflow and reducing the time spent on manual data entry. We knew we had to make this as smooth as possible. In addition to user feedback, we also looked closely at what our competitors were offering. This competitive analysis was eye-opening. It helped us identify gaps in the market and opportunities where we could provide more value. For instance, while some competitors offered basic reporting features, they needed more depth and flexibility than our users requested. This insight motivated us to enhance our reporting functionalities, ensuring they were comprehensive, easy to customize, and use.

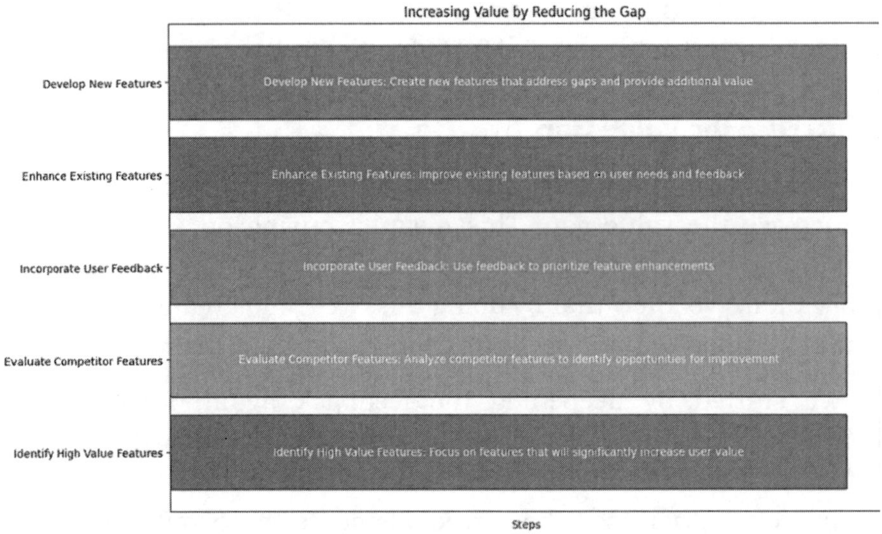

Figure 8.9 Increasing value by reducing the gap

We aimed to create a significant value gap between our application and existing solutions by focusing on these high-value features. This wasn't just about adding features for the sake of it but about ensuring every feature we developed provided substantial value to our users. One of the key outputs from this exercise was a prioritized list of features that would make it into our MVP. At the top of this list were real-time updates, customizable dashboards, and advanced data integration capabilities. These features were the ones that users found most valuable and would differentiate our application in the market.

Increasing the value gap with feedback and competitive analysis was a game-changing strategy. It ensured that our MVP would meet and exceed user expectations. It helped us focus our development efforts on what truly mattered and what would deliver the most significant impact. This approach boosted our confidence in the product we built and set a clear direction for the development team.

We knew exactly where to invest our time and resources, ensuring that every feature added maximum user value.

So, by identifying and focusing on high-value features, we created an MVP that was competitive and deeply resonated with our users' needs. This process was crucial in ensuring that our ESG management application stood out in the market and delivered exceptional user value.

4. Prioritization Techniques

After generating our prioritized list of features, we applied the MoSCoW method to zero in on what should be included in our MVP. This method helps us break down the features into four categories: must-have, should-have, could-have, and won't-have. It's a great way to ensure we focus on the essentials while examining future possibilities.

First up, the must-have features. These are the critical ones we need to include in our MVP. Real-time updates were cut here because users need immediate notifications about regulatory changes and real-time compliance status updates. Customizable dashboards are also essential, allowing users to personalize their interface with relevant information through widgets and an easy drag-and-drop system. Advanced data integration is another must-have, enabling seamless integration with various data sources and automating data entry and validation. Comprehensive reporting is critical, too, with customizable templates for different regulatory requirements and automated report generation with detailed analytics. Lastly, simplified data entry is a must to ensure users can easily manage their data, with error-checking and validation to reduce mistakes.

Moving on to the should-have features, these are important but only somewhat critical for the MVP. Flexible user permissions fall into this category, providing granular access controls and role-based permissions to streamline user management. Audit trails and compliance tracking are also important, as they offer detailed logs of user actions for audit purposes and monitor adherence to regulations.

Then, we have the could-have features. These are nice to have and enhance the user experience but aren't essential for the MVP. Interactive visualizations, such as graphs and charts, to visualize ESG metrics, trends, and interactive elements for deeper data analysis fit this category. AI-powered insights are another could-have, with predictive analytics to identify potential compliance issues and machine learning algorithms to provide actionable insights.

Finally, we have the won't-have features. These aren't necessary for the initial MVP but are great for future versions. User support and helpdesk integration fall into this category, including integrated support features like live chat, helpdesk tickets, and in-app tutorials and guides to assist users.

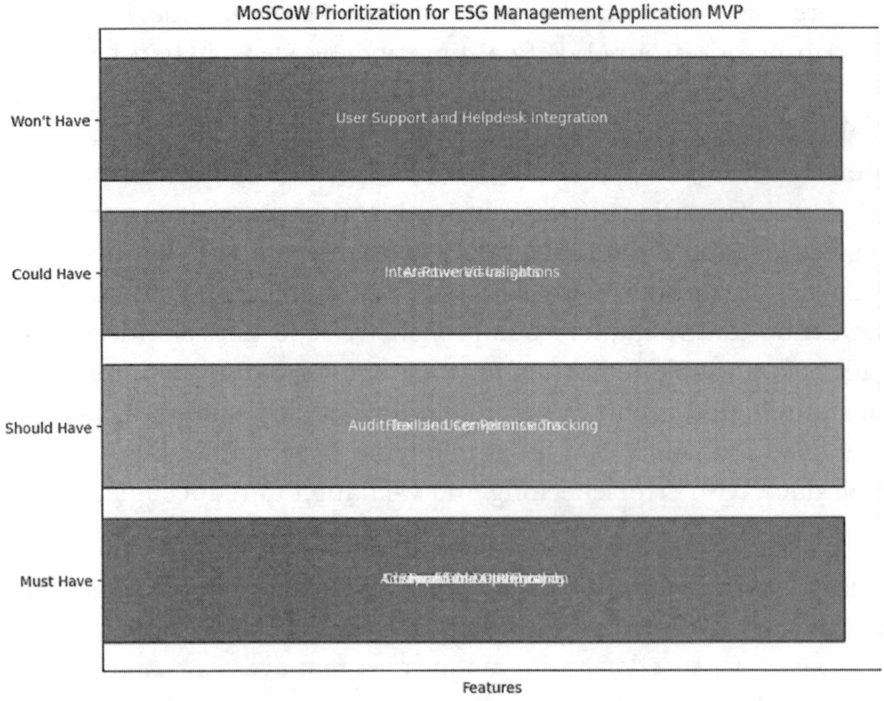

Figure 8.10 MoSCoW prioritization technique

By categorizing our features using the MoSCoW method, we can focus our development efforts on what's essential for our MVP. This way, we ensure we deliver maximum user value while planning for future enhancements. It's all about managing our resources effectively and meeting our users' critical needs immediately. This approach has helped us stay on track and clarify our priorities.

Kano Model

We applied the Kano model after prioritizing our features using the MoSCoW method. This approach helps us categorize features into three types: Basic Needs, Performance Needs, and Excitement Needs. It's a great way to ensure we meet user expectations and look for opportunities to delight them.

First, we looked at the basic needs. These are the features that our users expect to be there. If these aren't included, they're going to be unhappy. These must-have features for our ESG management application included real-time updates, which provide immediate notifications about regulatory changes and compliance status updates. Users also needed customizable dashboards where they could personalize widgets and easily arrange them with a drag-and-drop interface. Advanced data integration was another essential, ensuring seamless integration with various data sources and automating data entry. Comprehensive reporting, with customizable templates and automated report generation, was also a critical feature. Lastly, a simplified data entry system was a must to make data management user-friendly and reduce errors.

Then, we moved on to Performance Needs. These features increase user satisfaction in direct proportion to how well they're implemented. The more we enhance these features, the happier our users will be. For us, flexible user permissions fit this category, offering granular access controls and role-based permissions to streamline user management. Another critical performance feature was the audit trail and compliance tracking, which provided detailed logs of user actions for audit purposes and ensured adherence to regulations.

Finally, we considered the Excitement Needs. These are the features that users don't necessarily expect, but when they find them, they're thrilled. They can significantly boost satisfaction, even though their absence wouldn't cause dissatisfaction. Interactive visualizations like graphs and charts to visualize ESG metrics and trends and interactive elements for deeper data analysis were identified as exciting features. AI-powered insights also fell into this category, offering predictive analytics to identify potential compliance issues and machine learning algorithms to provide actionable insights.

We also identified features that we decided to exclude from our MVP. These were categorized as 'won't have for now.' For example, while valuable, user support and helpdesk integration weren't essential for the initial launch. This feature included integrated support like live chat and helpdesk tickets as well as in-app tutorials and guides to assist users.

By categorizing our features using the Kano model, we ensured that our MVP would meet the basic expectations, perform well, and potentially delight our users with unexpected features. This approach helped us stay focused on what truly matters and plan for future enhancements that can further elevate the user experience. It's all about balancing essential functionality with opportunities to exceed expectations and make our users happy.

RICE Scoring

After we categorized our features using the Kano model, we wanted to get more detailed with our prioritization. That's where the RICE scoring method came in handy. RICE stands for Reach, Impact, Confidence, and Effort, and it's a great way to quantify and compare the value of different features.

So, we decided to give each feature a score based on these four factors. We assumed a reach of ten for all the features, meaning we expected them to impact a similar number of users. Then, we rated the impact of each feature on a scale from 0.25 (minimal) to

3 (massive), estimated our confidence in these ratings from 0 to 1, and assessed the effort required to implement each feature in person-months.

For example, real-time updates scored very high. They weighed its impact as massive, with high confidence and moderate effort, giving it a top RICE score of nine. Similarly, customizable dashboards and simplified data entry both received high scores of 8, as they were features that users highly valued and would significantly enhance their experience.

We also looked at advanced data integration, which scored a bit lower due to the higher effort required, but it was still crucial. Features like flexible user permissions and audit trails were important, too, with scores reflecting their role in enhancing security and compliance tracking.

On the excitement side, features like interactive visualizations and AI-powered insights scored lower in terms of effort versus impact. However, they still made the list as nice to have additions that could wow users.

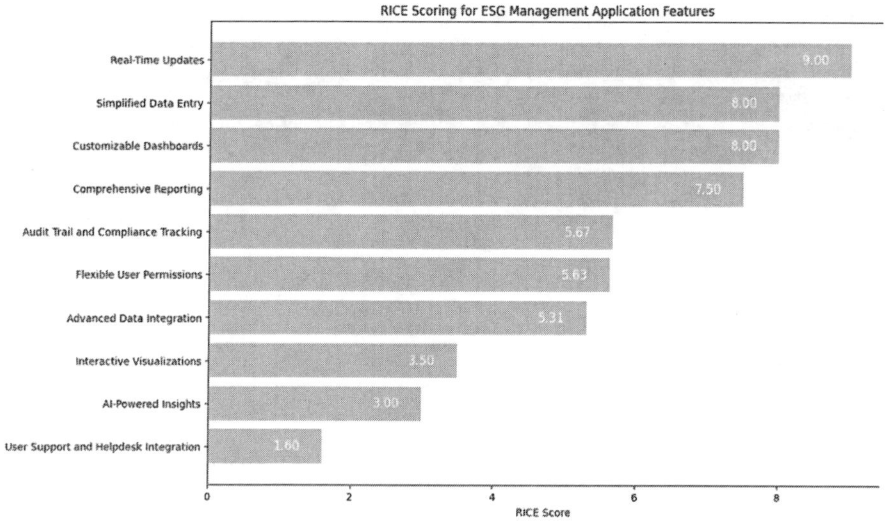

Figure 8.11 RICE Scoring for ESG management application features

Lastly, we had the user support and helpdesk integration, which had the lowest score. While useful, it wasn't a priority for the MVP, given the higher effort required and relatively lower immediate impact.

Once we had all the scores, we created a visual representation to help us determine which features should be our primary focus. We plotted them on a horizontal bar chart, sorting the features by their RICE scores. This visualization clarified which features were essential for the MVP and which could be considered for future updates.

RICE Formula:

$$\text{RICE Score} = \frac{\text{Reach} \times \text{Impact} \times \text{Confidence}}{\text{Effort}}$$

RICE for ESG Management Application:

Feature	Reach (0-10)	Impact (0-5)	Confidence (0-100%)	Effort (man-months)	RICE Score
Automated Regulatory Updates	8	5	80%	4	80
Data Integration Tool	7	4	70%	6	32.67
Simplified Interface	6	3	90%	3	54
Real-Time Dashboard Customization	5	3	80%	5	24
Advanced Notification Controls	4	3	70%	4	21
Additional Data Visualization Options	3	2	60%	3	12
Advanced Reporting Templates	4	2	50%	5	8

Step 3: Make Priorities Visible Using Impact vs. Effort Matrix

Impact vs. Effort Matrix:
This matrix helps visualize the prioritization by categorizing features into Easy Wins, Big Bets, Incremental, and Money Pits based on their impact and effort.

Category	Impact	Effort
Easy Wins	High	Low
Big Bets	High	High
Incremental	Low	Low
Money Pits	Low	High

Categorizing ESG Management Features:

Feature	Category
Automated Regulatory Updates	Big Bets
Data Integration Tool	Big Bets
Simplified Interface	Easy Wins
Real-Time Dashboard Customization	Big Bets
Advanced Notification Controls	Incremental
Additional Data Visualization Options	Incremental
Advanced Reporting Templates	Money Pits

Step 4: Prioritize Scopes Using MoSCoW

MoSCoW Method: This method categorizes features into Must-Have, Should-Have, Could-Have, and Won't-Have.

Applying MoSCoW to ESG Management Application:

Feature	MoSCoW Category
Automated Regulatory Updates	Must-Have
Data Integration Tool	Must-Have
Simplified Interface	Must-Have
Real-Time Dashboard Customization	Should-Have
Advanced Notification Controls	Should-Have
Additional Data Visualization Options	Could-Have
Advanced Reporting Templates	Won't-Have

Applying the RICE method gave us a clear, data-driven way to prioritize our features. It ensured we focused on the features that would deliver the most value to our users and make our ESG management application stand out.

5. Create a Prioritized MVP Roadmap

After sorting out our features using the RICE scoring method, we needed a straightforward way to determine which features should be included in our MVP. This is where our MVP roadmap comes in. We broke it down into phases to ensure we delivered the most critical features while monitoring what's coming next.

So, for Phase 1, we focused on the essential features. These are the must-haves, the backbone of our ESG management application. Right at the top, we have real-time updates. This feature scored a whopping 9, and it's easy to see why. Immediate notifications about regulatory changes and real-time compliance status updates are crucial for our users. Next up are customizable dashboards and simplified data entry, both scoring eight. Users need to personalize their dashboards to show the most relevant information, and they want an easy, error-free way to manage their data. Comprehensive reporting, with a score of 7.5 and advanced data integration at 5.31, rounds out this phase, ensuring users have robust tools for generating reports and integrating data seamlessly.

In Phase 2, we included essential features that, while not critical for the MVP, are still very important. Flexible user permissions, audit trail, and compliance tracking fall into this category. These features scored 5.63 and 5.67, respectively. They enhance security and help users monitor compliance more effectively.

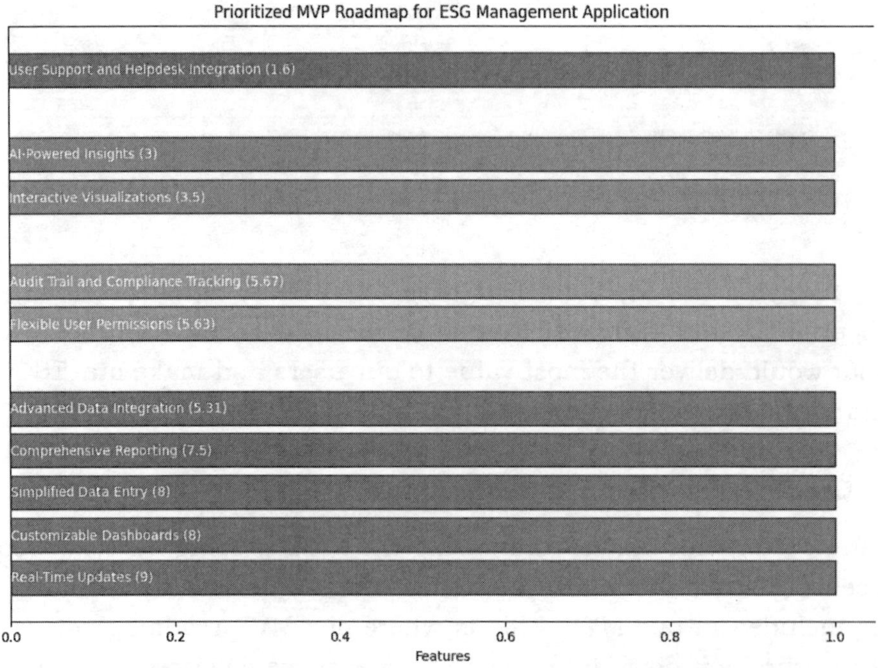

Figure 8.12 Prioritized MVP roadmap for ESG management application

Then, we move to Phase 3, which includes nice to have features. These features can significantly enhance the user experience but aren't essential for the MVP. Here, we have interactive visualizations and AI-powered insights. These features, scoring 3.5 and 3, respectively, can provide deeper insights and predictive analytics, which are great additions but can come later.

Lastly, we identified features we won't include in the MVP but could be considered for future updates. User support and helpdesk integration, with a score of 1.6, fits this category. While useful, it's not a top priority now compared to other critical features.

Visualizing this roadmap was helpful. We created a horizontal bar chart, plotting each feature within its respective phase. This clear layout made it easy to see our development focus and plan for future enhancements. It's like having a blueprint that guides us step-by-step, ensuring we build something valuable and aligned with our users' needs. By structuring our roadmap this way, we can confidently move forward, knowing we're prioritizing the right features and setting the stage for a successful ESG management application.

Chapter 9
Agile, Sprints, and More

The sun peeked over the horizon, casting a golden hue across my house in Hyderabad, India. The aroma of freshly brewed coffee filled the room, infusing me with a sense of readiness for the day ahead. Today was the day I would begin to craft the Product Requirements Document (PRD) for our ESG management application. The PRD wasn't just a document; it was the narrative that would bring our entire team onto the same page, align our goals, and pave the path for our product's success. It was the cornerstone of our journey into agile product development, which, as we quickly learned, was an iterative process at its core. Introducing Agile to our product development was a game-changer. Agile isn't about following strict rules but flexibility, adaptability, and continuous improvement. This approach allowed us to break down our product development into manageable chunks or sprints and tackle each with focus and determination.

From the outset, the agile, iterative nature proved invaluable. We started with sprint planning, setting clear goals, and defining the features we aimed to develop in each cycle. This was followed by daily stand-ups, where we could discuss progress, address any roadblocks, and make quick adjustments. It kept everyone in sync and allowed us to respond swiftly to new information or changing requirements.

Why Agile

When we first encountered the Cynefin framework, it helped us powerfully understand the challenges we might face while developing our ESG management application. The Cynefin framework categorizes problems into four domains: Obvious, Complicated, Complex, and Chaotic. Each type of problem requires a different approach to solve effectively, and understanding this helped us see why Agile was the best fit for our project.

Apparent problems are straightforward and have clear solutions. For us, these tasks included implementing a standard login feature or setting up a primary user interface. These tasks followed well-defined best practices, making them relatively easy to tackle. Complicated problems, on the other hand, require expert analysis and can have multiple correct solutions. Integrating various data sources to provide comprehensive ESG reports was an example of a complicated problem we faced. It required significant technical expertise and detailed planning but was ultimately solvable with the right approach.

Complex problems are where Agile truly shines. These problems, such as creating a dynamic dashboard that adapts to user inputs and displays real-time data, have many unknowns and interdependencies. Solutions to complex problems often emerge through experimentation and iterative development. This was an essential aspect of our project, as the requirements for ESG management are constantly evolving.

Chaotic problems are crises that require immediate action. These could include sudden regulatory changes that affect our application's compliance features or critical bugs that need urgent fixing. Agile's flexibility allowed us to quickly re-prioritize tasks and respond to these crises without losing sight of our overall goals.

Understanding that our project was inherently complex, we needed a development process to handle this complexity and uncertainty. This is where Agile came into play. Agile's iterative nature was perfect for a project like ours, where continuous iteration and refinement were necessary to meet user needs and keep up with changing regulations.

From the outset, Agile's iterative nature proved invaluable. We started with sprint planning, setting clear goals, and defining the features we aimed to develop in each cycle. This was followed by daily stand-ups where we could discuss progress, address any roadblocks, and make quick adjustments. It kept everyone in sync and allowed us to respond swiftly to new information or changing requirements.

One of the biggest reasons we chose Agile was the emphasis on user feedback. ESG requirements and best practices are dynamic; they change with new regulations, stakeholder expectations, and technological advancements. By incorporating regular feedback loops, Agile lets us stay in tune with our users' needs. After each sprint, we showcased our progress to stakeholders and gathered their input. This iterative process ensured we were always on the right track and could adjust before investing too much time in any one direction.

Sprint Planning

The initial planning phase of our project was both exhilarating and challenging. This was where we set our sprint goals and laid the foundation for the entire development process of our ESG management application. Picture the room filled with our newly stormed, normed, and formed team, buzzing with excitement and a touch of anxiety. This wasn't just another meeting; this was when our vision began to take concrete form.

With the PRD as our anchor, we began setting our sprint goals. Agile's sprint-based approach was perfect because it allowed us to break down the project into manageable chunks. Each sprint was like a mini-project with goals and deliverables, typically lasting two weeks. This meant we could focus intensely on a few features at a time, ensuring we got them right before moving on.

We leveraged Agile in Azure DevOps (ADO) to streamline our sprint planning. Setting up ADO was a game-changer, providing a centralized platform for seamlessly managing our backlogs, sprints, and tasks. We started by populating the product backlog in ADO with all the features and functions from the PRD. This gave us a clear overview of everything that needed to be done.

One of the most critical steps was prioritizing these features. We used the WSJF (Weighted Shortest Job First) method for this. WSJF helped us determine which features would provide the most significant benefit in the shortest time. We evaluated each feature based on its cost of delay and the effort required to implement it. This gave us a clear priority order, which we then reflected in ADO.

However, being a startup, we faced several challenges. One of the biggest was resource constraints. We had a small team and limited funds, so we had to allocate our resources strategically. Every decision had to count. Time was another major constraint. We were working against tight deadlines, and there was always more to do than hours in the day.

Team dynamics also posed a challenge. Our team was newly formed, and we were still getting to know each other's strengths and working styles. Building trust and effective communication was essential, but it took time. There was friction and misunderstandings, but we worked through them, knowing that a strong, cohesive team was crucial for our success.

Our first sprint goals were ambitious yet achievable. We decided to focus on building the application's core functionalities: the user login system, the primary user interface, and the foundational database structures. These were the building blocks upon which the rest of the application would be developed. Setting these as our initial goals made perfect sense because nothing else could function without them.

Table 9.1 Summary of Sprint Planning

Category	Details
Sprint Goals	- **Data Integration:** Establish secure connections to key ESG data providers and automate data import processes. - **Dashboard Development:** Create a functional, user-friendly dashboard with real-time data visualizations. - **KPI Definitions:** Identify and define critical key performance indicators (KPIs).
Tools Used	- **Azure DevOps (ADO):** A centralized platform for managing backlogs, sprints, and tasks. - **WSJF (Weighted Shortest Job First):** Method for prioritizing features based on the cost of delay and implementation effort.
Challenges	- **Resource Constraints:** Limited team size and budget require strategic resource allocation. - **Time Constraints:** Tight deadlines necessitated efficient time management. - **Team Dynamics:** A newly formed team requires time to build trust and effective communication.
Key Activities	- **Sprint Planning:** Set clear, actionable sprint goals aligned with the PRD. - **Prioritization:** I used WSJF to prioritize features and reflect them in ADO. - **Daily Stand-up Meetings:** Regular 15-minute check-ins to track progress and address issues.
Initial Sprint Focus	- **Core Functionalities:** Building the user login system, primary user interface, and foundational database structures.
Outcomes	- **Progress:** By the end of the first sprint, a basic but functional version of the ESG management application was developed. - **Feedback:** Conducted a sprint review with stakeholders and updated the backlog based on their input.
Reflection	- **Importance of Clear Goals:** Setting specific, actionable objectives provided direction and focus for the team. - **Agile Adaptability:** Agile flexibility allows for adjustments as needed, ensuring continuous progress.

In ADO, we created a sprint backlog from the prioritized features. Each team member was assigned specific tasks based on their expertise. Developers started coding the login features and setting up the database while designers worked on the UI mockups. Meanwhile, our project manager kept everything on track, ensuring we met our milestones and promptly addressed any roadblocks.

The daily stand-up meetings were a game-changer. We gathered for a quick 15-minute check-in every morning, using ADO to track our progress. Each person shared what they had accomplished the previous day, what they worked on that day, and any obstacles they faced. This constant communication kept everyone aligned and allowed us to address issues before they became major problems.

As the sprint progressed, we regularly revisited our goals in ADO to ensure we were on track. Agile's flexibility meant we could adjust as needed. If a particular feature proved more challenging than expected, we could re-prioritize tasks and allocate more resources to complete them. This adaptability was crucial in maintaining our momentum and ensuring continuous progress.

By the end of the first sprint, we had a basic but functional version of our ESG management application. We conducted a sprint review, showcasing our progress to the stakeholders. Using ADO, we gathered their feedback and updated our backlog accordingly. Their feedback was invaluable, highlighting areas that needed refinement and confirming that we were on the right track.

Reflecting on the initial planning phase, it was clear that setting clear, achievable sprint goals was the key to our early success. Leveraging Agile in ADO allowed us to streamline our planning and execution. Using WSJF to prioritize our features ensured we focused on delivering the most value quickly. This phase laid a solid foundation for the subsequent sprints, each building on the successes of the previous one. Agile's iterative approach ensured we were always moving one step at a time toward creating a robust and user-friendly ESG management application. Despite the challenges of limited resources, time constraints, and the dynamics of a newly formed team, we were able to navigate these obstacles and set our project on the path to success.

After scoring each feature, our top priorities emerged clearly: data integration, dashboard development, and KPI definitions. These core components would bring our application to life and deliver immediate user value. With priorities set, we crafted specific sprint goals. This involved translating our top features into clear, actionable objectives for the next two weeks. Our sprint goals were ambitious but achievable:

1. Data Integration: Establish secure connections to key ESG data providers and automate data import processes. This goal was to ensure that our application could seamlessly pull accurate and comprehensive data from various sources.
2. Dashboard Development: Create a functional, user-friendly dashboard. This included designing the layout, implementing real-time data visualizations, and ensuring the dashboard's responsiveness across different devices. The goal was to provide users with a clear and concise overview of their ESG metrics.
3. KPI Definitions: Identify and define critical key performance indicators (KPIs). This involved developing algorithms to calculate these KPIs from the integrated data and creating user-friendly interfaces for setting KPI targets and thresholds. The aim was to give users meaningful metrics to track their ESG performance.

Each team member was assigned tasks aligned with these goals based on their expertise. Developers focused on the technical aspects of data integration and dashboard implementation. Designers worked on the user interface, and data analysts tackled the KPI definitions.

As we finalized our sprint goals, the energy in the room was palpable. We knew we had a solid plan and clear objectives. Setting these goals provided a shared vision and focus for the entire team, ensuring everyone was aligned and knew exactly what needed to be accomplished. The sprint goals were now set in ADO, complete with a detailed sprint backlog and task board to track our progress. We scheduled our daily stand-up meetings and set milestones to keep us on track.

Reflecting on this sprint planning session, it was evident that clearly defined sprint goals were crucial to our success. By setting specific, actionable objectives, we provided a clear direction for the team, ensuring that our efforts were focused and aligned. This careful planning laid a strong foundation for a productive and successful sprint, moving us closer to delivering a robust and user-friendly ESG management application.

User Stories and Backlog Creation

During our sprint planning session, we sat down as a team to determine the specific features and improvements we wanted to implement over the next two weeks. Our focus was on three main areas: data integration, dashboard development, and defining KPIs. We needed to ensure our goals were clear and actionable, so we translated them into detailed user stories.

For data integration, we started by thinking about what our users needed. One essential story was, "As a data manager, I want to integrate data from external ESG data providers so that our application has comprehensive and up-to-date information." This meant identifying the right ESG data APIs, setting up secure connections, and ensuring the data flowed smoothly into our system. We also needed to automate these imports to keep the information current without manual effort. Another story was about mapping external data fields to our internal schema to keep everything organized and accessible.

Regarding the dashboard, we knew it had to be both functional and visually appealing. One user story that stood out was, "As a user, I want to view a real-time dashboard of my ESG metrics to monitor my performance at a glance." This involved designing the dashboard layout, implementing real-time updates, and ensuring it looked great on any device. We also wanted users to be able to customize their dashboards. For instance, a sustainability analyst might want to add, remove, or rearrange widgets to see the most relevant data. For the executives who needed to share their findings, we included a story about downloading dashboard reports in PDF format to maintain the integrity of the visuals.

Table 9.2 Summary of User Story and Backlog Creation

Category	**Details**
Focus Areas	- Data Integration: Ensuring seamless integration with external ESG data providers. - Dashboard Development: Creating a functional, customizable and visually appealing dashboard. - KPI Definitions: Allowing users to define and track custom KPIs specific to their organizational goals.
User Stories	- Data Integration: 1. "As a data manager, I want to integrate data from external ESG data providers so that our application has comprehensive and up-to-date information." 2. Mapping external data fields to internal schema. - Dashboard Development: 1. "As a user, I want to view a real-time dashboard of my ESG metrics to monitor my performance at a glance." 2. Customizable dashboard widgets for users. 3. Download dashboard reports in PDF format. - KPI Definitions: 1. "As a sustainability manager, I want to define custom KPIs based on our ESG data to track metrics specific to our organization's goals." 2. Testing KPI accuracy and reliability.

(*Contd.*)

Category	Details
Team Assignments	- Developers: Handle technical integration and coding. - Designers: Focus on UI/UX aspects of the dashboard. - Data Analysts: Define and calculate KPIs.
Acceptance Criteria	- Clear criteria for each user story to ensure tasks are completed correctly and meet user needs.
Tools Used	- Azure DevOps (ADO): Platform for setting sprint goals, creating the sprint backlog, and tracking progress.
Outcomes	- Detailed Sprint Backlog: Complete with user stories, assigned tasks, and acceptance criteria. - Team Alignment: Clear roles and responsibilities, ensuring everyone knew their tasks and objectives.
Reflection	- Importance of Well-Defined User Stories: Provided direction and ensured the team's efforts were focused on delivering real value to users.

Defining KPIs was another critical aspect. We needed to ensure users could track the most important metrics. We devised a story like, "As a sustainability manager, I want to define custom KPIs based on our ESG data to track metrics specific to our organization's goals." This meant providing an interface for users to set up and customize their KPIs, including setting targets and thresholds. Another critical story was for the data analyst, who needed to test these KPIs' accuracy and reliability to trust the presented data. We wanted to ensure the KPIs were calculated correctly and validated against known data sets.

As we fleshed out these user stories, we assigned tasks to team members based on their expertise. Developers would handle the technical integration and coding, designers would focus on the UI/UX aspects of the dashboard, and data analysts would work on defining and calculating KPIs. Each story had clear acceptance criteria to ensure we knew when a task was complete.

Setting these sprint goals felt like laying down the tracks for a train journey. We knew exactly where we were heading and the steps to take. By the end of the session, our goals were set in Azure

DevOps, complete with a detailed sprint backlog and task board to track our progress. The energy in the room was palpable; everyone knew their role and was ready to tackle the sprint head-on.

Reflecting on this planning session, it was clear that having well-defined user stories was crucial. They provided a clear direction and ensured our efforts focused on delivering real value to our users. With these goals in place, we felt confident and prepared to dive into the sprint, knowing that each step brought us closer to building a robust and user-friendly ESG management application.

Backlog Prioritization

So, there we were, sitting around the conference table, ready to tackle the task of prioritizing our backlog. It was a critical moment because we needed to focus on what would bring the most value to our users in the shortest amount of time. We started by looking at our Azure DevOps (ADO) product backlog. This was our master list of all the features and tasks we wanted to accomplish. The sheer volume of items was overwhelming, but we knew we had a solid process to sort through it all.

That's when we turned to the WSJF method—Weighted Shortest Job First. This method is excellent for prioritizing because it considers both the cost of delay and the effort required to implement each feature. We began by assigning values to each feature based on how critical they were (Cost of Delay) and how much effort it would take to complete them.

We started with data integration because accurate and up-to-date data was crucial for our users. We asked ourselves, "How painful would it be if this feature was delayed?" and "How much effort will this take?" For instance, integrating data from external ESG providers was vital but also complex, so we gave it a high Cost of Delay and a significant effort score.

Table 9.3 Summary of Backlog Prioritization

Category	Details
Objective	Prioritize the product backlog to focus on delivering the most value to users in the shortest time.
Tool Used	Azure DevOps (ADO): Used to manage the product backlog and track the prioritization process.
Prioritization Method	WSJF (Weighted Shortest Job First): A method that evaluates each feature based on the cost of delay and the effort required for implementation.
Key Features Prioritized	- Data Integration: Critical for providing accurate and up-to-date data, assigned a high cost of delay and effort score. - Dashboard Development: Essential for real-time data monitoring, with significant effort required. - KPI Definitions: Crucial for tracking performance metrics, prioritized based on their impact and required effort.
Process	- Assigned values to each feature based on the cost of delay and effort required. - Calculated WSJF by dividing the cost of delay by the effort required.
Outcome	- A prioritized list of features that would deliver the most significant value to users, guiding the team's focus for development.
Reflection	The WSJF method helped systematically sort through the backlog, making it easier to identify the most impactful features to develop first.

Then, we moved on to the dashboard development. Users needed real-time data at their fingertips, so the story "As a user, I want to view a real-time dashboard of my ESG metrics so that I can monitor my performance at a glance" was critical. We ranked this high on importance but recognized it would take a decent amount of effort to implement.

Defining KPIs was another critical area. We needed meaningful metrics for users to track their performance. The story "As a sustainability manager, I want to define custom KPIs based on our ESG data so that I can track metrics specific to our organization's goals" was essential. We again looked at the cost of delay and the effort needed to get this done right. After scoring each feature, we calculated the WSJF by dividing the Cost of Delay by the effort required. It was a bit like putting together a puzzle, but slowly, the priorities started to make sense.

Here's what we found:

- Mapping external data fields to our internal database schema topped the list. It had a high-impact but was relatively straightforward, making it a quick win.
- Automating regular data imports came next. They were essential for keeping data current, and automating them would save time and effort in the long run.
- Visualizing KPIs on the dashboard was also a high-priority. Users needed to see their metrics at a glance, and this feature was crucial for quick insights.
- Testing the accuracy and reliability of KPIs was equally important. Users needed to trust the data they were seeing.
- Integrating data from external ESG data providers was critical but more complex, so it was high on the list but slightly lower than the easier wins.
- Defining custom KPIs based on ESG data followed closely. It was essential, but it would take some effort to implement correctly.
- Viewing a real-time dashboard of ESG metrics was vital for user experience, but it required substantial work.
- Customizing dashboard widgets was necessary for personalization, but it wasn't as urgent as the core functionalities.

- Downloading dashboard reports in PDF format was a nice feature for sharing insights, but it wasn't a top priority compared to the others.

By the end of our prioritization session, we had a clear roadmap. We knew which features to tackle first to deliver the most value quickly. It was a huge relief to have this clarity and energized the team. We could now move forward confidently, knowing we focused on the right things at the right time.

Sprint Execution

So, our sprint goals were set, and our tasks lined up in Azure DevOps. It was time to get to work. Enter the daily stand-up meetings—our morning ritual that kept us all on the same page and moving forward despite the chaos that often comes with startup life.

Every morning, at precisely 9:30 AM (IST, of course), we'd gather in our cozy, somewhat chaotic office space in Bengaluru. Masala chai in hand, we'd circle up for our 15-minute stand-up. If you've ever seen an Indian startup in action, you know this is where the magic happens—or where things get hilariously off track.

The format was simple: each person would share what they did yesterday, what they planned to do today, and any obstacles. Sounds straightforward. Well, only sometimes. Picture this: Siva, our lead developer, starts his update. "Yesterday, I integrated the new ESG data provider and..."—he stops mid-sentence as our office's unofficial mascot, a street dog we named Brownie, decides it's the perfect time to bark at absolutely nothing. We all pause to watch the spectacle, laughter echoing in the room. Daily stand-ups with Brownie around are never dull.

Then there's Lasya, our UI/UX designer, who is full of creative energy but not a morning person. She starts her update with, "Today, I'm going to—oh, wait, what was I saying?" We all chuckle, handing her yet another cup of chai. It's the third one, but hey, who's counting?

Despite the interruptions and occasional hilarity, these stand-ups were crucial. They aligned everyone and allowed us to identify and address any blockers quickly. For instance, Praveen, our data analyst, mentioned he was stuck one morning because the API we were using had suddenly changed its format. Immediate chaos? Maybe. But within minutes, Siva and Praveen were huddled together, figuring out a solution.

But it wasn't all smooth sailing. As a startup, we faced our fair share of challenges during these meetings. There was the ever-present issue of resource constraints. With a small team, everyone wore multiple hats. One day, I'd manage the project; the next, I'd fix a bug or draft user documentation. Multitasking was our superpower, but it also meant that priorities could shift rapidly.

And then there was time. Or rather, the need for it. Deadlines loomed like the monsoon clouds, and every delay felt like a potential disaster. Our stand-ups often involved quick decision-making to re-prioritize tasks. "Okay, so the API issue is critical, Lasya. Can you hold off on the new dashboard design and help Praveen with data validation instead?" Flexibility and maintaining a sense of humor about the madness were vital. One memorable morning, we had a power outage just as we started our stand-up. We were standing in semi-darkness, lit by the glow of our laptops and the emergency exit sign. "Well," I said, trying to keep spirits high, "at least we're saving on electricity!" We all laughed and quickly moved the meeting to the nearby filter coffee stall, where the WiFi and dosas were more robust.

But, as is often the case in startups, our stand-ups sometimes veered off course. What was meant to be a quick status update occasionally turned into detailed discussions or impromptu requirement sessions. Siva might start discussing the integration challenges in detail, and before we knew it, half the team was deep into a technical debate.

I remember explaining a bug she encountered with the dashboard design. Praveen jumped in with potential solutions, and soon, they were dissecting the issue down to the pixel. We gently reminded everyone, "Guys, let's take this offline and get back to our updates. We need to keep the stand-up short and sweet!" It was a balancing act, keeping the meeting on track without stifling the collaborative spirit. Through all the challenges, our daily stand-ups became a cornerstone of our sprint execution. They kept us connected, fostered collaboration, and ensured that we tackled issues head-on. Plus, they gave us a chance to bond over the quirks and chaos of startup life.

Reflecting on those stand-ups, I realized that while they were sometimes chaotic, they were also where some of our best problem-solving happened. The open communication and quick pivots kept us agile and responsive, which is precisely what we needed to navigate the unpredictable journey of developing our ESG management application. And despite the occasional interruptions from Chintu or the need for extra chai, we always left those meetings with a clear plan and a sense of camaraderie that fueled our progress.

Sprint Reviews

After two intense weeks of coding, designing, and troubleshooting, it was time for our sprint review session. These meetings were crucial to our agile process, allowing us to showcase our progress and gather stakeholder feedback. Picture this: our team, a mix of excitement and nervous anticipation, gathered in our tiny conference room at our Miyapur home office. The aroma of fresh samosas and masala chai filled the air, which was an essential part of a good meeting.

Our sprint reviews were more than just a formality; they were an opportunity to celebrate our achievements, identify areas for improvement, and align our next steps with our stakeholders' expectations. We'd start by presenting what we had accomplished over the past sprint. Siva, our lead developer, would kick things off. "Alright, everyone, here's what we've got. We successfully integrated data from the new ESG providers," he'd say, pulling up a demo on the screen. Sometimes, though, Siva would bring up a screenshot instead of a live demo. "This part is almost done," he'd assure us, "just needs an hour more." We all knew Siva's 'one hour' could sometimes stretch a bit, but we appreciated his enthusiasm.

Next, Lasya would present the new dashboard features. She'd demonstrate the real-time data updates, customizable widgets, and sleek new design elements. "As you can see, users can now drag-and-drop widgets to customize their dashboard layout," she'd explain, her voice full of pride. Seeing the product come to life on the screen was always a thrill, and we'd often break into spontaneous applause.

Then, it was Praveen's turn. He'd dive into the KPIs we had defined and the visualizations we implemented. "Here are the new KPI charts. Users can now set custom targets and thresholds," he'd say, pointing to the colorful graphs on the dashboard. "And the best part? Thanks to the validation tests we ran, they're all accurate and reliable." This was often followed by a round of approving nods and a few celebratory high-fives.

But the real magic of the sprint review happened when we opened the floor to feedback. Our stakeholders—project sponsors and potential users—would weigh in on what they saw. "This is great progress," one would say, "but can we make the data import process even faster?" Another might ask, "Is adding more visualization options for the KPIs possible?"

Their feedback was invaluable. It validated our efforts and gave us new perspectives and ideas for improvement. I remember one review where a stakeholder suggested integrating a new data source we hadn't considered. It was a game-changing idea that we immediately added to our backlog.

However, our sprint reviews were only sometimes smooth sailing. Our new Scrum Master tended to accommodate delays by partially completing tasks within the current sprint and moving the remaining work to the next one. This practice led to some challenges. Often, we ended up with half-done features that couldn't be adequately demonstrated. The infamous 'it's almost done' became a common phrase, causing frustration for the team and our stakeholders.

This time, Siva presented a screenshot instead of a working feature, claiming, "It'll be done in an hour, I promise." Of course, that hour often turned into a day or even more. We also had instances where we had to chase team members for updates, scrambling to pull things together for the review. And yes, there were a few painful sprint reviews where we went empty-handed without significant progress.

These issues highlighted a critical need for better time management and task completion strategies. We realized that moving half-done work to the next sprint created a backlog of incomplete tasks, impacting our overall progress. During one particularly challenging sprint review, we decided to address this head-on.

"Okay, team, we need to change our approach," I said, trying to steer the discussion toward a solution. We agreed to be more realistic about our sprint goals and to break tasks into smaller, manageable chunks that could be completed within the sprint. The Scrum Master committed to holding us accountable and ensuring we didn't carry over unfinished tasks unless necessary.

Table 9.4 Summary of Sprint Review

Category	**Details**
Purpose	Review sprint progress, gather stakeholder feedback, celebrate achievements, and identify areas for improvement.
Setting	Sprint reviews are held in the Miyapur Home office's conference room, often accompanied by samosas and masala chai to create a relaxed atmosphere.
Key Presentations	- Siva (Lead Developer): Demonstrated data integration progress, often with a mix of live demos and screenshots. - Lasya (Designer): Showcased new dashboard features, including customizable widgets and real-time data updates. - Praveen (Data Analyst): Presented KPI definitions and visualizations.

Category	**Details**
Stakeholder Feedback,	- Feedback included requests for faster data import processes, additional visualization options for KPIs, and suggestions for integrating new data sources. - Stakeholder insights were valuable and often led to immediate updates to the backlog.
Challenges	- Task Delays: Issues with moving partially completed tasks to the next sprint, resulting in 'almost done' features that couldn't be adequately demonstrated. - Time Management: There is a need for better task completion strategies and more realistic sprint goals.
Improvements Made	- Task Management: The team committed to breaking tasks into smaller, manageable chunks and holding each other accountable to avoid carrying over unfinished tasks. - Sprint Goals: More realistic and achievable sprint goals were set to ensure better task completion and demonstration.
Outcomes	- Improved Sprint Reviews: Gradual improvement in the quality of sprint reviews, with fewer 'almost done' features and more completed work. - Enhanced Team Dynamics: The transparency and honesty during reviews fostered trust, collaboration, and a stronger team dynamic.
Reflection	Sprint reviews, despite occasional chaos, became a cornerstone of the agile process, promoting open communication, quick pivots, and effective problem-solving. These sessions kept the team connected, aligned and motivated, ultimately driving the successful development of the ESG management application.

Reflecting on these stand-ups, I realized that while they were sometimes chaotic, they were also where some of our best problem-solving happened. The open communication and quick pivots kept us agile and responsive, which is precisely what we needed to navigate the unpredictable journey of developing our ESG management application. And despite the occasional interruptions from Chintu or the need for extra chai, we always left those meetings with a clear plan and a sense of camaraderie that fueled our progress.

With these adjustments, our sprint reviews gradually improved. We saw fewer 'almost done' features and more completed, demonstrable work. It was a learning curve, but we became better at managing our time and expectations. The transparency and honesty during these sessions fostered trust and collaboration, ultimately strengthening our team dynamics.

Despite the occasional chaos, these sprint reviews became a cornerstone of our Agile process. They kept us connected, fostered collaboration, and ensured that we tackled issues head-on. Plus, they gave us a chance to bond over the quirks and chaos of startup life. Reflecting on those sessions, I realized that while they were sometimes chaotic, they were also where some of our best problem-solving happened. The open communication and quick pivots kept us agile and responsive, which is precisely what we needed to navigate the unpredictable journey of developing our ESG management application. And despite the occasional interruptions from Chintu or the need for extra chai, we always left those meetings with a clear plan and camaraderie that fueled our progress.

Sprint Demos

So, the sprint demo day arrived, and there was always a buzz of excitement. Our sprint demos were the moments we got to show off all the hard work we had put in over the past two weeks. The room was set up with a projector ready to display our latest features, and the aroma of fresh samosas and masala chai filled the air, making it feel more like a celebration than a meeting.

We started the demo with a brief introduction summarizing our sprint goals and aims. Our stakeholders included project sponsors, potential users, and, occasionally, a curious investor or two.

Siva, our lead developer, usually started the demo. "Alright, everyone, let's dive into the new data integration feature," he'd say, pulling up the application on the big screen. This time, thankfully, it wasn't just a screenshot. Siva navigated through the application, showing how data from the new ESG providers flowed seamlessly into our system. "As you can see, we've established secure connections, and the data is now being imported automatically," he explained, clicking through the demo. The live demo was always a nail-biter, but when it worked smoothly, it was pure satisfaction.

Next up was Lasya, our UI/UX designer. She was ready to showcase the enhancements to the dashboard. "Today, I'm excited to show you the new customizable dashboard widgets," she began, her eyes lighting up as she navigated through the interface. "Users can now drag-and-drop widgets, resize them, and create a layout that suits their needs." She demonstrated this live, moving widgets around and adjusting their sizes. Seeing the interface respond in real time to her actions was thrilling, and the room often applauded.

Table 9.5 Summary of Sprint Demos

Category	**Details**
Purpose	Showcase the progress made during the sprint, gather stakeholder feedback and validate the features developed.
Setting	The Sprint demo was held in the Miyapur Home Office's conference room, and samosas and masala chai created a celebratory atmosphere.
Key Demonstrations	- Siva (Lead Developer): Showcased data integration, highlighting secure connections and automatic data imports. - Lasya (UI/UX Designer): Demonstrated customizable dashboard widgets, allowing users to drag, drop, and resize elements. - Praveen (Data Analyst): Presented KPI definitions and visualizations with real-time updates.
Challenges Faced	- Incomplete Features: Instances where features were only partially functional or required further development. - Unexpected Delays: Siva's absence due to a family emergency caused delays. - Technical Issues: System downtime and unexpected API changes disrupted progress. - Task Overload: Some team members struggled to complete their demos on time.

(*Contd.*)

Category	Details
Feedback Received	- Stakeholder Engagement: Stakeholders provided valuable feedback, often leading to discussions and immediate backlog updates. Suggestions: Ideas, such as speeding up data import processes and adding more KPI visualization options, were frequently suggested.
Improvements Made	- Time Management: Focused on setting more realistic sprint goals and better task allocation. - Scrum Master Role: Played a key role in holding the team accountable and breaking down tasks into manageable pieces.
Outcomes	- Enhanced Alignment: The demos ensured alignment with user needs and expectations. - Spontaneous Innovation: New ideas, such as integrating unconsidered data sources, were quickly incorporated into the backlog.
Reflection	Sprint demos were more than just a showcase; they were crucial for validation, alignment, and fostering a collaborative spirit within the team. Despite the challenges, these sessions were key to building a user-centric ESG management application.

Praveen, our data analyst, then took the stage to demonstrate the KPI definitions and visualizations. "Here are the new KPI charts we've implemented," he said, pointing to the vibrant graphs on the screen. "Users can set custom targets and thresholds, and the visualizations update in real-time based on the latest data." Praveen would click through various examples, showing how easy it was to adjust settings and see immediate results. "And we've validated these KPIs thoroughly to ensure accuracy," he added, which was always reassuring for our stakeholders.

However, not every demo went off without a hitch. We faced several challenges, some of which were out of our control. For instance, there were times when Siva would start his segment with, "So, we almost finished this part..." and pull up a semi-functional demo. We'd watch him navigate the feature, only to encounter a bug or incomplete section. “It'll be done in an hour, I promise,” he'd say with a sheepish grin. We all knew Siva's ‘one hour’ could stretch a bit, but his commitment was never questioned.

One time, Siva had to take a couple of days of unexpected leave due to a family emergency. His absence threw us off balance since he was the main person handling the data integration. We had to scramble to cover his tasks, which caused delays and added stress to the team. It was challenging, but we pulled together, dividing his workload among the team and pushing through.

Data and unforeseen dependencies on other deliverables also existed that we hadn't accounted for. For example, our integration with a third-party API suddenly changed, which meant we had to rewrite parts of our code. This unexpected change was a real curveball and slowed us down significantly.

Then, there were the system down issues. In one particularly frustrating sprint, our central server went down right during a critical task. We spent hours on the phone with technical support, trying to get things back up and running. The downtime set us back, and we had to re-prioritize our tasks to recover lost time.

And then there were the times we had to chase team members for their demos. I remember one sprint when Lasya was swamped with multiple tasks. On demo day, she sheepishly admitted, “I don't have anything to show for the dashboard updates yet. Can we push this to the next sprint review?” It was a tough pill to swallow, but it was part of the learning process.

These moments highlighted the need for better time management and realistic sprint goals. We decided to take a more disciplined approach, ensuring that what we committed to was achievable within the sprint. Our new Scrum Master was crucial in holding us accountable and helping us break down tasks into manageable pieces.

Despite these hiccups, the feedback during our demos was invaluable. Our stakeholders were actively engaged, asking questions and offering suggestions. “This integration looks great, but can we speed up the data import process?" one might ask. Another would suggest, "Can we add more options for the KPI visualizations?"

Their feedback often led to lively discussions. We jotted down notes, updated our backlog in Azure DevOps, and prioritized these new insights for future sprints. The interactive nature of the demos ensured that we were always aligned with our users' needs and expectations.

One memorable demo was when a stakeholder suggested integrating a new data source we hadn't considered. The idea was so good that it sparked an immediate discussion, and we quickly added it to our backlog. This kind of spontaneous innovation was what made our demos exciting and forward-thinking. After the demo, we'd gather feedback and move into the retrospective part of the session. We'd discuss what went well and what could be improved. "The data integration was solid this time," Siva might point out. "But we need to allocate more time for testing," Praveen would add.

Reflecting on these sprint demos, I realized they were more than just a showcase of our progress. They were a critical touchpoint for validation and alignment, ensuring that we were building something valuable and user-centric. The transparency and collaborative spirit during these sessions fostered trust and camaraderie, essential to our startup's success.

And, of course, the shared laughs, the occasional hiccups, and the sense of accomplishment when everything worked made the journey all the more memorable. The demos were a testament to our hard work, resilience, and the collective effort of a passionate team dedicated to building a robust ESG management application.

Sprint Retrospectives

After the excitement of the sprint demo, we moved into one of the most crucial parts of our agile process: the sprint retrospective. This was our dedicated time to pause, reflect, and learn from the past two weeks. It was like a pit stop in a race, where the team regrouped, recharged, and adjusted to perform better in the next lap.

The atmosphere in the room was usually relaxed, with everyone enjoying some chai and snacks, ready to discuss our experiences. Our Scrum Master kicked things off, setting the stage for an open and honest conversation. "Alright, team, let's talk about what went well this sprint," she'd say, encouraging everyone to share their thoughts.

Reflecting on what went well was more than just a feel-good exercise. It was about identifying and leveraging our strengths to build a more efficient and effective team. Here are some key moments from our retrospectives that highlighted the importance of this reflection.

Siva, our lead developer, often started the discussion. "I think the way we handled the data integration, this sprint was a major win," he'd say. "We had clear API documentation, and our initial research paid off. Setting up the connections and automating the imports went smoother than expected." The team would nod in agreement, acknowledging the effort that went into planning and executing this task.

Lasya, our UI/UX designer, would chime in next. "I liked how we collaborated on the dashboard design," she'd add. "The brainstorming sessions were productive, and the feedback loop was quick. It helped us iterate on the designs faster and more efficiently." This was a great example of how open communication and teamwork led to better outcomes.

Praveen, our data analyst, highlighted the importance of the testing phase. "Our validation tests for the KPIs worked well," he said. We caught several potential issues early, which saved us a lot of time and rework later. The structured approach we took to testing made a big difference." This highlighted how meticulous planning and thorough testing were crucial to our success.

However, retrospectives weren't just about patting ourselves on the back. They were also about recognizing the processes and practices that contributed to these successes. For instance, we'd discuss how our daily stand-up meetings kept everyone aligned. Despite the occasional interruptions from Chintu, our office dog, or the extra chai breaks, these quick check-ins ensured that we were all on the same page and could address issues promptly.

There were also discussions about the tools and techniques that worked well. Using Azure DevOps to track our tasks and progress was frequently mentioned. "Having everything in ADO made it easy to see where we stood at any given time," someone would say. "It helped us stay organized and focused on our priorities." The clear visibility into our workflow was a significant factor in our efficiency.

Reflecting on what went well also meant recognizing individual contributions. "Siva, your quick fix on the API issue was a lifesaver," I'd say, highlighting his efforts. "And Lasya, your designs brought the dashboard to life. The users loved the customization options." Acknowledging these contributions boosted morale and encouraged everyone to keep giving their best. These positive reflections weren't just about raising our ego and creating a continuous improvement culture. By understanding what worked, we could replicate those practices in future sprints. It built confidence and fostered a sense of ownership and accountability within the team.

However, retrospectives also discussed what went wrong and how to improve. This balanced approach ensured we weren't just focusing on the positives and addressing our challenges head-on. For example, we'd discuss the unforeseen data dependencies that caused delays or the system down issues that disrupted our workflow. By analyzing these problems, we could devise strategies to mitigate them in future sprints.

One key takeaway from these sessions was the importance of adaptability. Startups are inherently unpredictable, and being able to pivot quickly was essential. Our retrospectives often revealed how flexibility in our approach helped us navigate through unexpected challenges. Whether it was Siva's last-minute fixes or Lasya's ability to juggle multiple design tasks, adaptability was a recurring theme in our discussions.

Table 9.6 Summary of Sprint Retrospectives

Category	**Details**
Purpose	Reflect on the past sprint, identify strengths, discuss challenges, and learn how to improve in the next sprint.
Setting	The retrospective was held in a relaxed atmosphere with chai and snacks, encouraging open and honest discussion.
Key Positive Reflections	- Data Integration Success: Siva highlighted the smooth handling of data integration due to clear API documentation and thorough planning. - Effective Collaboration: Lasya praised the productive brainstorming sessions that led to efficient dashboard design iterations. - Thorough Testing: Praveen emphasized how early validation of KPIs saved time and prevented rework.
Processes That Worked Well	- Daily Stand-up Meetings: Kept the team aligned and allowed for prompt issue resolution. - Azure DevOps (ADO): Provided clear visibility into tasks and progress, helping the team stay organized and focused on priorities.
Acknowledging Individual Contributions	Recognizing individual efforts boosted team morale and reinforced a culture of continuous improvement.
Challenges Discussed	- Unforeseen data dependencies: These caused delays and required strategic discussion on how to mitigate them. - System Down Issues: Disrupted workflow and highlighted the need for contingency plans. - Adaptability: The importance of being flexible and quickly adjusting to changes was a key takeaway.

(Contd.)

Category	Details
Key Takeaways	- Adaptability: The ability to pivot quickly in response to challenges was crucial. - Continuous Improvement: The retrospective reinforced the principles of Agile, fostering a culture of learning and growth. - Collaboration and Transparency: These principles were critical to the team's success and resilience.
Outcome	- The retrospectives strengthened the team, enhancing their ability to tackle challenges and adapt to the unpredictable nature of startup life. They also built a sense of camaraderie and made the process enjoyable and memorable.

Reflecting on these retrospectives, I realized they were more than just meetings. They were a vital forum for learning and growth. The candid conversations, honest feedback, and collective problem-solving strengthened our team. These sessions reinforced the principles of Agile—continuous improvement, collaboration, and transparency.

Ultimately, the retrospectives helped us build a robust and resilient team capable of tackling any challenge. They reminded us that while the journey was fraught with obstacles, our ability to reflect, learn, and adapt drove our success. And, of course, the shared laughs and camaraderie over chai and samosas made the whole process enjoyable and memorable.

CICD Pipelines

From the beginning, we knew maintaining a smooth and efficient development workflow was crucial for our startup's success. Implementing Continuous Integration and Continuous Deployment (CICD) was a game-changer for us. I remember the first time Siva, our lead developer, set up the pipeline. The excitement in the room was palpable. It was like watching magic unfold as our code automatically tested, integrated, and deployed.

The CICD pipeline worked wonders for us, integrating code from various developers into a shared repository multiple times daily. Each integration triggered automated build and testing sequences, catching issues early. This was vital in avoiding the dreaded 'it works on my machine' problem. Siva often developed a feature that worked perfectly on his laptop, but it would break when integrated with Lasya's UI updates or Praveen's data analytics code. Thanks to CICD, these conflicts were identified and resolved quickly.

What made our CICD approach even more novel was the initial demo feature. After every successful build, our pipeline deployed a demo version of our application to a staging environment. This meant we always had a live preview of the latest version of our app ready for stakeholders to see. Siva would proudly pull up the staging environment during sprint demos, showing real-time progress. It impressed our stakeholders and made our demos more dynamic and interactive.

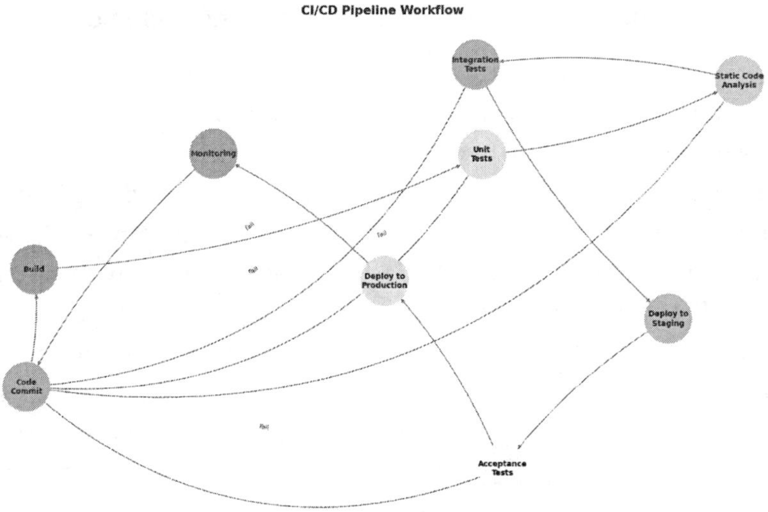

But we didn't stop at CICD. We understood the importance of managing technical debt. Using tools like SonarQube, we continuously analyzed our codebase for potential debt. This proactive approach helped us identify areas needing refactoring, like messy code or outdated dependencies. I recall a sprint where our debt analysis tool flagged performance issues in our data integration module. Initially, Siva was reluctant to spend time refactoring, but once we saw the potential impact on scalability and maintainability, we knew it was the right move. The result was a more efficient module that handled larger datasets without compromising performance.

Automated testing became another cornerstone of our development process. We set up comprehensive test suites using tools like Jenkins and Selenium, which ran with every code commit. This ensured that new changes didn't break existing functionality and improved our code quality. Lasya often mentioned how reassuring it was to have automated tests verifying the front-end elements. We integrated a complex feature to generate detailed ESG reports during one sprint. Manual testing would have been time-consuming and error-prone, but automated tests validated various scenarios rapidly, making our process much more efficient.

Documenting our code was another area where we excelled. We made it a priority from day one, using tools like JSDoc for JavaScript and Swagger for APIs to generate comprehensive documentation automatically. Each developer was responsible for writing explicit comments and documentation as they coded. I remember Praveen needing to extend a KPI calculation module initially developed by Siva. Praveen quickly understood the logic and dependencies thanks to the well-documented code, which made his modifications smooth. This practice facilitated smoother collaboration and ensured new team members could quickly onboard and contribute effectively.

Reflecting on our sprint retrospectives, these practices often came up. "Our CICD pipeline saved us this sprint," Siva would say. "We caught a critical bug early on and fixed it before it became a bigger issue." Lasya would add, "Automated tests caught issues I didn't even think to check manually. It's a game-changer." Praveen appreciated the documentation, saying, "I could dive into any module and start working without any roadblocks."

These integrated practices of CICD, technical debt management, automated testing, and thorough documentation were invaluable for our product development. They improved our efficiency and code quality and boosted our confidence and capability to deliver high-quality software. We took pride in our disciplined approach, proving that a startup could leverage best practices to build a robust and competitive product.

Table 9.7 Summary of CI/CD Pipeline

Category	**Details**
Purpose	To maintain a smooth and efficient development workflow, ensuring high-quality software delivery in a startup environment.
Key Practices Implemented	- Continuous Integration and Continuous Deployment (CICD): Integrated code from multiple developers into a shared repository, triggering automated build and testing sequences to catch issues early. - Technical Debt Management: Used tools like SonarQube to analyze and refactor code, ensuring scalability and maintainability. - Automated Testing: Set up test suites using Jenkins and Selenium, ensuring new changes didn't break existing functionality. - Comprehensive Documentation: Used tools like JSDoc and Swagger to generate detailed documentation, facilitating smoother collaboration and quick onboarding for new team members.
CICD Benefits	- Early Issue Detection: CICD helped catch and resolve integration conflicts quickly, preventing the 'it works on my machine' problem. - Live Demos: The CICD pipeline deployed a demo version of the application to a staging environment, allowing stakeholders to see real-time progress during sprint demos.

(*Contd.*)

Category	Details
Technical Debt Management	- Proactive Refactoring: Tools flagged potential issues, leading to timely refactoring and improved code performance and maintainability. - Example: Refactoring the data integration module enhanced its scalability and efficiency.
Automated Testing	- Efficiency and Quality Assurance: Automated tests ran with every code commit, improving code quality and reducing manual testing efforts. - Example: Automated tests validated complex ESG report generation, significantly speeding up the process and reducing errors.
Documentation	- Comprehensive and Accessible: Documentation tools generated thorough code documentation, facilitating easier collaboration and quick understanding of code for modifications. - Example: Well-documented code allowed Praveen to easily extend a KPI calculation module initially developed by Siva.
Reflections in Retrospectives	- CI/CD Pipeline: Praised for catching critical bugs early and enabling quick fixes. - Automated Testing: Recognized as a game-changer for catching issues that manual testing might miss. Documentation: Appreciated for enabling smooth collaboration and efficient problem-solving.
Outcome	These integrated practices significantly improved the team's efficiency, code quality and ability to deliver high-quality software. The disciplined approach demonstrated that a startup could successfully leverage best practices to build a robust and competitive product.

Iterative Development

One pivotal moment in our journey was releasing a beta version of our ESG management application. We were eager to get our product into the hands of real users, gather their feedback, and iterate based on their experiences. It was a nerve-racking yet exciting phase. By releasing a beta version, we knew we could validate our assumptions, identify bugs, and understand how users interacted with our application in real-time.

The beta release was limited to a select group of early adopters—users enthusiastic about ESG management and willing to provide honest feedback. These early adopters played a crucial role in shaping our product. We set up regular feedback sessions where we listened to their experiences, frustrations, and suggestions. Their insights were invaluable, guiding us in refining features, improving usability, and fixing bugs.

I vividly remember one of our first beta feedback sessions. Siva had just integrated a new data visualization feature, and we were eager to see how it was received. During the session, users pointed out that while the feature was powerful, it was too complex to navigate. They suggested simplifying the interface and adding more intuitive controls. We took this feedback to heart and iteratively improved the feature, making it more user-friendly and effective.

Seeking feedback from beta users wasn't just about identifying issues—it was about understanding their needs and preferences. For example, we learned that users wanted more customization options for their dashboards, which led us to prioritize and develop those features in subsequent sprints. This iterative process ensured that our product evolved in a way that genuinely met our users' needs.

However, as a startup, we faced significant challenges regarding A/B testing. We had limited users and time compared to larger companies with vast resources and a massive user base. A/B testing requires running multiple feature versions simultaneously and comparing user interactions, which can be resource-intensive and time-consuming.

We tried to implement A/B testing on a smaller scale. For instance, we tested two different designs for the KPI customization interface. However, with a limited user base, the results weren't as statistically significant as we hoped. Given our constraints, we quickly realized that while A/B testing could provide valuable insights, it wasn't always feasible for us.

Table 9.8 Summary of Iterative Development.

Category	Details
Purpose	Validate assumptions, identify bugs and gather user feedback to refine and improve the ESG management application.
Beta Release	- Released to a select group of early adopters who were enthusiastic about ESG management and willing to provide honest feedback. Regular feedback sessions were conducted to gather insights on user experiences, frustrations, and suggestions.
Key Feedback and Iterations	- Data Visualization Feedback: Users found the new data visualization feature powerful but complex. Based on their feedback, the interface was simplified and made more intuitive. - Customization Requests: Users requested more customization options for dashboards, leading to the prioritization and development of these features in subsequent sprints.
Challenges Faced	- A/B Testing Constraints: The limited user base and resources made it difficult to run statistically significant A/B tests. - Technical Debt: Bugs and performance issues were uncovered during the beta phase, requiring proactive technical debt management and refactoring to ensure a smoother user experience.
Alternative Approaches,	- Relied on qualitative feedback through user interviews, usability testing, and surveys to gather actionable insights, given the constraints of A/B testing.

Category	Details
Technical Practices	- Automated Testing: Comprehensive test suites using Jenkins and Selenium ensured that new changes didn't break existing functionality. - Documentation: Thorough documentation facilitated smooth collaboration and efficient problem-solving when addressing bugs and implementing changes.
Reflections in Retrospectives	- Beta Feedback: Recognized as a game-changer for catching issues early and making significant improvements. - User-Centric Design: Feedback on the dashboard design was invaluable, helping to prioritize features that users really wanted. - Automated Testing: Praised for catching issues that might have been missed manually.
Outcome	The beta release and iterative development process helped validate the product, identify critical improvements, and build trust with users. The disciplined approach to managing technical debt, automated testing, and documentation proved that a startup could leverage best practices to build a robust and competitive product.

Instead, we relied more on qualitative feedback and direct user interactions. We conducted detailed user interviews and usability testing sessions and collected feedback through surveys. Though less scientific than A/B testing, these methods provided rich, actionable insights that helped us make informed decisions.

The beta phase also highlighted the importance of technical debt management. As users explored the application, they uncovered bugs and performance issues we hadn't anticipated. Using tools like SonarQube, we continuously analyzed our codebase for potential debt and prioritized refactoring tasks in our sprints. This proactive approach prevented minor issues from escalating into more significant problems and ensured a smoother user experience.

Automated test management was another critical factor during this phase. With every piece of feedback and subsequent code change, we ran our comprehensive test suites using Jenkins and Selenium. This automated testing ensured that new changes didn't break existing functionality, maintaining the integrity of our product.

Documenting our code meticulously also proved invaluable. Each developer was responsible for writing explicit comments and documentation as they coded. This practice facilitated smoother collaboration, especially when addressing bugs and implementing feedback-driven changes. Praveen, our data analyst, often praised how easy it was to dive into any module and start working without roadblocks, thanks to the thorough documentation.

Releasing the beta version and actively seeking user feedback helped move from early adopters to a broader market. It validated our product, identified critical improvements, and built user trust. Pe promptly addressed their feedback and iteratively refined our application, demonstrating our commitment to delivering a high-quality product that met their needs.

Reflecting on our sprint retrospectives, these practices often came up. "The beta feedback was a game-changer," Siva would say. "We caught several issues early and made significant improvements." Lasya would add, "User feedback on the dashboard design was invaluable. It helped us prioritize and deliver features that users wanted." Praveen appreciated the automated testing, noting, "Automated tests caught issues I didn't even think to check manually. It's a game-changer."

Despite the challenges, the iterative development, beta feedback, and our disciplined approach to managing technical debt, automated testing, and documentation were critical differentiators for our startup. They improved our efficiency and code quality and boosted our confidence and capability to deliver high-quality software. We took pride in our innovative approach, proving that a startup could leverage best practices to build a robust and competitive product.

Embracing an iterative approach and valuing user feedback became part of our startup's DNA. These strategies guided us in making informed decisions, avoiding costly mistakes, and continually improving our product. In the fast-paced world of startups, this adaptability and responsiveness were invaluable assets that drove our growth and success. And, of course, the shared sense of accomplishment when we saw our efforts reflected in user satisfaction made the whole journey even more rewarding.

Managing Scope and Timelines

In the fast-paced world of startups, maintaining scope and timelines isn't just important—it's crucial for survival. Every day counts when you're racing against time to get your product to market and attract your first customers. This pressure was a constant reality for us, driving every decision and sprint we planned.

We knew sticking to our scope and timelines was essential from the beginning. We needed more resources, and delays could mean missing crucial opportunities. Our goal was clear: deliver a functional ESG management application that could secure our initial customer base and generate early revenue. However, achieving this goal took work.

One particular incident stands out vividly. We were preparing for a significant demo to potential investors and early adopters. This demo was critical; it had the potential to secure funding and attract our first customers. The pressure was on to showcase our product in the best possible light.

During one of our sprint reviews, Siva, our lead developer, proposed an enhancement to the data integration module. This was a great idea to improve the user experience. However, implementing it would have required significant work, and we were already tight on time. After a heated discussion, we decided to defer the change and focus on the demo preparation.

Looking back, this decision was both a blessing and a curse. On one hand, it allowed us to concentrate on polishing the features we already had, ensuring they were demo-ready and bug-free. The demo went smoothly, and the investors were impressed with our progress. It boosted our confidence and brought us closer to securing the desperately needed funding.

On the other hand, deferring the change meant we missed an opportunity to improve our product based on immediate feedback. In the weeks following the demo, we had to play catch up, integrating the deferred changes while pushing forward with new developments. It was a delicate balancing act, and while we managed it, the experience taught us the importance of making tough prioritization decisions.

Startups often operate on a tight budget, and we were no exception. Money was always a concern, and we had to make every rupee count. There were constant discussions about how to allocate our limited resources effectively. I remember one particularly challenging period when our cash flow was precariously low. We had to decide whether to invest in new development tools or save the money for essential expenses, like server costs and salaries.

Adding to our challenges was the issue of hardware. Siva, pivotal to our development efforts, needed a new MacBook to handle the heavy coding and testing workloads. It was a significant expense, and we debated it long and hard. Ultimately, we decided to go for it, recognizing that investing in the right tools for our key team members was crucial for maintaining productivity and quality.

These resource constraints required us to be creative and efficient. We leveraged free and open-source tools wherever possible, and each team member wore multiple hats. Lasya, our UI/UX designer, often doubled as a front-end developer, while Praveen, our data analyst, took on additional responsibilities for testing and documentation.

Despite these challenges, our commitment to maintaining scope and timelines was a testament to our resilience and determination. We knew every delay or deviation could have a ripple effect, potentially jeopardizing our chances of securing customers and funding. This sense of urgency kept us focused and disciplined.

In our retrospectives, we often reflected on these experiences. "Remember the demo prep crunch?" someone would say, eliciting groans and chuckles. "That was intense, but it paid off." We recognized the importance of making tough decisions, balancing short-term needs with long-term goals, and staying agile in unexpected challenges.

Maintaining scope and timelines wasn't just about meeting deadlines, survival, and growth. It required a clear vision, disciplined execution, and the ability to make strategic trade-offs. Our journey was filled with moments of doubt and tough choices, but these experiences forged our team's resilience and adaptability.

Reflecting on our startup journey, it's clear that managing scope and timelines, navigating financial constraints, and strategically investing our resources were critical to our success. These challenges shaped us, taught us valuable lessons, and ultimately helped us build a product that we were proud of and that met the needs of our customers. While the road was often rocky, the sense of accomplishment we felt when we achieved our milestones made every struggle worthwhile.

Collaboration and Communication

It was a Friday morning for Siva, Lasya, Praveen, and the rest of our team. Everyone was in a weekend mood, ready to wrap up their day for a weekend get-together at a local coffee shop. I was asked to join for a quick chat about an office escalation. It turned out that Lasya, our newly joined product manager, was still settling into her role and had a major complaint against the scrum team, especially Siva, our lead developer.

Lasya was frustrated that Siva wasn't listening to her suggestions and felt that the group's operation was chaotic. It was the second time I had heard an escalation about the team's performance in two months. Based on an earlier escalation, our previous scrum master was replaced with a new one, who was now asked to lead the product development. Hearing about another escalation surprised me and the team, as none of us, including Lasya, had raised the issue or at least hadn't brought the topic to the forefront.

As we sipped our coffees, it became clear that the root cause of the problem was a lack of proper leadership from the scrum master. The scrum master wasn't facilitating the sessions effectively and didn't involve Lasya in product management discussions before diving into technical details.

Whatever the outcome of Lasya's complaint, the key takeaway wasn't just about resolving it but understanding the underlying issue. In our startup, with the kind of agile scrum teams we are part of, it's common to hear stories highlighting how team conflicts can impact the product roadmap. It got me thinking about the importance of collaboration and communication in our workflow.

Recently, I've spent much time assessing and pondering the personality types of our product manager and the scrum team. Have you ever considered how this dynamic impacts product management? It is not just the product manager's personality but also how each team member's traits play a role in the product's evolution. I've noted my observations and wanted to share how these insights have shaped our approach to product management.

Our team's product manager typically aligns responsibilities based on the product group they oversee. It's a setup where everyone knows their role but collaborates closely. However, when communication breaks down, it can lead to significant friction. This was the case with Lasya and Siva.

Table 9.9 List of critical behaviors

Category	**Details**
Leadership	- Effective Facilitation: The Scrum Master needs strong facilitation skills to balance technical and strategic discussions. - Mediation: Ability to mediate conflicts and guide conversations toward compromise and resolution.

Category	Details
Communication	- Open Channels: Establish clear communication channels between product management and development teams. - Proactive Alignment: Pre-sprint meetings to align priorities and discuss potential roadblocks.
Collaboration	- Teamwork: Encourage collaboration and ensure that all team members' voices are heard and valued. - Cross-functional understanding: Team members should understand and appreciate each other's roles and contributions.
Feedback Culture	- Transparency: Foster a culture of open feedback during retrospectives, encouraging candid discussions about what worked and what didn't. - Continuous Improvement: Use feedback to identify and address issues early.
Resource Management	- Prioritization: Make disciplined decisions about resource allocation, focusing on tools and tasks that enhance productivity. - Balancing Scope and Timelines: Prioritize tasks to stay on track with project goals.
Conflict Resolution	- Addressing Friction: Recognize and address friction points between team members before they escalate. - Compromise and Flexibility: Encourage team members to compromise and remain flexible to find mutually beneficial solutions.
Empowerment	- Respect and Empowerment: Create an environment where all team members feel heard, respected and empowered to contribute their best work.
Adaptability	- Flexible Approach: Adapt processes and behaviors as needed to ensure smooth team dynamics and project success.

Siva, focused on coding and technical details, sometimes needed help seeing the broader product vision that Lasya was trying to convey. Conversely, Lasya felt sidelined when her strategic input wasn't considered in the daily scrums. Our new scrum master, tasked with mediating these interactions, hadn't yet found the balance between facilitating technical discussions and integrating Lasya's product insights.

One memorable incident occurred during a sprint planning meeting. Lasya had proposed a new feature based on user feedback, but Siva needed to be more open, citing technical constraints and tight timelines. The discussion quickly became heated, with neither side willing to budge. Our scrum master, instead of guiding the conversation toward a compromise, allowed it to stall, leaving the team divided and frustrated.

We realized that collaboration and communication had to be at the core of our agile process for it to work effectively in our startup. Regular meetings weren't enough; they needed to be structured to ensure everyone's voice was heard and valued.

To address this, we implemented a few fundamental changes. First, we ensured that our scrum master received additional training on facilitation techniques, focusing on balancing technical and strategic discussions. We also established more apparent communication channels. For example, Lasya and Siva started having pre-sprint meetings to align priorities and discuss potential roadblocks. This proactive approach allowed them to enter sprint planning sessions with a unified vision, reducing friction and misunderstandings.

Another significant change was fostering a culture of open feedback. During our retrospectives, we encouraged team members to share their thoughts candidly, highlighting what worked well and what didn't. This transparency helped us identify and address issues early, preventing them from escalating.

These changes didn't happen overnight, and there were plenty of challenges. Resource constraints were a constant hurdle. We were a startup, after all, and money was always tight. We sometimes had to make tough decisions about where to allocate our limited funds. For instance, when Siva needed a new MacBook for development work, we had a lengthy debate about whether we could afford it. Ultimately, we decided to invest in the right tools for our key team members, recognizing that this would ultimately benefit the entire team's productivity.

Another critical aspect was maintaining our scope and timelines. We had to be disciplined about prioritizing tasks and ensuring we stayed on track. There was a memorable incident in which we had to defer a significant feature change to focus on preparing for a crucial demo. While it felt like a setback at the time, it allowed us to deliver a polished presentation that impressed our stakeholders and secured much-needed funding.

Ultimately, the lessons we learned about collaboration and communication were invaluable. They reinforced the importance of working together, valuing each team member's contributions, and constantly striving to improve our processes. Despite the challenges, these efforts paid off, helping us build a robust ESG management application and fostering a strong, cohesive team.

Reflecting on our journey, I realize that the key to our success wasn't just about having the right tools or processes—it was about the people. It was about creating an environment where everyone felt heard, respected, and empowered to contribute their best work—more than anything, that drove our product's success and our team's growth.

Adapting to Changes

Flexibility and proactive problem-solving are hallmarks of successful startups. One of the most insightful exercises we adopted to enhance our team's flexibility was the post-mortem analysis. Inspired by practices from various leading companies, this exercise turned out to be a game-changer for us, allowing us to identify potential pitfalls before they become real issues.

Different companies approach post-mortem analysis in unique ways. For example, Google's Project Aristotle uses post-mortems to foster psychological safety within teams, encouraging members to speak openly about potential risks. Amazon, known for its rigorous approach to project management, uses post-mortems to simulate future failure scenarios and then brainstorm solutions. With its culture of freedom and responsibility, Netflix conducts post-mortems to identify risks and create a shared understanding of project goals and potential obstacles.

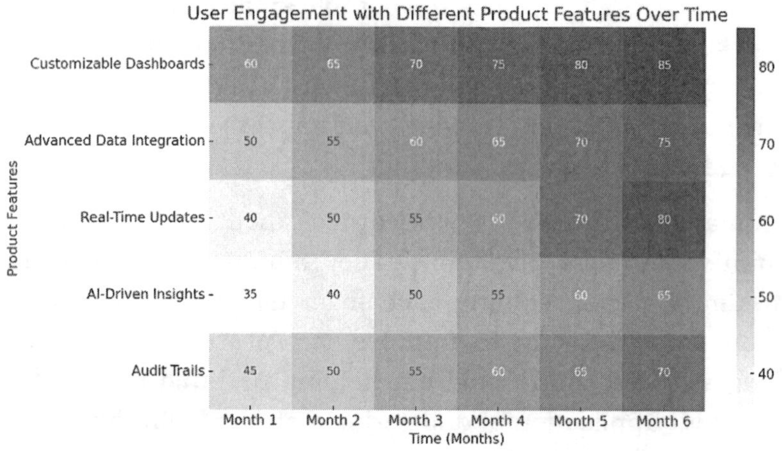

Taking a leaf from these companies, we implemented our version of a post-mortem analysis. We gathered the team and set the stage: "Imagine it's six months from now, and our ESG management application has failed. Let's list all the reasons why that might have happened."

The initial silence was telling, but the sticky notes filled the wall. Each note represented a concern quietly brewing in the back of our minds. Siva mentioned potential integration issues. Lasya pointed out the risk of misalignment in the product vision, and Praveen flagged concerns about user engagement and technical debt.

This exercise helped us surface several critical issues we had been reluctant to address. Lasya's point about misalignment was particularly eye-opening. She felt disconnected between what the development team was building and what the market needed. Siva's concern about technical debt was another crucial insight. Our rapid feature rollouts were accumulating hidden costs that could cripple us later.

Table 9.10 List of Key Requirements to Manage Adaptability in Product Development

Category	**Key Requirements**
Flexibility	- Post-Mortem Analysis: Adopt post-mortem exercises to identify potential pitfalls and address them before they become real issues. - Proactive Problem-Solving: Encourage a culture where team members can openly discuss risks and collaboratively brainstorm solutions.
Alignment on Product Vision	- Regular Communication: Establish one-on-one meetings between product management and development teams to ensure alignment on product goals and strategic direction.
Technical Debt Management	- Dedicated Sprints: Allocate specific sprints to address technical debt, focusing on refactoring code, updating dependencies, and improving maintainability. - Continuous Improvement: Regularly review and address technical debt to prevent it from hindering product development.
User Engagement	- Feedback Loop: Implement regular surveys and user interviews to gather insights directly from users, guiding feature development and retention strategies.
Integration and Documentation	- Clear Integration Protocols: Prioritize creating detailed documentation and establish clear integration protocols to reduce friction between different system components and ease onboarding of new developers.
Collaborative Culture	- Effective Communication Tools: Utilize tools like Slack and Azure DevOps to facilitate seamless communication and project management, reinforcing a collaborative work environment.
Risk Mitigation	- Foresight through Pre-Mortems: Use post-mortem analysis to anticipate potential problems, allowing the team to proactively address risks before they materialize.
Continuous Improvement	- Retrospective Reflection: Regularly reflect on both successes and challenges in retrospectives to reinforce effective practices and address issues early.

We didn't just stop at identifying what could go wrong; we also discussed what went well. This part of the exercise was equally important, highlighting our strengths and the strategies that worked for us. For instance, we recognized that our collaborative culture, facilitated by tools like Slack and Azure DevOps, was a significant asset. Our automated testing and continuous integration processes saved us countless hours and prevented numerous bugs from reaching production.

With a comprehensive view of our potential pitfalls and strengths, we moved on to actionable solutions. Here's how we tackled some of the critical issues:

1. Misalignment on Product Vision: We established regular one-on-one meetings between Lasya and Siva to ensure that the technical developments were aligned with the product's strategic goals. These meetings became a forum for open dialogue and helped bridge the gap between the product and development teams.
2. Technical Debt: We allocated specific sprints to address technical debt. Siva led this initiative, focusing on refactoring code, updating dependencies, and cleaning up any messy sections. This proactive approach significantly improved our codebase's maintainability and performance.
3. User Engagement: Praveen spearheaded the implementation of a feedback loop with our users. We started conducting regular surveys and user interviews to gather insights directly from the source. This data was invaluable in guiding our feature development and improving user retention.
4. Integration Issues: We prioritized creating more detailed documentation and establishing more apparent integration protocols. This reduced the friction between different parts of our system and made it easier to onboard new developers.

The benefits of this pre-mortem exercise were immediate and profound. It fostered a culture of openness and proactive problem-solving. By imagining our failures, we could confront and address our fears before they became reality. This mitigated risks and strengthened our team's cohesion and alignment.

Reflecting on what went well and what went wrong provided a balanced perspective. Acknowledging our successes gave us the confidence to tackle our challenges head-on. The insights we gained from discussing our strengths reinforced the working practices, such as using Slack for seamless communication and ADO for robust project management.

We often returned to the lessons learned from the pre-mortem in our retrospectives. "Remember in our retrospectives when we flagged that integration issue?" Siva would say. "Addressing it early saved us a lot of headaches," Lasya would add. "The regular check-ins helped us stay aligned on the product vision."

Other companies might use different methods, but the core idea remains post-mortem analysis is about foresight, collaboration, and continuous improvement. It became a crucial part of our strategy, allowing us to navigate the complexities of startup life with greater confidence and agility.

Ultimately, the post-mortem analysis was more than just an exercise—it was a catalyst for change. It demonstrated the power of flexibility and the importance of being proactive. By anticipating potential problems and celebrating our successes, we built a stronger, more resilient team capable of turning challenges into opportunities. As we moved forward, these lessons continued to guide us, ensuring that we remained adaptable and prepared for whatever lay ahead.

Final Frontier - Intriguing Dance of Personalities

It was a typical Friday morning, and the team—Siva, Lasya, Praveen, and I—eagerly looked forward to the weekend. We had planned a fun get-together at our favorite coffee shop. However, an office escalation needed our attention before we could slip into weekend mode. Lasya, our newly joined product manager, complained significantly against the scrum team, particularly Siva, our lead developer.

Now, Lasya was visibly frustrated and still finding her footing in her new role. "Siva isn't listening to my suggestions, and the team feels chaotic," she said, exasperated. This was the second time in two months I'd heard such complaints. Our previous scrum master had already been replaced due to similar issues, and here we were again.

As we sipped our coffees, the root cause of the problem started to crystallize. It wasn't just about Siva or Lasya but about how we managed our sessions. The new scrum master wasn't facilitating the meetings effectively and, crucially, wasn't involving Lasya in product management discussions before diving into the technical details.

Reflecting on Lasya's frustration, it became clear that resolving this wasn't just about fixing the immediate problem. It was about understanding the deeper issue at hand. Conflicts can significantly impact our product roadmap in the fast-paced world of ESG product management, where agile scrum teams are the norm. This situation got me thinking about the importance of collaboration and communication in our workflow.

Siva was intensely focused on coding and the technical nitty-gritty, sometimes missing the broader product vision that Lasya was trying to convey. On the other hand, Lasya felt sidelined when her strategic input wasn't being considered in the daily scrums. Our new scrum master, tasked with balancing these interactions, hadn't yet mastered integrating technical discussions with Lasya's insights.

One incident that stands out was during a particularly tense sprint planning meeting. Lasya proposed a new feature based on user feedback, but Siva pushed back, citing technical constraints and tight timelines. The discussion quickly heated up, with neither side willing to budge. Instead of guiding the conversation toward a compromise, our scrum master allowed it to stall. The team felt divided and frustrated. It was clear to me that for agile to work effectively in our startup, especially in the nuanced field of ESG product management, collaboration, and communication had to be at the heart of our process. Regular meetings alone weren't enough; they needed to be structured to ensure everyone's voice was heard and valued.

We decided to make some fundamental changes. First, we ensured our scrum master received additional training on facilitation techniques, focusing on balancing technical and strategic discussions. We also set up more apparent communication channels. Lasya and Siva started having pre-sprint meetings to align priorities and discuss potential roadblocks. This proactive approach helped them enter sprint planning sessions with a unified vision, reducing friction and misunderstandings.

Another significant change was fostering a culture of open feedback. During our retrospectives, we encouraged team members to share their thoughts candidly, highlighting what worked well and what didn't. This transparency helped us identify and address issues early, preventing them from escalating. I remember one retrospective where Praveen, our data analyst, spoke up about feeling out of the loop on some technical decisions that impacted his work. This honest feedback was invaluable. We adjusted our process to include Praveen more in those discussions, improving his work and our overall efficiency.

These changes didn't happen overnight, and there were plenty of challenges. Resource constraints were a constant hurdle. We were a startup, after all, and money was always tight. We sometimes had to make tough decisions about where to allocate our limited funds. For instance, when Siva needed a new MacBook for development work, we had a lengthy debate about whether we could afford it. Ultimately, we decided to invest in the right tools for our key team members, recognizing that this would ultimately benefit the entire team's productivity.

Another critical aspect was maintaining our scope and timelines. We had to be disciplined about prioritizing tasks and ensuring we stayed on track. There was a memorable incident in which we had to defer a significant feature change to focus on preparing for a crucial demo. While it felt like a setback at the time, it allowed us to deliver a polished presentation that impressed our stakeholders and secured much-needed funding.

Reflecting on our journey, I realize that the key to our success wasn't just about having the right tools or processes—it was about the people. It was about creating an environment where everyone felt heard, respected, and empowered to contribute their best work—more than anything, that drove our product's success and our team's growth.

So, as we moved forward with our ESG management application, we did so with a stronger sense of unity and purpose. We learned that conflicts, when handled constructively, could lead to better understanding and improved collaboration. We embraced agreeing to disagree, knowing it was a sign of a healthy, dynamic team, and that made all the difference.

Table 9.11 Summary table showcasing managing the personalities in product development.

Challenge	Description	How to Overcome
Lack of Effective Facilitation,	The scrum master was not effectively facilitating sessions, leading to unstructured meetings where product management and technical discussions were not well-integrated	- Provide additional training for the Scrum Master focused on facilitation techniques. - Ensure balanced discussions that integrate both technical and strategic inputs
Poor Communication and Collaboration	Miscommunication between the product manager (Lasya) and the lead developer (Siva) caused friction, with Lasya feeling sidelined and Siva focusing too much on technical details	- Establish clear communication channels, including pre-sprint meetings, to align priorities. - Encourage proactive discussions to reduce misunderstandings and improve collaboration
Resistance to Compromise	During a sprint planning meeting, the inability to find a compromise on feature implementation led to frustration and stalled progress	- Train the Scrum Master to guide conversations toward compromise and ensure that all voices are heard. - Foster a culture where team members feel comfortable discussing and resolving differences constructively
Resource Constraints	The startup faced tight budgets, making it challenging to allocate funds for necessary tools and resources, which sometimes delayed development	- Make strategic decisions on resource allocation, prioritizing investments that will enhance productivity and long-term success.

(*Contd.*)

Challenge	Description	How to Overcome
		- Balance immediate needs with future growth potential when allocating resources
Maintaining Scope and Timelines,	Balancing feature development with strict deadlines was difficult, sometimes requiring deferral of significant changes to meet critical deadlines, such as a major demo	- Prioritize tasks carefully and stay disciplined when maintaining scope and timelines. - Be prepared to make tough decisions about deferring features to meet critical deadlines and deliver polished presentations
Limited Feedback Loop	Team members, such as Praveen, felt out of the loop in discussions affecting their work, which impacted overall efficiency and alignment	- Foster a culture of open feedback, encouraging all team members to share their thoughts during retrospectives. - Adjust processes to ensure that all relevant team members are included in key discussions
Conflict Resolution	Conflicts between team members were not always handled constructively, leading to frustration and division within the team	- Encourage a culture of constructive conflict resolution, where differing opinions are valued and used to enhance understanding and collaboration. - Embrace the idea that agreeing to disagree can be healthy for team dynamics

Challenge	Description	How to Overcome
Creating a Respectful and Empowering Environment	Ensuring that all team members felt heard, respected, and empowered was crucial for maintaining morale and driving success	- Focus on creating an environment where everyone's contributions are valued. - Empower team members by involving them in decision-making processes and ensuring their input is considered in strategic and technical discussions

Celebrating Success and Next Steps

Celebrating successes, no matter how small, was vital to keeping our team motivated and united. One memorable celebration was after we reached a significant milestone with our ESG management application. The atmosphere was electric with excitement and pride, and we decided to throw an impromptu party to mark the occasion.

We gathered in the office and the aroma of freshly made samosas filled the room. Madhuri, our organization Director, had just bought a new MG Hector and she graciously offered to take us all for a drive. Piling into her car, we felt like we were on top of the world, our spirits high with the thrill of our achievement.

As we drove around the city, laughing and chatting, the reality of our accomplishments began to sink in. It wasn't just about the product; it was about the journey we had shared, the challenges we had overcome, and the team spirit that had gotten us this far. We started dreaming big—big. Someone joked about putting up a company billboard, and before we knew it, we were seriously discussing the logistics of setting one up on our house balcony. It was a hilarious yet symbolic gesture of how far we had come and how far we wanted to go.

Amidst the celebrations, I couldn't help but think about the road ahead. While everyone enjoyed the moment, I was already planning our next steps. I had a crucial demo coming up with a potential client in Switzerland. This demo was a make-or-break opportunity to showcase our product to a global market. The stakes were high, and I knew we had to nail it.

Marketing was also at the forefront of my mind. We needed a solid go-to-market strategy to attract customers and differentiate us from the competition. Balancing product development with consulting was a unique challenge. We wanted to leverage our consulting experience to enhance our product offerings, providing solutions that were not only innovative but also grounded in real-world insights.

Our go-to-market strategy had to be robust and multi-faceted. We planned to use a mix of direct sales, partnerships, and digital marketing to reach our target audience. The goal was to create a buzz around our product, leveraging our success stories and the positive feedback from our beta users. I was particularly excited about combining our product with consulting services, offering clients tailored solutions addressing their ESG needs. This hybrid approach would generate revenue and deepen our market understanding, fueling further innovation.

Chapter 10

Launching and Marketing the ESG Management Application

As I sit here, reflecting on the journey that has brought me to this pivotal moment, I can't help but feel a mix of pride and anxiety. Starting a business and developing a product from scratch is no small feat, especially when doing it for the first time with limited resources. Growing up in India, I always dreamed of creating something impactful that would make a real difference. And that dream led me to develop an ESG management application.

From the outset, I knew the road ahead would be challenging. We began with an exhaustive ESG market analysis, immersing ourselves in the complexities of environmental, social, and governance factors that companies must navigate today. Understanding the market was just the first step. We then mapped out the customer journey, pinpointing key touchpoints and pain points our application needed to address. This mapping helped us build a strategy that was not only robust but also deeply aligned with our vision of delivering genuine value to our users.

Next came the strategic management phase. We laid the foundation with a clear North Star, a compelling vision, and a mission statement to guide us through the stormy seas of product development. Crafting a strategy canvas, we ensured every decision was anchored in these guiding principles, keeping us accurate to our goals.

Planning the MVP was both exhilarating and daunting. We prioritized features, tackled high-risk hypotheses, and set clear sprint goals. Using agile principles, we broke down the development process into manageable sprints, allowing us to iterate quickly and adapt to feedback. This agile approach was the backbone of our journey, giving us the flexibility to pivot as needed. Developing the UI/UX was another critical milestone. We aimed to create a functional but also intuitive and engaging interface. Countless design sprints, usability tests, and iterations later, we had a user experience that resonated with our target audience.

Then came the beta product development phase. We poured our hearts into building a product that embodied our vision. Each line of code, every design element, and all the functionalities were meticulously crafted to meet our high standards. The beta version was our first tangible success, a testament to our hard work and dedication. But as we prepare for the product launch, reality sets in. Just one customer is willing to test our product before signing a contract. Our biggest worry is how to launch it effectively. We know we can't rely solely on product-led growth; the product isn't yet intuitive enough to stand independently. It requires detailed documentation and could be more user-friendly—improvements we have planned but haven't implemented yet. We're at a crossroads, needing to start somewhere despite knowing the product isn't perfect.

Our finances could be better, forcing us to rethink our approach. We can't afford an extensive marketing campaign, so we must be strategic and resourceful. This is a moment of hope and uncertainty. We've seen success and failure along the way, and now, more than ever, we need to leverage every bit of knowledge and experience we've gained.

As we stand on the brink of our product launch, I am filled with determination and trepidation. This journey has been anything but easy, but it has also been gratifying. In the chapters ahead, I'll share the strategies and tactics we've developed to navigate this crucial phase. We'll dive into our go-to-market plan, marketing strategies, and how we intend to gather and act on user feedback.

We'll explore frameworks like AARRR and the Bullseye method drawn from our first-hand experiences. This is where our efforts converge, and the real test begins. It's time to take that leap and make our mark in the ESG landscape. Let's embark on this final leg of the journey together, one step at a time.

Preparing Launch

As we neared the launch of our ESG management application, it was clear that we needed to meticulously prepare to ensure a smooth rollout. Every step we took in the final stages was crucial, considering our limited resources and the high stakes involved with our single potential customer ready to test the product.

We began by finalizing the key features of our application. This was a critical phase, during which we had to decide what would be included in the initial release. My childhood friend Dillesh played a pivotal role in this process. With his keen eye for detail and expertise in performance testing, Dillesh helped us ensure that our product was robust and ready for real-world use. He conducted rigorous performance tests, simulating heavy loads to ensure our application could handle stress without faltering.

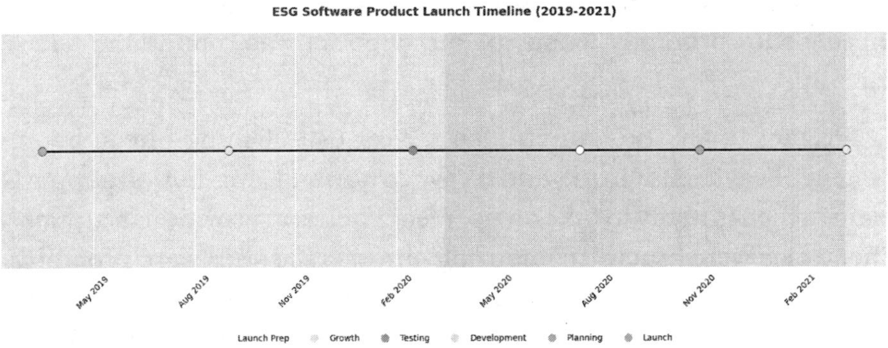

Figure 10. 1 ESG Software Product Launch Timeline (2019 – 2021)

Meanwhile, Siva, always the visionary, suggested additional features that he believed would enhance the product's usability.

While his ideas were excellent and aligned with our long-term vision, I had to take a stance against scope creep. We had to focus on our immediate goal: delivering a stable and functional product. It was a challenging decision, but necessary to maintain our launch timeline. Once our feature set was locked down, we moved into rigorous testing. This wasn't just about finding and fixing bugs, although there were plenty of those. It was also about ensuring the application could seamlessly handle real-world use cases. Our testing process included:

- **Functional Testing:** Ensuring each feature worked as intended.
- **Usability Testing:** Verifying that the user interface was intuitive and that users could navigate the application without confusion.
- **Performance Testing:** Ensuring the application can handle the expected load and perform efficiently under stress.
- **Security Testing:** Ensuring all data within the application was secure and met the necessary compliance standards.

During testing, we discovered several areas that needed refinement. Some features didn't perform well under heavy loads, and our test users highlighted a few usability issues. Thanks to Dillesh's thorough performance testing, we identified and addressed these issues promptly, ensuring our product was robust and user-friendly.

Preparing for the launch also meant establishing our support system. Lasya, Madhuri, and Praveen formed our initial support team, which is ready to take on user feedback and provide assistance. Their roles were crucial in ensuring our users' issues were promptly addressed. Lasya handled the helpdesk, Madhuri managed the knowledge base, and Praveen coordinated the feedback loop, ensuring we understood user experiences and challenges clearly.

Siva and I took on the role of implementation partners, working closely with our potential customers to set up the system. Our goal was to ensure that the application was seamlessly integrated into their existing processes and had all the support they needed to make the most of our product. We also knew that our product wasn't entirely intuitive yet and that users would need detailed guidance to maximize its capabilities. We developed user manuals, quick start guides, and video tutorials to help users get up and running. This documentation was crucial because we couldn't provide extensive hands-on support due to limited resources.

Table 10.1 Checklist: Preparing for the Launch of ESG Management Application

1. *Finalize Key Features*
    - *Lock down the feature set for the initial release.*
    - *Prioritize stability and functionality over additional features.*
    - *Avoid scope creep to maintain the launch timeline.*
2. *Conduct Rigorous Testing*
    - *Functional Testing: Ensure each feature works as intended.*
    - *Usability Testing: Verify that the user interface is intuitive and user-friendly.*
    - *Performance Testing: Simulate heavy loads to ensure the application can handle stress without performance issues.*
    - *Security Testing: Ensure data security and compliance with necessary standards.*
3. *Refine and Fix Issues*
    - *Address performance issues and usability concerns identified during testing.*
    - *Implement refinements based on feedback from test users and performance testing results.*

4. *Establish Support System*
    - *Form an initial support team to handle user feedback and assistance.*
    - *Assign roles:*

- *Helpdesk: Manage user inquiries and issues.*
- *Knowledge Base: Develop and maintain documentation.*
- *Feedback Loop: Coordinate user feedback and ensure its effectively communicated to the team.*

1. *Develop User Documentation*
    - *Create user manuals, quick start guides, and video tutorials.*
    - *Ensure documentation is clear and helps users maximize the product's capabilities.*
2. *Coordinate Implementation*
    - *Work closely with potential customers to ensure seamless integration into their existing processes.*
    - *Provide necessary support for system setup and initial use.*
3. *Set Up Monitoring Tools*
    - *Implement tools to track product performance and user interactions post-launch.*
    - *Use real-time data to inform immediate improvements and future updates.*
4. *Prepare Marketing Strategy*
    - *Develop a modest marketing plan within budget constraints.*
    - *Leverage social media, reach industry influencers, and use content marketing.*

   - *Create blog posts, whitepapers, and case studies to generate interest.*

5. *Hold Daily Stand-Up Meetings*
   - *Ensure all team members are aligned and aware of their roles and responsibilities.*
   - *Address any last-minute concerns or issues.*

6. *Launch Day Preparations*
   - *Confirm that the team is ready to address any issues that arise.*
   - *Monitor the application closely as it goes live.*
   - *Be prepared to iterate based on real-time feedback and data.*

Post-Launch

- *Continuously gather feedback and make necessary adjustments.*
- *Monitor product performance and user satisfaction.*
- *Plan for future updates based on user needs and feedback.*

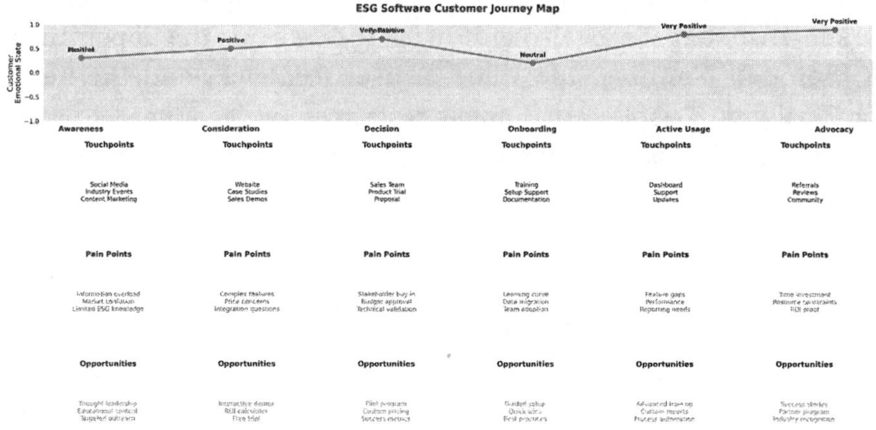

Figure 10. 2 ESG Software Customer Journey Map

As launch day approached, we coordinated with our team to ensure everyone knew their roles and responsibilities. Communication was vital; we needed to be ready to address any issues that might arise swiftly. We held daily stand-up meetings to keep everyone aligned and to tackle any last-minute concerns. One of the most critical steps was setting up monitoring tools to track the product's performance and user interactions post-launch. This would allow us to gather real-time data and feedback, helping us make informed decisions about immediate improvements and future updates.

Given our budget constraints, we also developed a modest marketing plan. Our strategy included leveraging social media, reaching out to industry influencers, and using content marketing to generate interest. We created blog posts, whitepapers, and case studies to highlight the benefits of our application and attract potential customers.

On launch day, the excitement and nervousness were palpable. We knew this was just the beginning, and actual work was about to start. As we flipped the switch and our ESG management application went live, we were ready to monitor, support, and iterate based on the feedback we received. This preparation phase was intense, but it was also gratifying. It taught us the importance of thorough planning, the value of user feedback, and the need for flexibility. Despite our limited resources, we managed to pull together and prepare for a successful launch, setting the stage for the next chapter of our journey.

Go-To-Market Strategy

As we prepared to launch our ESG management application, it was clear that a well-thought-out go-to-market strategy was crucial for our success. With limited resources and the need to make a significant impact, we turned to our business model canvas to guide our approach, helping us identify key markets and segments and craft a compelling value proposition for our target personas.

Identifying Key Markets and Segments

Using the business model canvas, we broke down our approach into distinct, actionable segments:

1. **Customer Segments**: We identified the primary customer segments that would benefit most from our ESG management application. These included:

Table 10.2 Checklist: Go-To-Market Strategy for ESG Management Application

1. *Identify Key Customer Segments*
    - *Large Enterprises:*
        - *Target companies with extensive ESG reporting requirements.*
        - *Focus on businesses with resources to implement robust management systems.*
    - *Mid-sized Firms:*
        - *Target is rapidly growing businesses needing scalable ESG management solutions.*
    - *Consulting Firms:*
        - *Target ESG consultants looking for tools to help clients manage and report ESG metrics efficiently.*
2. *Craft Tailored Value Propositions*
    - *For Large Enterprises:*
        - *"Streamline your ESG reporting and ensure compliance with global standards effortlessly."*
    - *For Mid-sized Firms:*
        - *"Scalable ESG management solutions that grow with your business."*
    - *For Consulting Firms:*
        - *"Enhance your client services with a powerful tool for comprehensive ESG management."*

3. *Identify Effective Channels*
    - *Direct Sales:*
        - *Use personal outreach through networking and direct marketing to target large enterprises.*
4. *Digital Marketing:*
    - *Utilize SEO, content marketing, and social media campaigns to reach mid-sized firms and consultants.*
        - *Partnerships:*
    - *Collaborate with industry influencers and ESG consulting firms to leverage their networks and establish credibility.*
5. *Build Strong Customer Relationships*
    - *Personal Assistance:*
        - *Provide dedicated support for large enterprises with personalized onboarding and training sessions.*
    - *Self-Service:*
        - *Develop detailed documentation, tutorials, and resources to help mid-sized firms and consultants start independently.*
    - *Communities:*
        - *Create user communities and forums for customers to share insights, ask questions, and provide feedback.*
6. *Leverage the Business Model Canvas*
    - *Regularly review and update the business model canvas to ensure alignment with market needs and strategic goals.*
    - *Use the canvas to guide decision-making and prioritize efforts in each customer segment.*

Table 10.3 Go-to-Market Strategy for ESG Application Management.

GTM Component	**Strategy**	**Actions**	**Expected Outcomes**
Market Positioning	Establish strong market presence in the ESG space	- Leverage key partnerships with industry leaders - Highlight unique capabilities of the application in sustainability and ESG management - Use thought leadership	- Increased brand recognition - Higher trust and credibility within the market
Sales & Partnerships	Drive sales through strategic partnerships and targeted initiatives	- Partner with sustainability consultants and technology providers - Offer specialized advisory and implementation services	- Expanded customer base through partner networks - Increased sales opportunities through trusted partners
Customer Engagement	Enhance customer experience and engagement through personalized solutions	- Implement tailored onboarding experiences - Provide continuous updates based on customer feedback - Offer premium support options	- Higher customer satisfaction and retention - Reduced churn rates
Product Development	Continuously evolve the product to meet emerging sustainability standards and customer needs	- Regularly update the application with new features - Integrate AI and analytics for better decision-making - Align product with evolving regulations (e.g., CSRD)	- Product remains relevant and competitive - Better compliance with new sustainability reporting standards

(Contd.)

GTM Component	Strategy	Actions	Expected Outcomes
Revenue Generation	Increase revenue through diverse pricing models and premium offerings	- Introduce tiered subscription plans - Offer premium features for advanced users - Upsell additional services and support packages	- Improved Average Revenue Per User (ARPU) - Increased revenue through upselling and premium offerings
Market Expansion	Expand into new markets and customer segments	- Target industries with high sustainability demands (e.g., agriculture, manufacturing, logistics) - Utilize cloud and AI technologies to scale the solution globally	- Entry into new geographic and industry markets - Enhanced scalability and global reach of the application
Awareness & Advocacy	Build brand awareness and encourage customer advocacy	- Launch targeted marketing campaigns - Highlight success stories and customer testimonials - Foster a community of engaged users	- Increased organic referrals - Enhanced community engagement and brand loyalty
Regulatory Compliance	Ensure the application is aligned with the latest sustainability regulations and standards	- Regular updates to comply with regulations like CSRD - Provide detailed reporting features that meet legal requirements	- Higher customer trust - Compliance with international standards
Technical Enablement	Equip partners and customers with the necessary technical knowledge to maximize application benefits	- Offer comprehensive training programs - Provide access to learning paths and certifications for partners - Develop a rich set of documentation and resources	- Empowered partners and customers - Increased adoption and effective use of the application

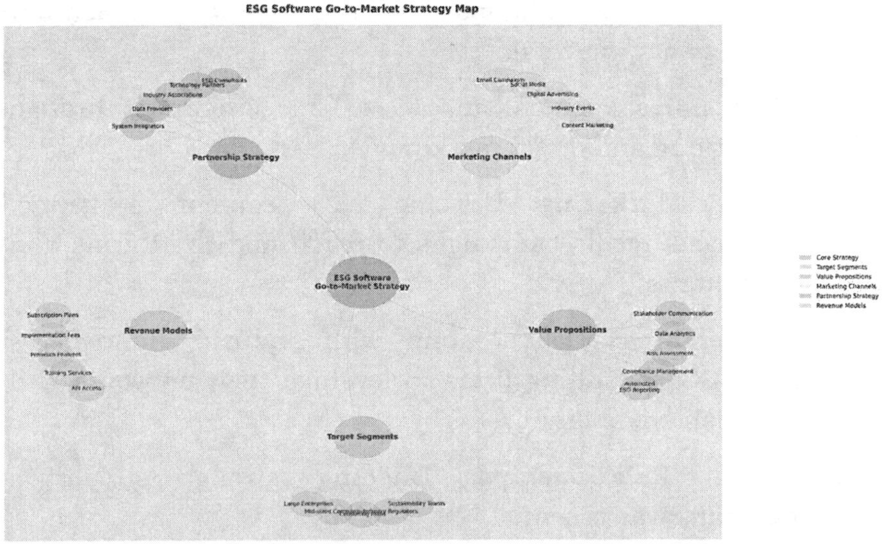

Figure 10.3 ESG Software Go-To-Market Strategy map.

Large Enterprises: Companies with extensive ESG reporting requirements and resources to implement robust management systems.

- **Mid-sized Firms**: Businesses proliferating and need scalable solutions for ESG management.
- **Consulting Firms**: ESG consultants looking for a tool to help their clients manage and report on ESG metrics efficiently.

2. **Value Propositions**: We crafted specific value propositions tailored to our target segments. This was crucial in ensuring our messaging resonated with their unique needs and challenges.
   - **For Large Enterprises**: "Streamline your ESG reporting and ensure compliance with global standards effortlessly."
   - **For Mid-sized Firms**: "Scalable ESG management solutions that grow with your business."
   - **For Consulting Firms**: "Enhance your client services with a powerful tool for comprehensive ESG management."

3. **Channels**: Identifying the most effective channels to reach our target segments was vital.
    - **Direct Sales**: Personal outreach to large enterprises through networking and direct marketing.
    - **Digital Marketing**: Utilizing SEO, content marketing, and social media campaigns to reach mid-sized firms and consultants.
    - **Partnerships**: Collaborating with industry influencers and ESG consulting firms to leverage their networks and establish credibility.
4. **Customer Relationships**: Building strong, supportive relationships was essential.
    - **Personal Assistance**: Providing dedicated support for large enterprises through personalized onboarding and training sessions.
    - **Self-service**: Developing detailed documentation and tutorials to help mid-sized firms and consultants start independently.
    - **Communities**: Creating user communities and forums where customers could share insights, ask questions, and provide feedback.

Table 10.4 Revenue Stream Assessment using ESG Application Management

Revenue Stream	Strategy	Actions	Expected Outcomes
Software Sales	Leverage the ESG Management Application to drive direct software sales	- Offer tiered subscription plans to cater to different customer segments - Provide premium features for advanced users	- Steady revenue stream from subscriptions - Increased Average Revenue Per User (ARPU)
Consulting Services	Provide expert consulting services to help clients implement and optimize their ESG strategies	- Offer advisory services to help clients navigate sustainability regulations and reporting standards - Provide implementation and integration support	- High-margin revenue from consulting engagements - Strong client relationships leading to long-term contracts
Knowledge Management	Develop and share thought leadership content to establish credibility and attract clients	- Create white papers, case studies, and thought leadership articles - Host webinars and workshops on sustainability and ESG management	- Recognition as a thought leader in the ESG space - Increased inbound leads and consulting opportunities
Expert Advisory Services	Position yourself as a go-to expert in ESG and sustainability by offering specialized advisory services	- Offer strategic advisory services to C-level executives - Provide custom-tailored solutions based on deep industry knowledge and best practices	- Premium consulting fees for expert advice - Strong market positioning as an industry leader

(*Contd.*)

Revenue Stream	Strategy	Actions	Expected Outcomes
Training and Certification	Offer training programs and certifications to partners and clients to deepen their expertise in ESG management	- Develop certification programs for partners and clients - Offer specialized training sessions and workshops	- Additional revenue from training programs - Enhanced credibility as an educational leader in the field
Integrated Solutions	Bundle software, consulting, and training into comprehensive solutions to address complex client needs	- Create bundled offerings that include software, consulting, and training services - Provide ongoing support and continuous improvement programs	- Higher contract values through bundled services - Stronger client loyalty and reduced churn
Community Engagement	Build and lead a community of ESG professionals and enthusiasts to foster knowledge sharing and networking	- Create an online platform for community interaction and resource sharing - Organize industry events and forums	- Establishment as a central hub for ESG knowledge - Increased brand visibility and loyalty among professionals

Crafting the Value Proposition

We delved deep into our target personas' specific pain points and needs to craft compelling value propositions. We aimed to ensure that our ESG management application provided clear, tangible benefits that would resonate with each segment.

1. **Large Enterprises**:

    - **Pain Points**: Complex ESG reporting requirements, high regulatory scrutiny, and the need for robust data management.

- **Value Proposition**: Our application offered a comprehensive solution that streamlined data collection, ensured compliance with global standards, and provided powerful analytics and reporting tools. This meant less time spent on manual processes and more accurate, reliable ESG reports.

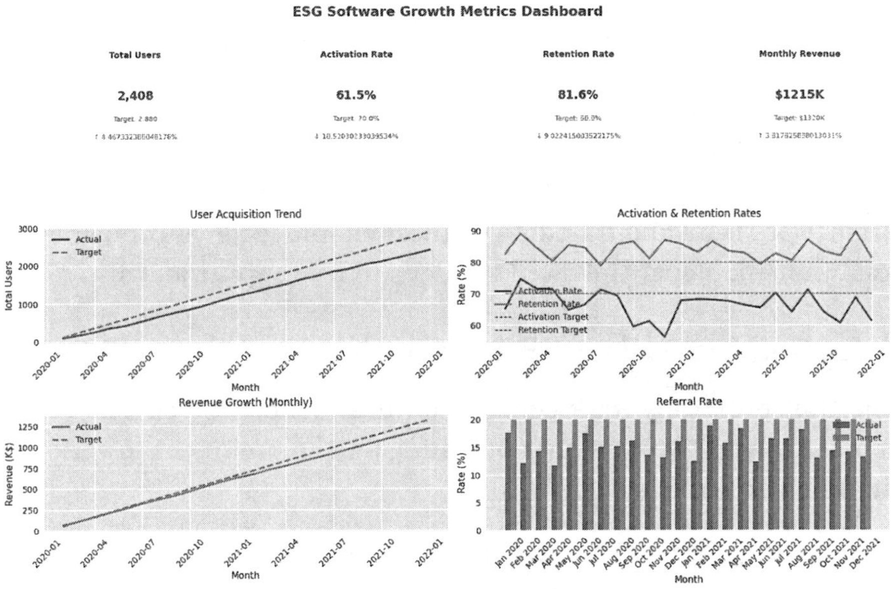

Figure 10.4 ESG Software Growth Metrics Dashboard

2. **Mid-sized Firms**:
   - **Pain Points**: Limited resources for ESG management, need for scalable solutions, and pressure to comply with emerging regulations.
   - **Value Proposition**: We provided an affordable, scalable solution that could grow with their business. The application was user-friendly, required minimal setup, and offered automation features to reduce the burden on their teams.
3. **Consulting Firms**:
   - **Pain Points**: Need for efficient tools to manage multiple clients, provide accurate ESG reporting, and offer value-added services.

- **Value Proposition**: Our application enabled consultants to manage and report on ESG metrics for multiple clients from a single platform. It offered robust data integration, customizable dashboards, and detailed reporting capabilities, enhancing the value it could provide to its clients.

Bullseye Framework Adoption and Key Observations

When we started growing our ESG management application, we knew we needed a robust framework to focus our efforts. That's when we turned to the Bullseye Framework, which helped us systematically test and refine our growth strategies. The Bullseye Framework is all about finding the best channels for your business, and we meticulously followed its steps to narrow our focus.

Adopting the Bullseye Framework

The Bullseye Framework consists of three concentric circles, each representing different stages of testing and commitment to various marketing channels:

1. **Outer Ring:** This is where we brainstormed and listed all potential marketing channels. It's a wide net that includes every conceivable way to reach our customers.
2. **Middle Ring:** From the outer ring, we selected a few promising channels to test. These channels showed some potential and were worth exploring further.
3. **Bullseye:** The innermost circle represents the channels that have proven to be the most effective. We decided to focus our primary efforts on these channels.

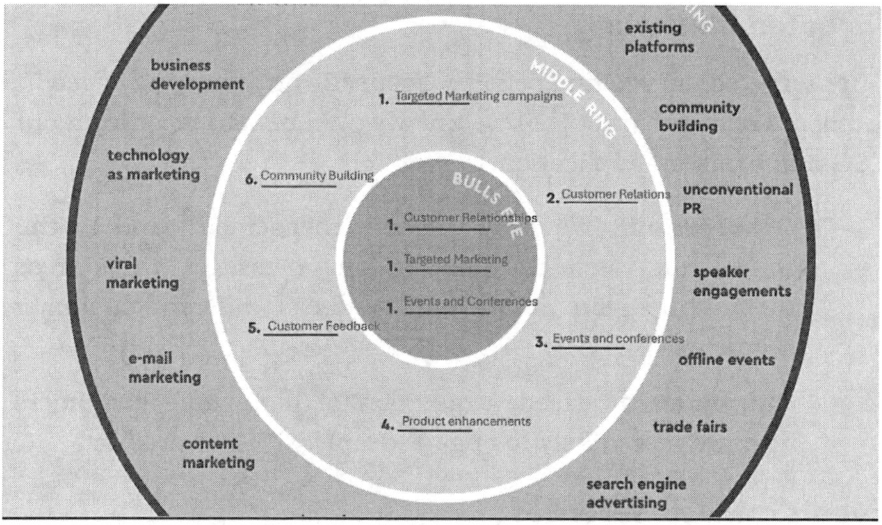

Figure 10.5 Bulls Eye Framework

Our Bullseye and Key Observations

After extensive brainstorming, testing, and analysis, we narrowed our Bullseye to three key channels: Customer Relationships, Targeted Marketing, and Events and Conferences. We describe how these channels contributed to our growth and share our observations.

Customer Relationships

We found that building strong customer relationships was crucial for our growth. This included regular check-ins, personalized support, and actively gathering feedback.

- **Observation:** Users who felt valued and supported were likelier to stick with our product and recommend it to others. The feedback loop helped us improve the product and strengthened our customer bond.
- **Outcome:** High user retention rates and a steady stream of referrals from satisfied customers.

Targeted Marketing

Our targeted marketing efforts focused on reaching specific segments of our market that we knew would benefit most from our ESG management application.

- **Observation:** We saw higher engagement and better conversion rates by tailoring our messages to address the unique pain points and needs of different customer segments.
- **Outcome:** Increased acquisition of high-value customers who are more likely to engage deeply with our product.

Events and Conferences

Participating in industry events and conferences proved an effective way to showcase our product and network with potential customers and partners.

- **Observation:** Face-to-face interactions at events allowed us to build trust quickly and provided valuable opportunities for live demos and immediate feedback.
- **Outcome:** We formed several strategic partnerships and acquired key customers with significant influence in their respective industries.

Middle Ring Strategies

While the Bullseye channels received the most focus, our middle ring included other strategies that also played an essential role in our growth. These included:

1. **Targeted Marketing**: Beyond just the focused efforts in the Bullseye, this included broader campaigns and experimental marketing tactics.
2. **Customer Relationships**: Continued effort to deepen and expand our relationships with existing customers.

3. **Events and Conferences**: Participate in broader events to maintain visibility and relevance.

4. **Product Enhancements**: Ongoing improvements based on user feedback to ensure our product remains competitive and valuable.

5. **Customer Feedback**: Systematic collection and analysis of feedback to drive continuous improvement.

6. **Community Building**: We want to create a community around our product where users can share insights, support each other, and feel a sense of belonging.

Personal Reflections

Reflecting on our journey using the Bullseye Framework, it's clear how vital this structured approach was to our success. Initially, we cast a wide net, considering every possible channel. This was both exciting and daunting, as the possibilities seemed endless. However, we could maximize our impact by systematically narrowing down and focusing on the most promising channels without spreading ourselves too thin.

The framework guided us to invest our time and resources wisely, ensuring our efforts aligned with the channels that brought the highest returns. Customer relationships, targeted marketing, events, and conferences emerged as our key growth drivers, each contributing uniquely to our overall strategy.

In particular, the emphasis on customer relationships helped us build a loyal user base that stayed with us and became advocates for our product. Targeted marketing allowed us to reach the right audience with the right message, significantly improving our conversion rates. Lastly, participating in events and conferences gave us the visibility and credibility needed to form strategic partnerships and attract critical customers.

The middle ring strategies supported our core efforts, ensuring we continuously improved and connected with our users.

Combining the Bullseye focus and the middle ring support, this holistic approach created a dynamic and effective growth strategy that propelled us forward.

In conclusion, adopting the Bullseye Framework was a game-changer for us. It provided the clarity and direction needed to navigate the complexities of market growth, allowing us to focus on what truly mattered. This journey has been a testament to the power of strategic thinking, iterative testing, and unwavering commitment to our goals. These principles will remain at the heart of our growth strategy as we evolve.

Implementation and Execution

With our value propositions defined and our target segments identified, we implemented our go-to-market strategy.

1. **Marketing and Outreach**: We created targeted marketing campaigns for each segment. For large enterprises, this meant personalized outreach and high-touch engagement. For mid-sized firms and consultants, we leveraged digital marketing strategies, including content marketing, SEO, and social media campaigns, to generate interest and drive leads.
2. **Sales Enablement**: We equipped our sales team with the tools and training to communicate our value propositions effectively. This included detailed product demos, case studies, and ROI calculators to help potential customers see the tangible benefits of our application.
3. **Customer Onboarding and Support**: We developed a comprehensive onboarding process to ensure a smooth transition for new customers. This included detailed user manuals, video tutorials, and dedicated support from our team. Lasya, Madhuri, and Praveen were crucial in providing initial support and gathering user feedback, ensuring that any issues were quickly addressed.

4. **Continuous Improvement**: Based on the feedback we received from our initial users, we continuously iterated on our product and our marketing strategies. This iterative approach allowed us to stay agile and responsive to our customers' needs, ensuring we always delivered maximum value.

We could craft a strategic and practical go-to-market strategy by leveraging our business model canvas. This approach ensured we targeted the right customers with the right messages, ultimately setting the stage for a successful product launch.

Onboarding Experiences

As we prepared to launch our ESG management application, one of our key priorities was ensuring a seamless onboarding experience for our users. Given our diverse customer segments and their varying needs, we designed three distinct onboarding strategies: Simplified Onboarding, Partner-Assisted Onboarding, and Phased Implementation. Each approach was tailored to provide the right level of support and guidance, ensuring our users could get up and running quickly and efficiently.

Simplified Onboarding

Simplified Onboarding was designed for mid-sized and consulting firms that needed a straightforward, self-service approach. These users often had limited resources and preferred an onboarding process that was quick and easy to follow.

1. **User Manuals and Quick Start Guides**: We developed comprehensive user manuals and quick start guides that provided step-by-step instructions on setting up and using the application. These resources were designed to be clear and concise, allowing users to get started without extensive technical support.
2. **Video Tutorials**: We created a series of video tutorials to complement the written guides. These videos covered the

application's basics, from initial setup to advanced features. Users could watch these tutorials at their own pace, making learning and implementing the application's functionalities easy.

3. **Interactive Walkthroughs**: We integrated interactive walkthroughs within the application itself. These guided tours helped users navigate the interface and perform critical tasks like data entry and report generation. The interactive nature of these walkthroughs ensured that users could learn by doing, which is often more effective than passive learning.

Partner-Assisted Onboarding

We offered partner-assist onboarding for large enterprises and organizations with more complex needs. This approach involved a more hands-on, personalized experience, leveraging our network of implementation partners.

1. **Dedicated Support Team**: Lasya, Madhuri, and Praveen formed our dedicated support team, ready to provide one-on-one assistance. They helped users with everything from initial setup to troubleshooting, ensuring that issues were promptly addressed.
2. **Customized Training Sessions**: We organized customized training sessions tailored to the specific needs of each organization. These sessions, led by our implementation partners, covered advanced features and provided in-depth training on maximizing the application's potential.
3. **Implementation Workshops**: We conducted workshops to ensure a smooth integration with existing systems. These workshops, facilitated by our partners, helped users map out their processes and configure the application to meet their unique requirements.
4. **Ongoing Support and Check-ins**: After the initial setup, we continued to provide ongoing support. Regular check-ins

with our support team ensured that users were progressing well and could get help with any new challenges.

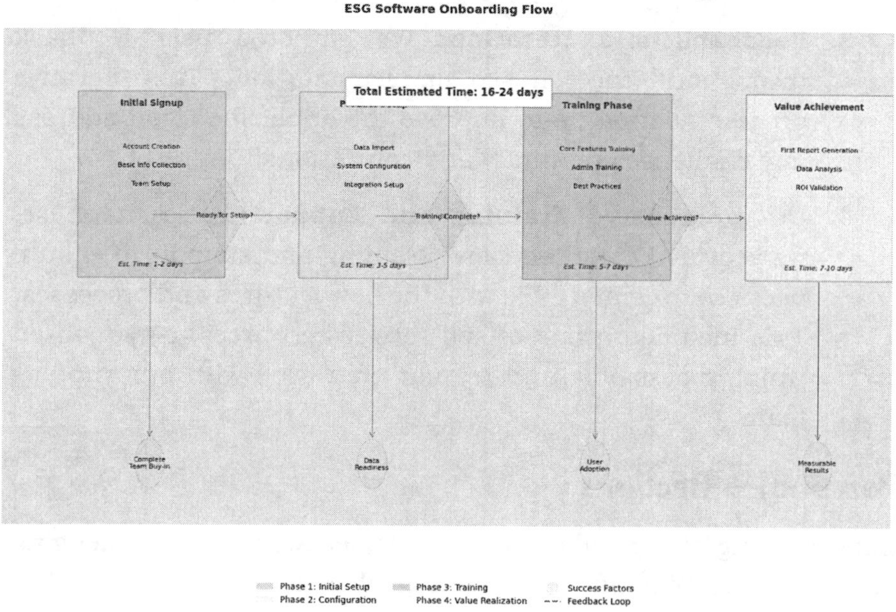

Figure 10.6 ESG Software Onboarding Time

Phased Implementation

We recommended a phased implementation approach for organizations with highly complex requirements or those looking to roll out the application gradually. This strategy allowed for a more controlled deployment, minimizing disruption and ensuring a smooth transition.

1. **Initial Pilot Phase**: We started with a pilot phase, where the application was implemented in a limited scope. This allowed the organization to test the application in a real-world environment, gather feedback, and make necessary adjustments before a full-scale rollout.
2. **Incremental Rollout**: We planned an incremental rollout based on the insights gained from the pilot phase. Each phase focused on a specific set of features or user groups,

allowing for gradual adoption and minimizing the risk of potential issues.

3. **Feedback and Iteration**: We gathered user feedback throughout the phased implementation. This iterative process allowed us to improve the application and address any challenges promptly and continuously.
4. **Comprehensive Training and Support**: At each phase, we provided comprehensive training and support to ensure users were comfortable with the new features and processes. This included a mix of self-service resources, personalized training sessions, and regular check-ins with our support team.

Personal Reflections

Implementing these onboarding strategies was both challenging and rewarding. Simplified Onboarding allowed us to efficiently serve smaller firms and consultants who needed to get started quickly with minimal handholding. Partner-assisted onboarding provided large enterprises with a high-touch, personalized experience, ensuring they received the necessary support to leverage the application entirely. Phased Implementation offered a flexible approach for complex deployments, allowing organizations to adopt the application at their own pace.

Lasya, Madhuri, and Praveen played crucial roles in making these onboarding experiences successful. Their dedication and expertise ensured that our users felt supported and valued, regardless of the complexity of their needs. Siva and I, as implementation partners, worked closely with our customers to ensure the application was seamlessly integrated into their existing processes.

Reflecting on this journey, I realize that the success of our onboarding strategies was a testament to the power of adaptability and customer-centric thinking. By tailoring our approach to meet the unique needs of our users, we delivered a positive onboarding experience, setting the stage for long-term success and satisfaction.

Growth Strategies Post-Launch

After the initial launch of our ESG management application, it became clear that maintaining momentum and driving growth would require a multi-faceted approach. We couldn't rest on our laurels; we needed to expand our offering, leverage existing platform capabilities, forge strategic partnerships, and focus on innovation through R&D. Here's how we tackled each of these strategies post-launch.

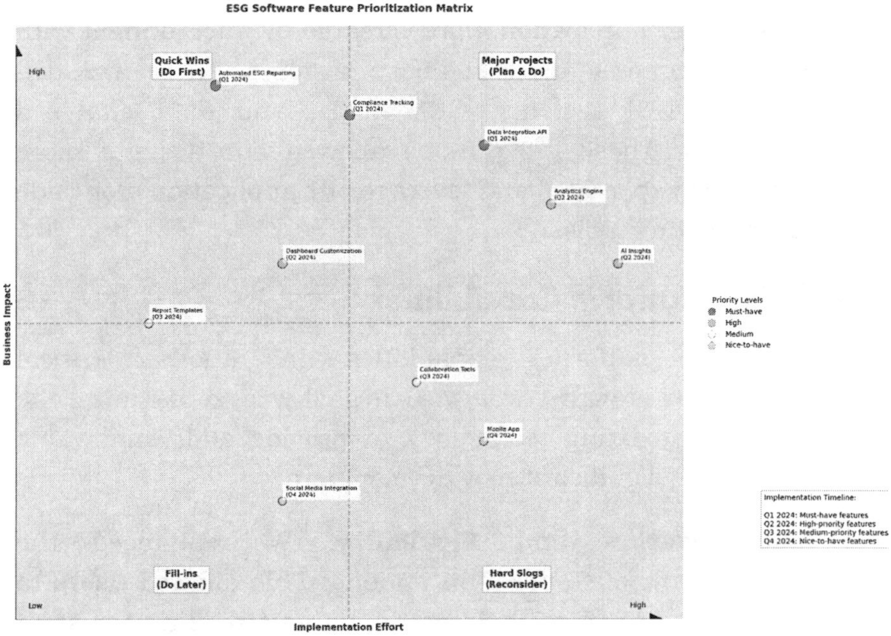

Figure 10.7 ESG Software Feature Prioritization Matrix

Expansion of ESG Suite

The first step in our growth strategy was to expand our ESG suite. Although the initial version of our application was robust, we knew additional features and capabilities could provide even more value to our users.

1. **User Feedback and Market Research**: We started by gathering detailed feedback from our initial users and conducting market research to identify the most

sought-after features. This helped us prioritize the development of new modules and functionalities.

2. **New Modules**: We introduced several new modules based on the insights. These included advanced analytics for deeper insights, automation tools to streamline reporting processes, and enhanced collaboration features to improve team coordination.

3. **Integration with Other Systems**: We also focused on making our application more versatile by integrating it with other commonly used business systems. These included popular ERP systems, CRM tools, and data analytics platforms. These integrations allowed our users a more seamless experience and leverage our application alongside their existing tools.

Leveraging Platform Capabilities

Leveraging our platform's capabilities was another critical component of our growth strategy. Our goal was to maximize the potential of our existing technology to provide additional value without requiring significant new development.

1. **Customization and Flexibility**: We enhanced the application's customization options. This allowed users to tailor the system to their needs without requiring custom development work. Users could create custom dashboards, reports, and workflows, making the application more adaptable to various business processes.

2. **Scalability Improvements**: We focused on improving the scalability of our platform to support larger enterprises and more complex deployments. This involved optimizing our infrastructure and ensuring our application efficiently handled increased data volumes and user loads.

3. **Enhanced Security Features**: As data security concerns increased, we invested in bolstering our platform's security capabilities. This included advanced encryption, multi-

factor authentication, and comprehensive audit trails to help users comply with stringent regulatory requirements.

Strategic Partnerships

Forming strategic partnerships was crucial for expanding our reach and enhancing our product offering. By collaborating with other organizations, we could tap into new markets and provide more comprehensive solutions to our users.

1. **Industry Partnerships**: We established partnerships with leading ESG consulting firms. These firms could leverage our application to provide enhanced services to their clients, and in return, we gained valuable insights and access to their extensive client networks.
2. **Technology Alliances**: Partnering with technology providers allowed us to integrate our application with other leading platforms. For instance, our collaboration with a primary cloud service provider enabled us to offer a more scalable and secure hosting environment, enhancing the overall user experience.
3. **Joint Ventures and Co-Marketing**: We also explored joint ventures and co-marketing opportunities with complementary product providers. This expanded our product suite and increased our visibility in the market through shared marketing efforts.

Focused Innovation on R&D

Innovation through focused R&D was the final pillar of our growth strategy. We knew continuous improvement and staying ahead of industry trends were essential for long-term success.

1. **Dedicated R&D Team**: We formed a dedicated R&D team to explore new technologies and innovations. This team focused on developing cutting-edge features and staying abreast of the latest trends in ESG and sustainability.

2. **User-Centric Development**: Our R&D efforts were heavily influenced by user feedback. We maintained an ongoing dialogue with our users, involving them in beta testing new features and gathering their input to ensure our developments aligned with their needs.

3. **Exploring Emerging Technologies**: We invested in exploring emerging technologies such as artificial intelligence and machine learning. These technologies had the potential to revolutionize ESG management by providing predictive analytics, automated insights, and advanced data processing capabilities.

4. **Innovation Labs and Hackathons**: We regularly organize innovation labs and hackathons to foster a culture of innovation. These events encourage our team to think creatively and develop new ideas that can be incorporated into our product roadmap.

Personal Reflections

Reflecting on our journey post-launch, I see that these growth strategies played a crucial role in driving our success. Expanding our ESG suite allowed us to provide more value to our users while leveraging our platform capabilities to ensure we made the most of our existing technology. Strategic partnerships opened new doors, broadened our reach, and focused innovation through R&D, keeping us at the forefront of the industry.

The road was only sometimes smooth, and there were numerous challenges along the way. Balancing immediate user needs with long-term strategic goals required careful planning and execution. However, our team's dedication and resilience enabled us to navigate these challenges and continue growing.

This multi-faceted approach to growth helped us expand our product offering and market presence and reinforced our commitment to delivering a top-tier ESG management solution. It has been a learning journey, adaptation, and relentless pursuit of excellence. As we look to the future, we remain committed to driving innovation and providing unparalleled value to our users.

Initial user Feedback:

We've come a long way in developing and refining our ESG management application. Remember those early days when we were grappling with market analysis, trying to nail down customer journey maps, and meticulously planning our MVP? It's been quite a journey, and today, looking at the market report, it's heartening to see our efforts bearing fruit.

Our product has received positive feedback, particularly its comprehensive feature set and user-friendly interface. One standout aspect is how we've integrated various ESG functions into a single platform, making it a go-to solution for many companies looking to streamline their ESG reporting and management processes.

Users have praised the application for its robust data integration capabilities, which allow them to pull data from multiple sources seamlessly. This feature has been a game-changer for many of our clients, who previously struggled with disparate systems and manual data entry. Reporting automation has also been highlighted as a significant benefit, saving users time and reducing potential errors.

However, it's not all roses. We've also received constructive feedback on areas where we can improve. Some users have mentioned that the initial setup can be complex, requiring more detailed documentation and support. Given the comprehensive nature of our tool, we anticipated this, and it's reassuring to know that our support team's efforts are being recognized and appreciated.

One aspect that consistently comes up in the feedback is the application's performance and scalability. For larger organizations, in particular, we need to ensure that the platform handles large volumes of data efficiently, which is crucial for their operations. This scalability has given us an edge in the market, positioning our application as a reliable solution for mid-sized and Small enterprises.

We needed to work on our strategic partnerships role to enhance our market presence. Collaborations with industry leaders not only expand our reach but will also add credibility to our offering. Another key highlight from the initial assessment is our focus on user satisfaction. The users see the continuous updates and improvements, and users appreciate that we listen to their needs and make necessary adjustments to enhance their experience. This feedback loop has been critical in maintaining high satisfaction rates and reducing churn.

Table 10.5 Summary of User Feedback for the ESG Management Software

Feedback Category	**User Comments**	**Suggested Improvements**	**Action Plan**
User Interface (UI)	Users found the UI to be generally intuitive but noted that certain elements were not as user-friendly as expected.	- Simplify the navigation. - Enhance the visual appeal of the dashboard.	- Redesign key interface elements based on user feedback. - Conduct A/B testing to validate UI changes.
Performance	Some users experienced slow load times, particularly with large datasets.	- Improve data processing speed. - Optimize the application for better performance with large datasets.	- Implement backend optimizations. - Conduct stress tests to ensure performance improvements under various conditions.

Feedback Category	**User Comments**	**Suggested Improvements**	**Action Plan**
Feature Set	Users appreciated the core features but requested more advanced analytics and reporting capabilities.	- Add more customizable reporting options. - Introduce predictive analytics features.	- Develop and integrate advanced reporting and analytics tools. - Provide tutorials and documentation for new features.
Customer Support	Users expressed satisfaction with customer support but mentioned that response times could be improved during peak times.	- Implement a more responsive support system during peak hours. - Consider a 24/7 support option for premium users.	- Increase support staff during peak hours. - Explore AI-driven support tools for faster response times.
Documentation & Training	Users found the documentation helpful but requested more in-depth tutorials and use case examples.	- Develop comprehensive tutorials and case studies. - Offer webinars and interactive training sessions.	- Create new content focused on practical use cases. - Schedule regular webinars and workshops to cover different aspects of the application.
Integration Capabilities	Users appreciated the existing integration options but requested support for additional third-party tools and platforms.	- Expand integration capabilities to include more third-party tools. - Improve the API documentation for easier integration by developers.	- Prioritize integration with the most requested third-party tools. - Revise API documentation and provide examples to assist developers.

(*Contd.*)

Feedback Category	**User Comments**	**Suggested Improvements**	**Action Plan**
Pricing & Value	Some users felt that the pricing was slightly high for the feature set offered.	- Consider offering more flexible pricing plans. - Introduce a tiered pricing model to cater to different user needs.	- Review current pricing structure and adjust, as necessary. - Explore the introduction of a tiered pricing model with added benefits at higher tiers.
Overall Satisfaction	Most users expressed overall satisfaction with the product but highlighted areas where continuous improvements could enhance their experience.	- Focus on continuous improvement based on regular user feedback. - Ensure that the product evolves in line with user needs and industry standards.	- Establish a regular feedback loop with users to gather ongoing insights. - Plan and execute regular updates and enhancements based on the collected feedback.

Reflecting on this journey, it's clear that every step we took—from market analysis to the strategic planning of our MVP to gathering and acting on user feedback—has been crucial. The AARRR framework has provided a structured approach to our growth, guiding us through acquisition, activation, retention, revenue generation, and referrals.

We must continue leveraging these insights and maintaining the momentum as we progress. The positive reception of our product is a testament to our team's hard work and dedication. It's been a challenging but rewarding journey, and I am excited about the future of our ESG management application.

Growth Analysis Using the AR Framework

Reflecting on our journey of launching and growing the ESG management application, I realized that applying the AARRR framework—acquisition, Activation, Retention, Revenue, and

Referral—has been instrumental in strategizing our growth. Inspired by the insights and strategies illustrated in the attached image, here's an in-depth analysis of each stage.

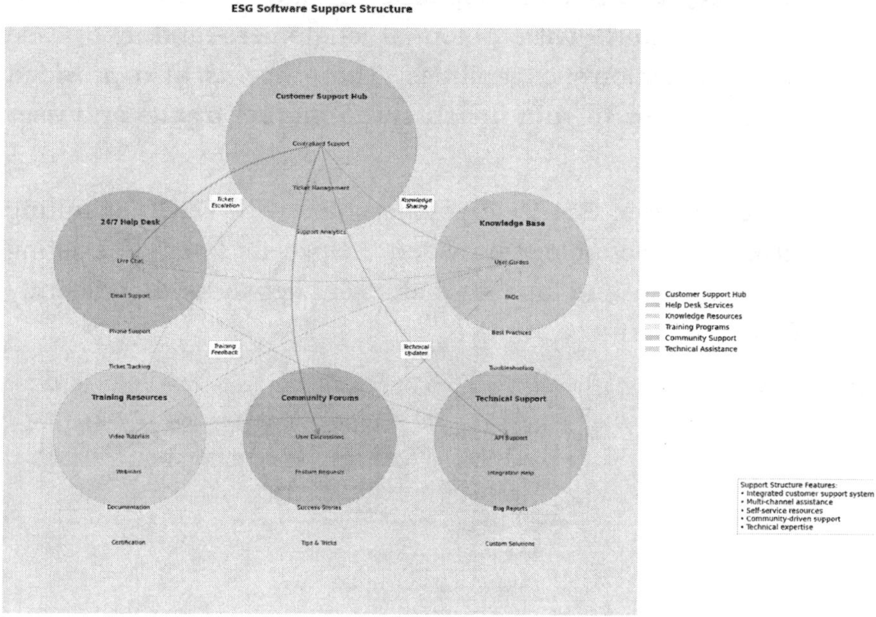

Figure 10.8 ESG Software Support Structure

Acquisition

Key Findings:

- Targeted marketing
- Industry events
- Partnerships

Strategies:

To acquire users, we focused on increasing our visibility and attracting our target audience through several channels:

- **Targeted Marketing**: We implemented highly targeted marketing campaigns focusing on our key segments. This included digital marketing efforts like SEO, content marketing, and social media campaigns to reach mid-sized firms and ESG consultants.

- **Industry Events**: Participating in industry events allowed us to network with potential customers and showcase our application's capabilities. These events also provided opportunities to gain insights into market trends and user needs.
- **Partnerships**: Strategic partnerships with ESG consulting firms and technology providers helped us leverage existing relationships and tap into their client networks, significantly expanding our reach.

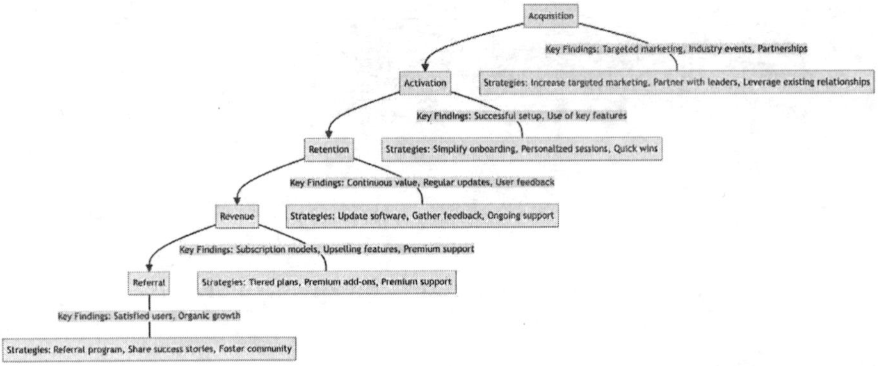

Figure 10.9 AR framework

Activation

Key Findings:

- Successful setup
- Use of critical features

Strategies:

Activation was about ensuring new users could quickly realize the value of our application. We focused on simplifying the initial user experience to drive engagement:

- **Simplified Onboarding**: We provided detailed user manuals, video tutorials, and interactive walkthroughs to help users get started quickly.
- **Personalized Sessions**: We offered personalized training sessions and support for larger enterprises to address their needs.
- **Quick Wins**: Highlighting quick wins and easy-to-use features during the initial setup helped users experience immediate benefits, increasing their likelihood of continued use.

Retention

Key Findings:

- Continuous value
- Regular updates
- User Feedback

Strategies:

Retention was critical for our growth, and we focused on delivering continuous value to our users:

- **Continuous Value Delivery**: We ensured our application provided ongoing value through regular updates and new features based on user feedback.
- **User Feedback Loop**: Actively gathering and acting on user feedback helped us identify areas for improvement and keep our users engaged.
- **Ongoing Support**: Our dedicated team provided exceptional support, ensuring users felt supported and valued, which was crucial for retention.

Revenue

Key Findings:

- Subscription models
- Upselling features
- Premium support

Strategies:

To drive revenue, we implemented various monetization strategies:

Table 10.6 Growth analysis using the AARRR Framework

AARRR Stage	Key Findings	Strategies	Personal Reflections
Acquisition	- Targeted marketing - Industry events - Partnerships	- Targeted Marketing: Focus on digital marketing (SEO, content marketing, social media) aimed at mid-sized firms and ESG consultants. - Industry Events: Networking and showcasing the application at industry events. - Partnerships: Collaborating with ESG consulting firms and technology providers to expand reach.	Applying a targeted approach in acquisition allowed us to strategically position ourselves in the market, leading to effective user acquisition and visibility within key segments.

AARRR Stage	**Key Findings**	**Strategies**	**Personal Reflections**
Activation	- Successful setup - Use of critical features	- Simplified Onboarding: Provided user manuals, video tutorials, and interactive walkthroughs. - Personalized Sessions: Tailored training and support for larger enterprises. - Quick Wins: Emphasized easy-to-use features and immediate benefits to drive early engagement.	Focusing on a seamless activation process helped users quickly realize value, increasing early engagement and setting a positive tone for continued use.
Retention	- Continuous value - Regular updates - User feedback	- Continuous Value Delivery: Regular updates and new features based on feedback. - User Feedback Loop: Actively gathered and acted on user feedback. - Ongoing Support: Provided exceptional customer support to maintain user engagement and satisfaction.	Retention efforts ensured we maintained strong user relationships, keeping our application relevant and valuable through ongoing support and continuous improvements.
Revenue	- Subscription models - Upselling features - Premium support	- Subscription Models: Offered different plans for various segments. - Upselling Features: Introduced premium add-ons and advanced features. - Premium Support: Provided premium support packages for additional revenue.	Implementing diverse revenue strategies allowed us to cater to various customer needs while maximizing revenue opportunities through upselling and premium offerings.

AARRR Stage	Key Findings	Strategies	Personal Reflections
Referral	- Satisfied users - Organic growth	- Referral Program: Incentivized users to refer the product. - Sharing Success Stories: Highlighted user success stories and case studies. - Fostering Community: Built a community for users to share insights and encourage word-of-mouth referrals.	Leveraging satisfied users as advocates helped drive organic growth, with referrals contributing significantly to our expansion and community building efforts.

- **Subscription Models**: We used different subscription plans to cater to various customer segments, from mid-sized firms to large enterprises.
- **Upselling Features**: We introduced premium add-ons and advanced features that users could purchase to enhance their experience.
- **Premium Support**: Providing premium support packages for an additional fee helped us generate more revenue while offering enhanced value to users needing extra assistance.

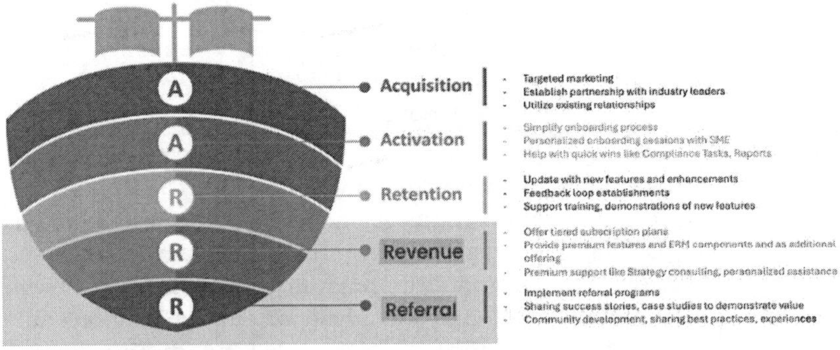

Figure 10.10 ESG Management - AARRR Framework

Referral

Key Findings:

- Satisfied users
- Organic growth

Strategies:

Referrals played a significant role in our growth, driven by satisfied users who advocated for our product:

- **Referral Program**: We created a referral program to incentivize users to spread the word about our application.
- **Sharing Success Stories**: Highlighting user success stories and case studies showcased the benefits of our application and encouraged others to try it.
- **Fostering Community**: Building a community around our product where users could share insights and best practices fostered a sense of belonging and encouraged word-of-mouth referrals.

Personal Reflections

Applying the AARRR framework provided a structured approach to our growth strategy, helping us identify and focus on the most impactful activities at each stage of the customer lifecycle. This structured approach allowed us to systematically acquire, activate, retain, generate revenue from, and encourage user referrals.

The journey wasn't without its challenges, but each step in the AARRR framework guided us toward sustainable growth. Each element played a crucial role in our success, from targeted marketing efforts to forming strategic partnerships and continuously delivering value. By listening to our users and iterating based on their feedback, we could refine our product and strategies, ensuring we met their needs and exceeded their expectations.

Overall, the AARRR framework helped us build a strong foundation for our ESG management application, driving growth and ensuring we stayed aligned with our goals and user needs. This approach has set us up for continued success as we navigate the competitive landscape and strive to make a meaningful impact in the ESG space.

OKRs and More

Elaborating on OKRs and Initiatives for ESG Management Application

Reflecting on our journey, it's clear that achieving sustainable growth for our ESG management application requires a strategic approach. We leveraged the OKRs (Objectives and Key Results) framework to set clear goals and initiatives. Here's a detailed look at our objectives, key results, and the initiatives that have guided our path forward.

Increase Market Presence

Objective: Increase Market Presence

Key Results:

- Secure five new partnerships with industry leaders by Q2.
- Increase mentions in industry publications by 20% by Q2.
- Achieve a 30% growth in overall market presence by Q4.

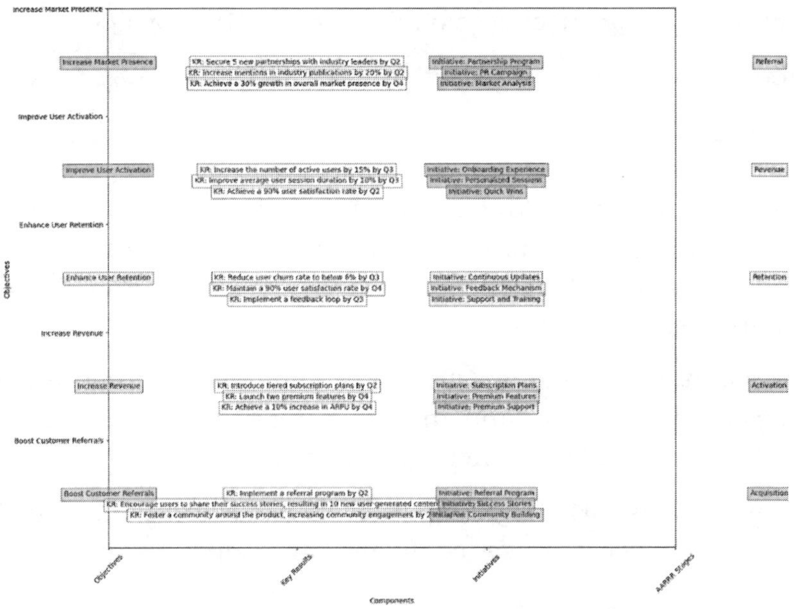

10.11 OKRs for ESG management application

Initiatives:

- **Partnership Program:** We actively sought partnerships with industry leaders who could help us expand our reach and credibility. These partnerships provided us with access to new markets and valuable industry insights.
- **PR Campaign:** We launched a targeted PR campaign to increase our visibility in industry publications. This involved press releases, interviews, and thought leadership articles.
- **Market Analysis:** Conducting a thorough market analysis helped us identify key trends and opportunities, enabling us to tailor our marketing efforts effectively.

Improve User Activation

Objective: Improve User Activation

Key Results:

- Increase the number of active users by 15% by Q3.

- Improve average user session duration by 10% by Q3.
- Achieve a 90% user satisfaction rate by Q2.

Initiatives:

- **Onboarding Experience:** We focused on simplifying the onboarding process to ensure users could get started quickly and effectively. This included interactive walkthroughs and comprehensive guides.
- **Personalized Sessions:** Offering personalized training sessions helped users understand the full potential of our application and how it could meet their specific needs.
- **Quick Wins:** Highlighting easy-to-achieve results during onboarding boosted user confidence and engagement.

Enhance User Retention

Objective: Enhance User Retention

Key Results:

- Reduce user churn rate to below 6% by Q3.
- Maintain a 90% user satisfaction rate by Q4.
- Implement a feedback loop by Q3.

Initiatives:

- **Continuous Updates:** We regularly updated the application with new features and improvements based on user feedback, keeping our product relevant and valuable.
- **Feedback Mechanism:** Implementing a robust feedback loop allowed us to gather user insights continuously and make necessary adjustments promptly.
- **Support and Training:** Ongoing support and training ensured that users could maximize the application's benefits, enhancing their overall experience and satisfaction.

Increase Revenue

Objective: Increase Revenue

Key Results:

- Introduce tiered subscription plans by Q2.
- Launch two premium features by Q4.
- Achieve a 10% increase in ARPU (Average Revenue Per User) by Q4.

Initiatives:

- **Subscription Plans:** We introduced tiered subscription plans to cater to different user needs and budgets, broadening our market appeal.
- **Premium Features:** Launching premium features provided additional value to users willing to pay for advanced functionalities, driving higher revenue.
- **Premium Support:** Offering premium support packages for an additional fee provided an additional revenue stream while enhancing user satisfaction.

Boost Customer Referrals

Objective: Boost Customer Referrals

Key Results:

- Implement a referral program by Q2.
- Encourage users to share their success stories, resulting in ten new user-generated content pieces by Q3.
- Foster a community around the product, increasing community engagement by 20% by Q4.

Table 10.7 OKRs and Initiatives for ESG Management Application

OKR Stage	Objective	Key Results	Initiatives	KPIs to Track	Personal Reflections
Increase Market Presence	Increase Market Presence	- Secure five new partnerships with industry leaders by Q2. - Increase mentions in industry publications by 20% by Q2. - Achieve a 30% growth in overall market presence by Q4.	- Partnership Program: Sought partnerships to expand reach and credibility. - PR Campaign: Launched targeted PR campaigns, including press releases and interviews. - Market Analysis: Conducted thorough market analysis to identify trends and opportunities.	- Number of new partnerships - Mentions in industry publications - Market share growth percentage	Strategic efforts in partnerships and PR campaigns greatly increased our visibility and market presence, validating the importance of a well-planned market presence strategy.
Improve User Activation	Improve User Activation	- Increase the number of active users by 15% by Q3. - Improve average user session duration by 10% by Q3. - Achieve a 90% user satisfaction rate by Q2.	- Onboarding Experience: Simplified the onboarding process with interactive walkthroughs. - Personalized Sessions: Offered tailored training sessions to meet specific needs. -	- Number of active users - Average session duration - User satisfaction score	Focusing on user activation through personalized onboarding and quick wins was crucial for ensuring early user engagement and satisfaction, setting a strong foundation for user retention.

Enhance User Retention	Enhance User Retention	- Reduce user churn rate to below 6% by Q3. - Maintain a 90% user satisfaction rate by Q4. - Implement a feedback loop by Q3.	Quick Wins: Highlighted easy-to-achieve results to boost confidence and engagement. - Continuous Updates: Regularly updated the application based on feedback. - Feedback Mechanism: Implemented a feedback loop to gather insights. - Support and Training: Provided ongoing support and training to enhance user experience and satisfaction.	- Churn rate - User satisfaction score - Number of feedback loop iterations	The focus on continuous updates and robust feedback mechanisms helped maintain user satisfaction and reduce churn, emphasizing the value of ongoing user engagement and support.
Increase Revenue	Increase Revenue	- Introduce tiered subscription plans by Q2. - Launch two premium features by Q4. - Achieve a 10% increase in ARPU by Q4.	- Subscription Plans: Introduced tiered plans to cater to different user needs. - Premium Features: Launched premium features for additional revenue.	- Number of new subscriptions - Revenue from premium features - ARPU (Average Revenue Per User)	The introduction of tiered subscription plans and premium features allowed us to diversify our revenue streams and provided additional value to users, driving overall revenue growth.

OKR Stage	Objective	Key Results	Initiatives	KPIs to Track	Personal Reflections
Boost Customer Referrals	Boost Customer Referrals	- Implement a referral program by Q2. - Encourage user-generated content, aiming for ten new pieces by Q3. - Increase community engagement by 20% by Q4.	- Premium Support: Offered premium support packages as an additional revenue stream. - Referral Program: Created a referral program to incentivize existing users. - Success Stories: Shared user success stories to encourage referrals. - Community Building: Fostered a community around the product to enhance engagement and loyalty.	- Number of referrals - User-generated content count - Community engagement rate	Building a community and encouraging referrals not only drove growth but also fostered a sense of belonging among users, validating the effectiveness of community-driven growth strategies.

Initiatives:

- **Referral Program:** We created a referral program that incentivized existing users to refer new customers, leveraging their networks to drive growth.
- **Success Stories:** Sharing user success stories highlighted the practical benefits of our application and encouraged others to try it.
- **Community Building:** Building a community around our product helped foster engagement and loyalty. Users could share insights and best practices and support each other, creating a robust support network.

Personal Reflections

Implementing these OKRs and initiatives has been a transformative journey. Each objective required a concerted effort, strategic planning, and relentless execution. Our focus on increasing market presence, improving user activation, enhancing retention, driving revenue, and boosting referrals has allowed us to build a strong foundation for sustainable growth.

The partnership program and PR campaigns significantly increased our visibility, while personalized onboarding sessions and continuous updates ensured our users remained engaged and satisfied. We were introducing tiered subscription plans and premium features, diversifying our revenue streams and providing additional value to our users.

Building a community and encouraging user referrals have been particularly rewarding. Seeing our users become advocates for our product validated the hard work and dedication we put into creating a valuable and impactful application.

As we continue to grow, these OKRs and initiatives will guide us, ensuring we stay aligned with our goals and deliver exceptional user value. This structured approach has helped us navigate the complexities of the market and fostered a culture of continuous improvement and customer-centricity.

Reflecting on the journey and looking forward

As I sit here in my favorite coffee shop, the aroma of freshly brewed coffee mingling with the sounds of baristas working their magic, I reflect on our journey with the ESG management application. It's been quite the ride. We've come a long way from those early days of brainstorming and market analysis to the intense MVP development and iterative testing phases.

Lately, my thoughts have been drifting toward the potential of AI in ESG. Imagine harnessing the power of AI and Generative AI, including ChatGPT, to generate insights that could transform how businesses manage their environmental, social, and governance responsibilities. The possibilities are endless, and it excites me to consider integrating these advancements into our product to make it even more powerful and user-friendly. Table 10.8 outlines my vision for an advanced ESG management application to leverage advanced technologies like AI, Generative AI, Elastic Search, native APIs, 3rd party Risk management applications. This approach helps enhance data accuracy, streamlines processes, and provides deep insights, empowering organizations to navigate the complexities of ESG management with confidence and precision.

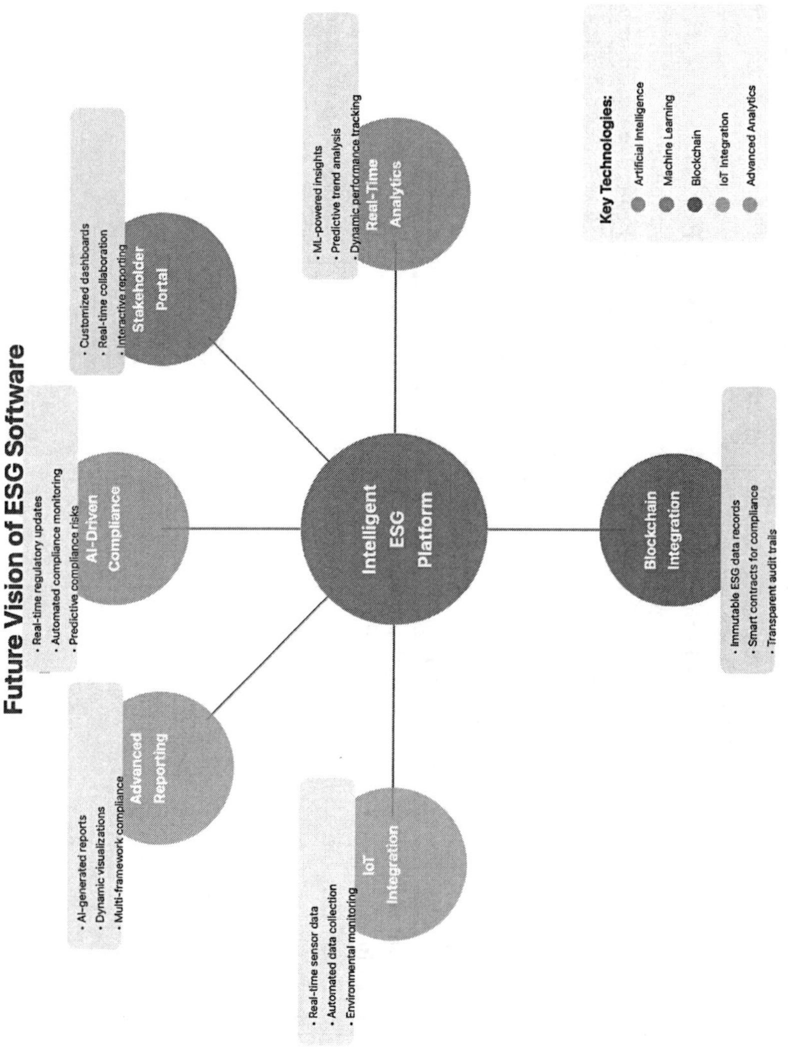
Future Vision of ESG Software
Intelligent ESG Platform
AI-Driven Compliance
• Real-time regulatory updates
• Automated compliance monitoring
• Predictive compliance risks
Stakeholder Portal
• Customized dashboards
• Real-time collaboration
• Interactive reporting
Real-Time Analytics
• ML-powered insights
• Predictive trend analysis
• Dynamic performance tracking
Advanced Reporting
• AI-generated reports
• Dynamic visualizations
• Multi-framework compliance
IoT Integration
• Real-time sensor data
• Automated data collection
• Environmental monitoring
Blockchain Integration
• Immutable ESG data records
• Smart contracts for compliance
• Transparent audit trails
Key Technologies:
Artificial Intelligence
Machine Learning
Blockchain
IoT Integration
Advanced Analytics

Table 10.8 Summary Future State ESG Management Application

Component	**Description**	**Key Features**	**Expected Benefits**
AI-Powered Analytics	Integrate AI to enhance data processing, analysis, and decision-making capabilities.	- Automated data classification and tagging - Predictive analytics for ESG trends - AI-driven risk assessment and management	- Faster and more accurate analysis - Enhanced decision-making capabilities - Proactive risk management
Generative AI for Reporting	Utilize Generative AI to create customized reports and insights based on user input and data patterns.	- Automated report generation with natural language explanations - Personalized insights and recommendations based on ESG data - Adaptive learning for report improvements	- Time-saving in report generation - Tailored insights for different user roles - Continuous improvement of reporting quality
Elastic Search Integration	Implement Elastic Search to optimize data retrieval and scalability across large datasets.	- Real-time search and filtering of ESG data - Scalability for large and complex datasets - Full-text search capabilities across all ESG documents and data sources	- Improved data accessibility and retrieval speed - Scalable solution for growing data needs - Enhanced user experience in data navigation

Dynamic Dashboard	Develop dynamic, customizable dashboards that allow users to visualize key ESG metrics and trends in real-time.	- Drag-and-drop widget customization - Real-time data visualization - Integration with various data sources and APIs	- Personalized user experience - Real-time monitoring of ESG metrics - Improved decision-making with up-to-date information
Advanced Reporting Capabilities	Provide advanced reporting features that are customizable, with the ability to create, save, and share report templates.	- Customizable reporting templates - Dynamic report generation based on user-selected criteria - Shareable reports with real-time collaboration features	- Streamlined reporting processes - Consistent and standardized reporting across the organization - Enhanced collaboration on reporting tasks
Template Management	Enable users to create, manage, and apply templates for common ESG tasks, reports, and workflows.	- Library of pre-built templates for various ESG activities - Template customization and sharing - Automatic application of templates to new projects	- Reduced setup time for new projects - Consistency in ESG management processes - Increased efficiency and productivity in recurring tasks
AI-Driven Insights & Alerts	Leverage AI to generate insights and alerts based on real-time data and predictive models.	- Real-time alerts for potential ESG risks and opportunities - AI-driven recommendations for ESG strategy - Automated compliance checks against regulations	- Proactive management of ESG risks and opportunities - Improved compliance with evolving regulations - Enhanced strategic planning capabilities

Component	Description	Key Features	Expected Benefits
Collaboration & Communication	Integrate collaboration tools to facilitate communication and project management within the platform.	- Integrated chat and discussion forums - Shared project workspaces with document collaboration - Task management and assignment features	- Improved team collaboration on ESG projects - Streamlined communication within the platform - Enhanced project management and execution
Compliance Management	Enhance compliance tracking and management with AI-driven automation to ensure adherence to ESG regulations and standards.	- Automated compliance checks - Real-time updates on regulatory changes - Integration with regulatory databases for up-to-date compliance information	- Reduced risk of non-compliance - Simplified compliance management - Up-to-date adherence to global ESG standards
Scalability & Cloud Integration	Ensure the platform is scalable and cloud-integrated to support growing data and user demands.	- Cloud-native architecture for scalability - Integration with major cloud platforms (AWS, Azure, Google Cloud) - Automatic scaling based on usage and data load	- Seamless handling of increasing data volumes - Cost-effective scaling - Flexibility in deployment and usage
Advanced IoT Integration	Integrate IoT devices for real-time environmental data collection and monitoring across supply chains and operations.	- Real-time monitoring of emissions, energy use, and other ESG metrics - Automated data collection from IoT sensors - Integration with existing IoT ecosystems	- Enhanced data accuracy and real-time tracking - Proactive identification of ESG issues in operations - Improved operational efficiency

3rd Party API Native Integration	Provide native integration with 3rd party APIs to expand the platform's functionality and connect with external data sources and services.	- Seamless integration with popular 3rd party tools and services - Pre-built connectors for leading ESG data providers - API management dashboard	- Expanded functionality without custom development - Easy access to external data and services - Faster implementation of integrated solutions
Enterprise Risk Management (ERM)	Integrate comprehensive ERM tools to manage and mitigate risks associated with ESG factors across the enterprise.	- Centralized risk management dashboard - AI-driven risk prediction and mitigation strategies - Integration with enterprise risk databases	- Improved risk visibility and control - Proactive management of potential risks - Better alignment of ESG strategies with overall enterprise risk
Supply Risk Management	Incorporate advanced supply risk management features to monitor and mitigate risks within the supply chain related to ESG factors.	- Real-time supply chain risk monitoring - Predictive analytics for supply chain disruptions - Integration with supplier risk data and third-party risk assessments	- Enhanced visibility into supply chain risks - Reduced supply chain disruptions due to ESG factors - Strengthened supplier relationships

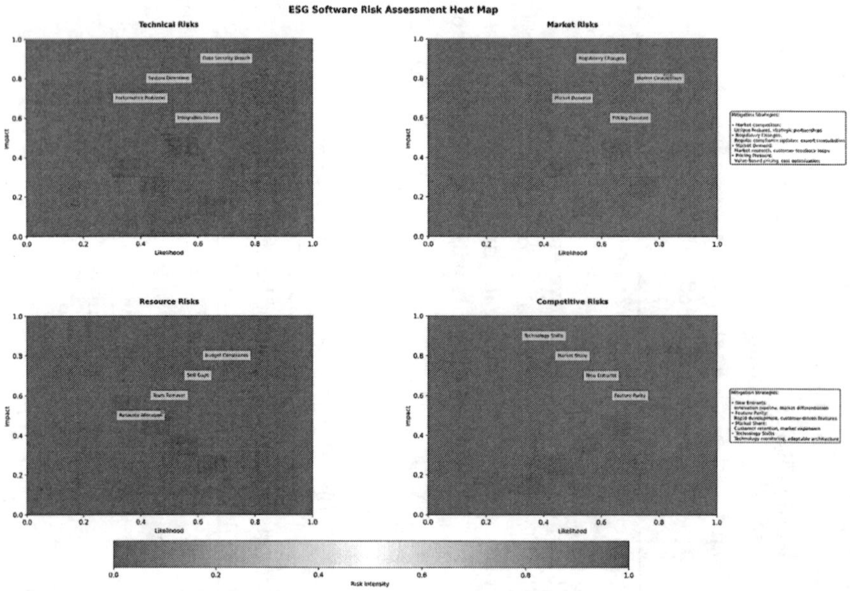

Figure 10.12 ESG Software Risk Assessment heat map

But let's take a step back and consider where we are now. Our product has been well-received, with users appreciating its comprehensive features and user-friendly interface. However, we've also identified some areas for improvement—complex onboarding processes, better user training and support, and aligning the product more closely with customer workflows. These are challenges but also opportunities for us to refine and enhance what we've built.

One thing that's become clear is the importance of understanding our users better. We've got to dig deep, conducting thorough customer interviews, collecting structured feedback through surveys and questionnaires, and analyzing how users interact with our software. This feedback will be invaluable in helping us identify specific issues and prioritize them for improvement. We also need to make the onboarding process smoother and more intuitive. Implementing guided tutorials and walkthroughs, offering comprehensive training programs, and providing robust support channels will help new users get up to speed quickly and reduce the initial learning curve. It's all about making their journey with our product seamless.

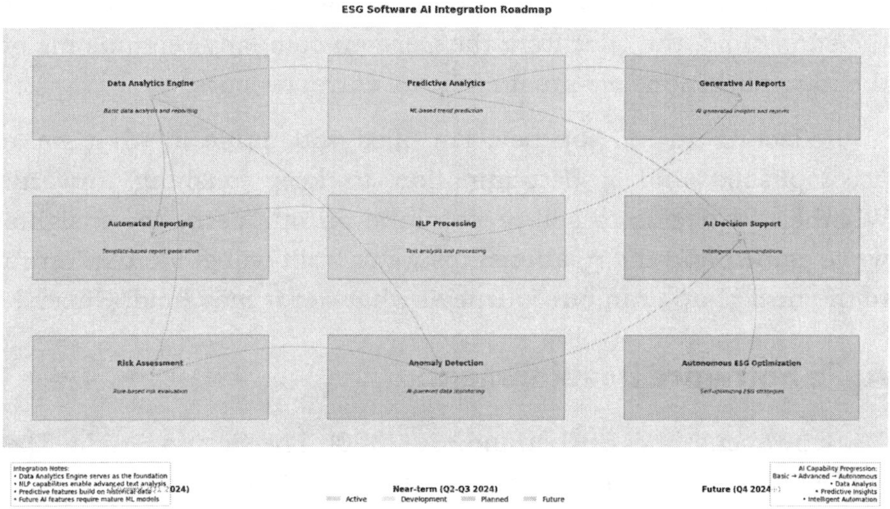

Figure 10.13 ESG Software AI Integration Roadmap

As I sip my coffee, I can't help but think about the next steps. We've been offered the chance to sell our idea to a more prominent company in Germany. This is tempting, given the financial pressures we've been facing and the constant need to stretch our resources. But there's also a part of me that believes in the potential of what we've built and wants to see it through.

So, what's next? We'll address the adoption issues by simplifying onboarding, enhancing training, and ensuring our product aligns more closely with customer workflows. We'll dive deeper into customer insights through interviews, surveys, and data analysis to gather actionable feedback. And, of course, we'll continue to improve the user experience based on this feedback, making necessary adjustments to the interface and overall functionality. Strengthening our support mechanisms will also be crucial. By providing real-time assistance, we can ensure our users feel supported and valued every step of the way. It's about building a relationship with them and showing that we're not just a software provider but a partner in their ESG journey.

As I sit here, lost in thought, the future feels daunting and exciting. There's so much potential in what we've created, and integrating AI to enhance our product's capabilities is thrilling. At the same time, the offer from the German company reminds me of the tough decisions we must make as entrepreneurs.

Reflecting on our journey, I'm filled with pride in what we've accomplished and a determination to keep pushing forward. Whether we decide to sell or continue on our path, the insights we've gained and the relationships we've built will guide us. Here's to the next chapter in our journey—whatever it may hold. Cheers!

Agile Software Development:

1. Schwaber, K., & Sutherland, J. (2020). The Scrum Guide: The Definitive Guide to Scrum: The Rules of the Game.
2. Cohn, M. (2004). User Stories Applied: For Agile Software Development. Addison-Wesley Professional.

ESG and Sustainability:

1. Eccles, R. G., & Klimenko, S. (2019). The Investor Revolution. Harvard Business Review, 97(3), 106-116.
2. Whelan, T., Atz, U., Van Holt, T., & Clark, C. (2021). ESG and Financial Performance: Uncovering the Relationship by Aggregating Evidence from 1,000 Plus Studies Published between 2015 – 2020. NYU Stern Center for Sustainable Business.

Product Management:

1. Cagan, M. (2017). Inspired: How to Create Tech Products Customers Love. John Wiley & Sons.
2. Perri, M. (2019). Escaping the Build Trap: How Effective Product Management Creates Real Value. O'Reilly Media.

Software Development Practices:

1. Martin, R. C. (2019). Clean Agile: Back to Basics. Pearson Education.
2. Fowler, M. (2018). Refactoring: Improving the Design of Existing Code. Addison-Wesley Professional.

DevOps and CI/CD:

1. Kim, G., Humble, J., Debois, P., & Willis, J. (2016). The DevOps Handbook: How to Create World-Class Agility, Reliability, and Security in Technology Organizations. IT Revolution.
2. Forsgren, N., Humble, J., & Kim, G. (2018). Accelerate: The Science of Lean Software and DevOps. IT Revolution.

User Experience and Design:

1. Krug, S. (2014). Don't Make Me Think, Revisited: A Common Sense Approach to Web Usability. New Riders.
2. Norman, D. (2013). The Design of Everyday Things: Revised and Expanded Edition. Basic Books.

Business Strategy:

1. Osterwalder, A., & Pigneur, Y. (2010). Business Model Generation: A Handbook for Visionaries, Game-Changers, and Challengers. John Wiley & Sons.
2. Ries, E. (2011). The Lean Startup: How Today's Entrepreneurs Use Continuous Innovation to Create Radically Successful Businesses. Crown Business.

AI and Machine Learning in Software:

1. Géron, A. (2019). Hands-On Machine Learning with Scikit-Learn, Keras, and TensorFlow: Concepts, Tools, and Techniques to Build Intelligent Systems. O'Reilly Media.

2. Hulten, G. (2018). Building Intelligent Systems: A Guide to Machine Learning Engineering. Apress.

Data Management and Analytics:

1. Davenport, T. H., & Harris, J. G. (2017). Competing on Analytics: Updated, with a New Introduction: The New Science of Winning. Harvard Business Review Press.

2. Provost, F., & Fawcett, T. (2013). Data Science for Business: What You Need to Know about Data Mining and Data-Analytic Thinking. O'Reilly Media.

Team Management and Leadership:

1. Lencioni, P. (2002). The Five Dysfunctions of a Team: A Leadership Fable. Jossey-Bass.

2. Sutherland, J. (2014). Scrum: The Art of Doing Twice the Work in Half the Time. Crown Business.